PRAISE F[...]
BEIJING BA[...]

"Wang's memoir feels akin to a captivating documentary, sh[...] camera, which greedily takes in the changing landscape of Beijing and the dynamic daily life of ordinary Chinese. . . . If [Wang] set out looking for trouble when she moved to China, it seems she also found her voice along the way. This affectionate memoir . . . will provide a deeper understanding of Beijing at a time when it is increasingly difficult to discern its true character through the impenetrable smog."
—*Chicago Tribune*

"Humorous . . . Wang is at her best when describing the characters who inhabit Beijing's periphery."
—*The New York Times Book Review*

"A rebellious daughter who scandalized her immigrant-Chinese family near Washington, DC, by moving to Beijing after college, Wang lends punky, snarky humor to her improbable tale of accommodating to the traditional ways of the home-country relatives whom she moves in with, while also finding her way into the local filmmaking avant-garde and shooting a documentary about a fast-fading art form—Peking opera."
—*Elle*

"In her drifter memoir of leaving home in order to find it, Chinese American author Val Wang struggles between head and heart as she tries to make a living— and a life—in Beijing, burdened by the expectations of her forebears yet buoyed by the spirit of youth. In the process, she shows us a China full of contradictions: at once glamorous and grungy, ancient and modern, ambitious and loafing."
—*Mother Jones*

"[*Beijing Bastard*] weaves a strange patchwork of longing familiar to anyone who has ever had a dream but was too afraid to seize it. . . . By fleeing to China, Wang desired to prove herself. But it's in losing her dreams and recrafting them at the end that she discovers what five years in China had done to her."
—*The Washington Post*

"A coming-of-age story that combines observations of Beijing with the culture clashes of West and East, Wang's memoir gives readers insight into the city's artistic subcultures, while exploring her own Chinese roots."
—*The Asian Review of Books*

"Damn, that Val Wang can write real good. I couldn't get enough of her *Beijing Bastard*. This is the kinda book that makes you want to pack an extra lung and move to China."
—Gary Shteyngart

Beijing Bastard

INTO THE WILDS
OF A CHANGING CHINA

Val Wang

AVERY

an imprint of Penguin Random House

New York

An imprint of Penguin Random House LLC
375 Hudson Street
New York, New York 10014

First trade paperback edition 2015
Copyright © 2014 by Valerie Wang

Most Avery books are available at special quantity discounts for bulk purchase for sales promotions, premiums, fund-raising, and educational needs. Special books or book excerpts also can be created to fit specific needs. For details, write SpecialMarkets@penguinrandomhouse.com.

ISBN 978-1-592-40942-6 (paperback)

Printed in the United States of America
10   9   8   7   6   5   4   3   2   1

Designed by Spring Hoteling

For my family

Contents

Part Six

You take delight not in a city's seven or seventy wonders
but in the answers it gives to a question of yours.

—*Italo Calvino*, Invisible Cities

Part One

Chapter One

I H_T_ CH_N_S_ SCH__L

On the very first page of a book about Christopher Columbus that my dad is reading to me, there is a word I don't know. I am squeezed next to him in the creaky maroon recliner where he does all his reading. Every new word opens up new worlds to me. This one has a long, slow sound to it and looks so different than it sounds.

"What is a *journey*?" I ask. He looks surprised and pauses before answering.

"A *journey* is a long trip," he says.

"A long trip!" What a disappointment. But as we read further into the book, I see what he means. A trip is what happens when I go with my mom to the store, or when we visit my grandparents in Virginia, five hours away. But a journey is when you sail into uncharted waters searching for something you've seen with only your innermost eye. You cross perilous seas, lose half your crew to scurvy, and discover a place that will later be called America.

I'm not sure why this memory etched itself so deeply into my mind. Maybe I was starting to realize that my parents had made a journey like that years before. Maybe my dad had even told me that he too had come to America on a boat.

My parents had both been born in China in the early 1940s and just before the Communist takeover in 1949 had both fled with their families to Southeast Asia. Before the age of eighteen, they had immigrated separately to New York, where they met and married. They moved to Washington, D.C., in the late 1960s, and then months before my older brother was born in 1973, they moved to a beige colonial with brown shutters on a cul-de-sac in the D.C. suburbs, where I grew up and where they still live today. Throughout my childhood in the 1980s, as China opened up to the world, my parents promised we would visit the motherland when I turned thirteen.

They bought the suburban house and quarter-acre lot when it was no more than an empty field; the area had been farmland just years before. Our house had no past, only a future, and perhaps that's how they wished to see their lives too. *You can be anything you want to be in life*, my mom always told us.

When asked in second grade to draw a picture of what I wanted to be when I grew up, I drew myself sitting by a sunny window, my fingers on the keys of a typewriter.

Shortly after moving into their new house, my parents planted twenty-nine white pine trees around the perimeter of the bare yard to separate the house from the identical houses around it, the saplings so tiny that my then-tiny brother accidentally trampled one to death, so the story goes. For years my parents had lived in small homes filled with too many people, and planting the pine trees was a grandiose gesture marking out the kingdom where they hoped to live happily ever after. Over the next twenty or so years, the pine trees grew taller than the house, shielding our yard from the sun and the neighbors. "Good fences make good neighbors," declared my dad once. We were each proud in our own way of the dark line of trees. I liked the feeling they gave me that I was growing up in a forest.

The suburbs allowed my parents to create for the first time an orderly world that they had total control over. The rhythms of our yard ran like clockwork. The forsythias were the first to bloom in the spring, then the three dogwood trees in the front and the petite red maple tree in the back. Summer brought perfect, perfumed roses, and sugar snap peas and tomatoes from the vegetable garden, and many empty hours for me to spend alone under the sheltering cave of the forsythia bushes, a space too small for adults. A big chive patch grew all year round. Cardinals and blue jays came regularly to the pine trees. While other families around us hired gardeners and landscapers, my parents tended the yard by themselves. My dad trimmed the hedges and aerated the lawn with a machine that made the rounds among the Chinese families in our area. My mom mowed and watered the lawn and put herself in charge of patrolling its borders. When rabbits began ravaging her vegetable garden, she chased down a marauding baby bunny and trapped it under a pail, oblivious to its mother's screams, and let it go by a nearby creek. ("Who should be eating the crunchy snow peas—the rabbit's baby or my baby?" she asked.) Hornets stung my allergic dad, and so she swaddled herself head to toe in protective outerwear, ripped their nest from its moorings, and threw it out with the evening's trash. Once when mowing the lawn, she spotted a snake in the grass. My brother and I ran over to see, and he, with a vast storehouse of knowledge gleaned from the *World Book,* declared it to be a common, harmless garter snake. "Oh, a garden snake," she said, and ran it over with the lawnmower. It was not wise to cross my mother.

My mom peppered my childhood with stories of her own childhood so fantastical and vivid I felt as if I'd experienced them firsthand. She remembered only snapshots from her early childhood in China: the frightening smell from her grandfather's long opium pipe, the grand car that chauffeured her to kindergarten, the huge house built with money from the jade and timber trades. When she was four, in 1949, a cargo truck smuggled her and her family out of China in the middle of the night; she remembers struggling to keep her younger siblings quiet in the back. They carried nothing of value but the jade jewelry sewn into her mother's belt. Her parents, having never worked a day in their lives, ran a teahouse called Airplane in Shwebo, Burma, as they raised seven children in a two-room house. Burma seemed even wilder than China: Poisonous snakes slithered free in the streets, green mangoes grew in her family's backyard and were eaten sour and sprinkled with salt, an annual water-splashing festival took over the streets of the city.

For high school, my mom went to a Chinese boarding school an overnight train ride away in Rangoon. When she was a senior, a mysterious man called her, saying he was a friend of her uncle's in America and asking her to meet him at a hotel, a nice hotel. Her uncle had left to study in America in the 1930s before she was born and when war broke out in China, his father had told him not to return. He had lost contact with his family in China and had heard only that they had fled to Burma, so when he found out his friend was going to Rangoon on business, he asked him to track them down. The man gave my mom her uncle's address in New York as well as a gift from him, a small Gruen watch. She wrote him a letter, and several months later she flew to New York alone to live with his family. On cold winter mornings, while waiting for the city bus to take her to Queens College, she would buy a single bagel from the shop by the bus stop and hold it in her hands to warm them. Her parents and six younger siblings didn't immigrate to the States until a decade later.

Her stories opened up amazing, faraway worlds that seemed a part of mine, even if they couldn't have been more distant.

Many other Chinese immigrants had also moved to the D.C. area, and it allowed my parents to administer to my brother and me a nearly lethal dose of "Chinese" culture. As regular as church, we attended Chinese School every Sunday, from the first week of kindergarten to the last of high school, learning Mandarin Chinese. Potomac Chinese School was held in the rented classrooms of Herbert Hoover Junior High School, with my mom and other parents working as teachers doling out homework, tests, and report cards and ranking us as they had been ranked growing up.

On one test, I wrote I H_T_ CH_N_S_ SCH_ _L, *Wheel of Fortune*–style, and the teacher filled in the missing vowels.

I also performed in a Chinese dancing troupe whose signature piece, performed at the Kennedy Center and the National Theatre as well as at a random crab house off the interstate, was a lyrical evocation of tea harvesting, in which we plucked invisible tea leaves off of imaginary vines and delicately placed them into real straw baskets, in between sequences of trotting in a line, pausing, snapping open and closed sequined pink silk fans, and then trotting again. When our bookings fell in direct proportion to the waning of our cuteness, I immediately switched to karate, which my brother was already learning, and eight years and eleven broken boards later, I was a black belt. Of course I took piano lessons too, de rigueur for a proper suburban Chinese-American upbringing, and took tennis lessons because my parents had heard that the tennis court was where all the real deals got made in America.

Growing up, we spent a lot of time with my dad's extended family, a rigidly hierarchical Confucian family headed by Yeye, my grandfather. He was a classic patriarch—arrogant, overbearing, awe-inspiring, never attired in less than a three-piece suit and hat. When I saw Ayatollah Khomeini on TV thundering angrily at masses of people, I mistook him for Yeye, just doing his day job as a history professor. Yeye made no secret of the fact that he liked my brother more because he would carry on the family name. (My mom, on the other hand, made a point of treating us equally.) My brother, as the Number One Son of the Number One Son, bore a heavy burden to live up to the values exemplified by Yeye: hard work, integrity, filial obligation. I, as the youngest of the clan, felt pulled in two directions: Of course I wanted to measure up but I also wanted to poke fun at their pious values and disrupt their precious order. Youngest siblings are natural contrarians; subverting the rules of the family is one of the few ways we can wield power.

Yeye would always demand I answer the same question: "Are you Chinese or American?" I thought it a silly choice, but because I knew he wanted me to say Chinese, I always said American.

China seemed impossibly distant. Yeye had been born in Hunan, like Chairman Mao, but instead of becoming a Communist became an ardent Nationalist. He had studied his way out of the provinces, first to a top university in Beijing, then abroad in the 1920s, earning a doctorate in comparative government from Columbia University. He returned to China in the 1930s to help build the new nation. Once when visiting Shanghai, he was invited to dinner by a friend and his wife, who brought along her younger sister to accompany him. Smitten, he invited the three of them out for dinner again the next night. After the young woman returned home to Beijing, he followed a few days later to ask her father for her hand in marriage. They married, bore three children, and, after moving around the country with the Nationalists, returned to Beijing and bought a courtyard house in 1946. Then just before the Communists took over in 1949, the family fled, first to Hong Kong briefly, then Jakarta, Indonesia, for almost a decade, where Yeye edited *The Free Press,* a Chinese newspaper. In the late 1950s, he moved the family to the States, leaving them on the Upper West Side of New York while he taught at universities around the country. Nainai took the English name Lily. Her older sister, who went by Mabel, made it to the States via Macau and also ended up on the Upper West Side, several blocks away. She too had left behind a courtyard house in Beijing.

Yeye eventually found a position in the history department of Hampton University. Every Easter and summer vacation, we went to visit them in their little green bungalow in Hampton. Nainai always had a box of fresh brownies ready, crisp on the top, tender inside. For Christmas, they came to our house, and as Nainai lay on the guestroom bed reading the Chinese newspaper, I would climb in with her and point out all the familiar characters that jumped out at me from the gray blur of stories. She would sing me Chinese songs in an exaggerated, old-timey voice that made me laugh. But she also had a sternness that intimidated me. When I was six and out with her alone, I was too scared to ask to go to the bathroom and ended up soaking the faux sheepskin lining of my boots.

Yeye had constant conflicts with my parents about what language to speak to us at home. He lectured us about using "ear training" to learn Chinese, while my parents spoke English to us out of fear that otherwise we would fall behind in school. They spoke mostly Chinese with each other. I am embarrassed to say I mocked Yeye's accent, parroting his "eaah training."

Though my family had succeeded in making a life in the States, I always wondered about China. Poems and myths I read in Chinese School implanted in a secret compartment of my mind hazy images: a boat on a lake at dusk . . . a festival . . . I was there, lighting paper lanterns and setting them afloat on the lake . . . ghosts of drowned women rising from the water . . . My family also watched National Geographic specials about China together; I was haunted by an image of a live monkey's head held in a vise, cracked open like a coconut and its brains scooped out and eaten fresh as a roadside snack. The romantic and the ghoulish mixed into a potent brew in my mind and I was eager to see this place in person. I imagined that it would be like visiting a large museum of ancient civilization that would cleanly elucidate some deep truths about my family. I was thirteen in the summer of 1989; after the Tiananmen Square Massacre, my parents never spoke again about visiting China.

It was during my teenage years that my relationship with my parents fell apart. I found the hermetically sealed environment of our suburban home suffocating, my go-go Chinese-American lifestyle of nonstop studying unbearable, my parents ceaselessly dictatorial. The community I'd grown up in was stifling—everyone knew whose children went to Harvard and whose got pregnant, whose families were getting ahead in America and whose were falling behind. My successes or failures were theirs as well, and nothing was ever enough for them. It turned out that we could be anything we wanted to be in life—as long as it was a doctor or a lawyer. My older brother followed all the rules; he got into an Ivy League college and would go on to be a lawyer, support Republican tax cuts, and never date. For a while I copied him exactly. I earned my black belt, attended a math and science magnet school, became the editor of my high school newspaper. Though I mimed the right actions, my heart wasn't in it. All I knew was the simple urge to do the opposite of what I was supposed to do: date white boys, talk nonstop on the phone, agitate for a driver's license. I idolized Georgia O'Keeffe and had a crush on Andre Agassi and imagined myself their lovechild: an ascetic, passionate being trying to break free from the repression of the East Coast and a world where deals were made on the tennis court.

At around this time, Yeye and Nainai left Virginia and moved into an apartment in a retirement community not far from us and they added to the chorus of disapproval; in fact, Yeye must have been its original source, as my parents' successes and failures ultimately reflected back on him. When I was present in the room, they criticized me in the third person. It was their job to talk and mine to listen. Nainai stayed in Yeye's shadow for the most part and bore the brunt of his increasing irascibility. I remember being confused when he called her a *fantong,* or a rice bucket, until my mom told me it also meant "imbecile." But Nainai never became meek. She had been born into a wealthy, educated family in Beijing and to show for it carried herself with a haughtiness I later associated with native New Yorkers. The gentle and humorous Nainai of my childhood faded away and in her place was an imperious matriarch full of dissatisfactions she could communicate with a single look.

When I dated a boy who resembled in my mom's eyes a Hispanic drug dealer and whose radical leftist parents were getting a divorce because their open marriage was falling apart, my mom routinely hung up on him when he called our house, riffled through my journals seeking dirt, and once delivered a succinct four-word safe-sex talk to me: *Don't ruin your life.* My parents sensed me going my own way and instead of

{ 11 }

loosening their grasp, they tightened it. The "drug dealer" had actually
been a straight-A student who eventually went to Harvard, though my
mom had accurately sniffed out his beliefs in wanton drug use, free love,
and Marxism. After my parents caught me alone at his house, something
snapped in our relationship. Being Chinese was obviously the root of my
problems, and so I began to hate all things Chinese, or what I imagined
to be Chinese.

I went off to a liberal arts college, where I became a leftist, a feminist,
and a vegetarian; shaved my head; and veered off the doctor/lawyer tra-
jectory into English and Women's Studies. My parents insisted I go to the
number-one-ranked liberal arts college, instead of to my first choice,
Oberlin (ranked twenty, down from fourteen), which my dad likened to
"marrying an alcoholic and going on a honeymoon on a sinking ship."
While I was away at college, he frequently sent me photocopies of Ann
Landers columns that he found relevant to my life. One letter I particularly remember came from a dad who wrote in wondering how to deal
with his daughter whom he characterized as "very smart but with no
common sense." "No common sense" my dad had highlighted in yellow
and underlined twice in red. I too was an avid Ann Landers reader and
my personal favorite column came from a young Asian-American woman
who wrote in wondering how to deal with her parents who kept her under
virtual house arrest. The letter had been signed, "Oppressed, Repressed
and Depressed." I clipped it out and taped it into my journal. I don't remember what advice Ann Landers gave either of them, probably to seek
counseling. But that wasn't our way, to say our problems out loud to a
total stranger.

In short, the peace my parents had found in the suburbs was not
mine to inherit. I didn't feel as though I belonged there, or anywhere yet,
and I itched to travel to exotic places far away to look for what was missing in my life.

So I went to Sweden. I went in my junior year of college, taking a
break from the manicured New Englandness of Williams College, but to

my dismay found it was even cleaner, colder, darker, and more orderly than the places I'd come from. The alienation I felt from my family seemed to extend to the rest of humanity and I spent most of my time watching films alone. One night I went to see a film purely because I had deciphered in its description the words *kinesisk rockstjärna*—Chinese rock star. There wasn't much to *Beijing Bastards*. You could take a character from column A, put him or her in a setting from column B, and make him or her do something from column C, and you'd pretty much have it.

A	B	C
hooligans	*concrete apartments*	*drinking*
rock star Cui Jian	*rock concerts*	*fucking*
knocked-up girls	*train tracks*	*cursing*

But the film opened an escape hatch into a world mirror opposite of the version of China I had grown up with, where we were all nerdy, overachieving droids with no errant desires of our own who lived out the script as it had been handed to us, marching through the Ivy Leagues into respectable professional careers.

I had rarely put any thought into what contemporary China was like, and when I did, it took a huge mental leap to imagine the farmers and petty bureaucrats of my supposed motherland—even my own relatives seemed impossibly foreign. But to my surprise, I recognized myself in those characters on-screen and, through them, the filmmaker who had created them. I was young and alienated too, also drifting without narrative, and like the filmmaker, I just wanted to find a way to get the moment down on paper—by writing, by filming, by any means necessary.

Back in the States, I stumbled across an article about the "Sixth Generation" of filmmakers in China who shot gritty underground films in Beijing, including the director of *Beijing Bastards*, Zhang Yuan. The filmmakers had even written a manifesto that declared their aim: "To present a more truthful and more expansive document on the life of the Chinese people." After making *Beijing Bastards,* Zhang Yuan was labeled a disseminator of "spiritual pollution" and the government banned him from making feature films. To avoid censorship, the Sixth Generation directors all made films without official permission, funded mostly by Europeans and screened only outside of China, mostly in Europe.

These filmmakers became my heroes. I wanted to meet them. I wanted to make films like them. I liked the way that having a camera in my hand gave me an excuse to poke into people's lives and go where I wasn't sure I was welcome. Everyone I knew in New York was starting to shoot their own documentaries with these affordable new digital video cameras.

When Nainai's older sister offered up her apartment in New York to her relatives the summer before my senior year, I eagerly took her offer. It was a rent-controlled two-bedroom apartment on the Upper West Side where Great-Aunt Mabel had raised her family after they immigrated to the States more than forty years before. The lease was in the name of a Chinese man long dead; the rent was two hundred and seventy-three dollars a month plus the cost of an anonymous cashier's check. She was moving to Seattle to be near her son Johnny. I planned to live there that summer while interning at a publishing house and then move back after graduating, but without notice she "sold" the apartment to a perfect stranger for a thousand dollars. Having robbed me of my ancestral rent-controlled birthright, Great-Aunt Mabel then had me live with this person, her false heir—a horsy Chinese-American woman with an ugly boyfriend and a bad temper—for the entire summer and instructed us to tell anyone who asked that we were her granddaughters.

After graduating, moving back to New York was the logical next step, but I balked. Without my rent-controlled apartment, the future seemed like a terrifying void of boring office jobs and unfulfilled dreams. Even finding overpriced housing was deathly cutthroat. I'd heard a story of a friend of a friend who'd had to resort to desperate measures: She had an inside person working at *The Village Voice* who would call her before the paper went to press and whisper to her the details of apartments for rent, and I didn't know anyone at *The Village Voice*. Plus, I'd lived in New York long enough to know that the city was just like a guy I was dating there: shiny and mesmeric as mercury and just as elusive. Slipping away right as I reached for it. I longed to be somewhere I could touch and be touched by.

Around this time I read *Things,* a novel by Georges Perec about a young couple that decamps from their blissful life in Paris and moves to Sfax, an obscure seaside city in Tunisia because—as I carefully copied into my journal—because Paris had become "a shrunken universe, a world running out of steam, opening onto nothing." It was exactly how I saw life in New York unfolding if I moved there. Perec went on: "Puns, boozing, walks in the woods, dinner parties, endless discussions about films, plans, gossip had long stood in for adventure, history and truth."

Adventure, history, and truth. I liked the sound of that.

Suddenly, I knew beyond a doubt what I was meant to do: Go to Beijing, find the filmmakers, and make a documentary about them. I wanted to kick my nerdy upbringing to the curb and chase that vision of myself that had flitted across the screen in *Beijing Bastards.* Imagine the street cred I'd have if it worked out! This wasn't a plan that anyone with any common sense would have hatched. Luckily, I had none.

When my parents heard the news that I was moving to the country they'd fled almost fifty years before, they were less than happy. Things may be different today, but in the late 1990s no one in their right mind was moving to China.

"How about graduate school in English, Val?" asked my mom. "A job in publishing in New York? You had that summer internship."

"It was great because it helped me figure out that I didn't want to work in publishing in New York."

"What is your Five-Year Plan?" my dad demanded, as if I ran my life like a socialist dictatorship.

"Five years?" I said. "I can barely think about the next five minutes!"

"Why go to China? Do you know how dirty the bathrooms are there?"

"I thought you would be happy. You made me learn Chinese growing up and whatnot."

"You were pampered growing up," said my mom. "You'll see when you get there."

"You'll hate it there," my dad assured me.

Before I left, each took me aside for a private talk.

"Val, I want you to watch out for men who will want to marry you for a green card."

"Oh, Mom," I said after I'd stopped laughing. "I don't even like Chinese guys."

Her expression shifted. "Val, don't be so close-minded. If you find a nice one who you think can make it in America, don't say no just because he's Chinese. Keep an open mind."

My dad warned me about corruption. "China is a place governed by relationships, not by the law. People will do favors for you and expect you to do favors in return," he said. "Your Yeye had hated that about China and you have no experience dealing with it."

I nodded.

"Plus, the customer service there is terrible," he said. "Terrible."

To them, me moving to China was a step backward that would un-ravel all the work they'd put into my life. They had achieved the Chinese-American dream: steady job, house in the suburbs, children through good colleges. I was supposed to repeat the pattern. I didn't tell my parents that my dream was to make a documentary, to be an artist.

My dad also told me that Nainai still owned a courtyard house in Beijing. He had lived in it for two years of his childhood and all he re-membered was that it was located on a wedge of land between two roads. He didn't know much more than that.

As for Yeye, he found out on his deathbed that I was going to China; I never knew what he thought about it. I know only that he believed he could never go back to China because as soon as he stepped off the plane he would be captured and executed, even though we told him that anyone who might kill him was probably already dead.

The only member of my family who wholeheartedly approved of my decision was Nainai. "Life is slower in China. People don't rush around like they do in America," she said in a tender voice I wasn't accustomed to hearing. "You'll love it there."

Chapter Two

Fresh Tensions in U.S.–China Relations

I awoke with a start.

"*Zao,*" said Bobo. Good morning. I was lying in bed, earplugs in my ears, airline eyeshade over my eyes, but they were no match for the big color TV two feet behind my head, which Bobo had just turned on, loud. Bobo is Nainai's eldest brother's eldest son and was the relative in Beijing with whom she kept in closest contact. When I had moved to Beijing the week before, Bobo had graciously allowed me to stay with his family until I found my own apartment. He, his wife, their son Xiao Peng, and their daughter-in-law Xiao Lu lived in half of a small courtyard house in the old city. I slept on a folding cot in the living room.

"*Zao,*" I croaked out. I pulled off my eyeshade and looked at my watch. Six o'clock. *Zao* means both "good morning" and "early." *Early. Way too early for the TV to be on that loud.* I lay still. My cot was wedged between the TV and a long couch that was covered in a sheet as if its owners were away on a long trip. The room had high ceilings, and across from the couch were a wide window and a tall door trimmed in lime green, which opened onto a walkway that opened onto a courtyard. Morning light straggled in and the air was heavy with coal soot. Bobo and Bomu were dressed and ready to go, except that they didn't ever go anywhere. They were both retired teachers in their sixties and seemed to spend most of their time inside this dim, cluttered room watching TV, as if making up for a whole lifetime lived without it. Bobo is my dad's cousin, and his turning on the TV briefly reminded me of my dad's long-ago habit of waking me on Saturday mornings by flashing my bedroom light and clapping crisply, but Bobo seemed even sterner and more unyielding than my dad, with no apparent soft spot in his heart for me. Bomu was equally formidable. Slim and beautiful, she had big, sad, quietly judgmental eyes and she rarely smiled.

On the surface, we were excruciatingly polite to one another. Though I had always been the rebellious one in the family, with a flick of the switch into Chinese I had been instantly transformed into an obedient daughter who said whatever she sensed the other person wanted to hear. I could tell that my relatives were thinking much more than they were saying too, and the air was close with unspoken feelings.

"Not going to work today?" Bobo asked. I should have sprung lightly out of bed, but this morning I had had enough of the role-playing. I had come to China to get farther away from my family, not closer, and had somehow ended up living with these humorless old people who were proving to be a concentrated version of all the irksome traits of my parents. Plus, the house's indoor plumbing was limited to a cold tap, so I hadn't showered in days and the itch of my uncleanliness made me cranky. *Let them see the real me,* I thought.

I paused dramatically and said in my most acidic tone, "*Of course* I'm going," before burying my face in the pillow. I willed the darkness to take me away—preferably to a soot-free apartment with a flush toilet, a hot shower, and no relatives. We had exchanged only a few choice words, but they were enough to uncork the bottle of gripes that we had all been filling for the days I'd been living with them. And who knew what tiffs had been simmering between them and my relatives in America for years?

In the ringing silence, I could hear Bobo's thoughts loud and clear: *Disrespectful, ungrateful, spoiled American.* I shot back with my own: *Domineering Confucian overlords.*

I was tired of sleeping on other people's couches. I'd been doing it for two months already as I waited in New York for the sacred Z Visa that would allow me to work in Beijing. First on the couch (and in the bed) of my ex(ish)-boyfriend in Park Slope, who was two years older than I and whom I was madly in love with and who I was slowly realizing did not love me in return (was congenitally incapable of love, he claimed, wires got crossed somewhere).

When he kicked me out, I moved to the raw Williamsburg loft of three of my male college friends, one of whom was another ex. He was training to be a French chef, another was a sushi chef, and the third was broke and living off his parents while he procrastinated about making any decisions about his life. I too ran out of money but, refusing to ask my parents for any, went to a temp agency and ended up as a temp at the temp agency. My friends rented a sunny corner of the loft to a male painter who produced larger-than-life-size canvases of pinkish nudes with huge cocks. I slept on a soggy mattress positioned between the huge, looming cocks and a gigantic fan with exposed blades. It was summer and the loft had been full of clusters of coeds who inexplicably found my friends sophisticated and worth sleeping with. I wondered if they did it just so they could hang around the loft, which had great views of Manhattan. It was hard to tell. Everyone began sleeping with everyone else's ex-girlfriend (except for me), and as the loft had no walls, only translucent partitions, the situation quickly deteriorated. I couldn't wait to leave and have a room of my own far, far away.

Now I was here. After a few minutes of silent standoff with Bobo, I swung my legs over the cot and sat up. I put on my jacket and my shoes and discreetly unrolled a few squares of the plump roll of white toilet paper I had secreted in my bag. I refused to use their toilet paper, which had roughly the look and feel of tree bark and was constantly migrating around the house, first under a pair of glasses on the bookshelf, then on the dining table.

I passed through the walkway, lined with eight or nine cages each filled with a small, twittering bird, and went outside into the courtyard. Soft morning sunlight lit up the crooked gray paving stones and green plants of the small space, which was surrounded on four sides by the weathered wood of the house, painted a faded maroon. The yard was crowded with handmade brick planters and potted plants, cylindrical coal briquettes stacked underneath the windows, sturdy bikes covered by worn plastic tarps, and laundry lines hung with giant bloomers billowing gently in the morning breeze. Black soot dusted everything. I drew a deep breath of crisp fall air and my bad mood dissipated. I couldn't wait to move out, but I would miss this charming, ramshackle oasis in the middle of the city.

Then the wind shifted and I caught a whiff of the slight, sweet miasma from the outhouse at the center of the courtyard. I held my breath and plunged into the small brick hut that contained only a porcelain squatter, a spigot, and a dirty little red bucket. When I had first gotten to Beijing, Bomu had been worried that the soft American cousin wouldn't be able to handle the outhouse and had apologized profusely for the inconvenience. Ha! I was tough. I could handle anything. But my soft American backside was another matter, hence the secret roll of TP.

As I walked back inside, I thought back to my first jet-lagged night in Beijing, when I had fumbled my way out to the courtyard in the middle of the night to escape the stuffy, sleepless house. The cool air on my cheeks had come as a relief. I had sat on the edge of a brick planter filled with bamboo, put on my headphones, and pressed play on my Walkman; single guitar notes dropped like cooling lozenges into my ears as Elliott Smith's mournful voice spun my insides into taffy.

There's nothing here that you'll miss
I can guarantee you this is a cloud of smoke

I had looked up, above the tiled roofline, above the skeletons of trees, up to the single tall apartment building looming in the darkness, its lights all extinguished. I had felt like the only one awake on this side of the world. I had looked up to the expanse of dark, starless sky opening above my head and breathed in the entirety of the heavens.

Trying to occupy space
What a fucking joke
What a fucking joke

After my early-morning blowout with Bobo, I took the subway to work. I worked as an editor for *City Edition,* a new English-language magazine. At the end of college, I had written a grant to make the documentary about the filmmakers, and when it didn't come through, I'd decided to move to China anyhow. I'd found a job teaching English for a year in Tianjin, a city not far from Beijing, and this year had made the leap to the big city.

The *City Edition* office was located down a maze of unnamed streets that seemed to have been tossed down to earth as haphazardly as pick-up sticks. I walked past a hotpot restaurant, past an enormous billowing smokestack, and through a black metal gate bedizened with five or six bronze plaques proclaiming the very long names of the various state agencies housed within, the largest of which was the enigmatic "Office of Defense Conversion." Inside the gate was our six-story building, covered entirely in white tile like the inside of a bathroom. There was no elevator, and so of course we were on the top floor. In the hallway on the way to the office was the public squatter toilet.

The routine of putting out a magazine was relentless. Every two weeks we produced a magazine of twenty-eight pages. Twenty thousand copies of it were distributed for free at bars and hotels around town. I was the only editorial staff aside from my American boss Sue, who was often preoccupied with writing reports on obscure topics like soybean futures to finance the magazine. My job was to compile and design the twelve-page Entertainment Guide, write restaurant and art reviews, compile shopping guides, handle freelancers, copyedit stories, and if all that got done, write my own articles. Every issue, I went down a list and called every art gallery, aquarium, bar, cinema, club, shooting range, teahouse, and theater in town to see if they had events. The graphic designers laid out the magazine on computers that kept crashing because of the pirated software. After we checked the proofs of the magazine, it was sent to the printers, and the deliverymen distributed the magazine around town via tricycle. Once the paper was out, we did it all over again.

Like many start-ups, the magazine lacked basic organization. While I was in the States waiting for my visa, Sue had hired Leo to fill in for me. Leo was a recent engineering grad from Africa, and even though I'd arrived to take over, he still hung around the office every day, his awkwardness quickly turning to desperation. Sue told me that there'd been a coup in his home country, and because his father had been high up in the government, he couldn't go home. She didn't have the heart to tell him that his job was over and that she couldn't sponsor his visa.

Most of the staff was women, from the Americans heading the departments down to the squadron of petite and bilingual Chinese staff, mostly saleswomen in pencil skirts and tiny pumps. The women had all chosen English names—Amy, Jean, June, Shannon, Shirley, Susan. There was also our intern Jade, a Chinese-American woman around my age who had come to Beijing to study Chinese at Capital Normal University. Now her course was ending and she needed to find a job, preferably in photography. Though I was the one on staff, Jade was the more confident and put-together one. Her hair was long and straight, her perfectly ovoid face as milky smooth as a porcelain doll's, and her figure voluptuous. She made me see myself clearly: how sensible my shoes and clothes were, how short and nest-like my hair, how un-made-up my face. We gravitated toward each other, despite (or perhaps because of) our differences.

Sue had started the magazine with a buff Chinese man in his

midthirties who had chosen for himself the English name Max. I wasn't sure what he did at the magazine save for storm in and out of the office looking terribly busy, issuing the odd edict, and cutting a swath of testosterone through our nest of estrogen. He was also the one who dealt with the censors. Since *City Edition* was registered as a Chinese newspaper, we were subject to strict but amorphous regulations; one misstep could shut down the paper. The only other men in the office were a rotating squadron of petite and monosyllabic deliverymen and the American web designer Scott, chunky with the goatee, ponytail, and labyrinthine imagination of a role-player. He spent most of his time out on the balcony smoking and once casually asked me if I wanted to write about human smuggling, as he knew someone at the Canadian embassy who was smuggling people through Canada. At night a local gym teacher, Lao Li, Frankensteinian in build, slept on a little couch in our advertising room. It wasn't clear why we needed a night watchman, who exactly was going to be breaking into our offices or why.

Sue was bilingual, frighteningly smart, and alarmingly tactless. She had moved to Beijing in her twenties like me, gotten married to a Chinese man almost twenty years her senior, moved back to D.C., and then back to Beijing in her thirties to run the US-China Business Council, which she had recently quit to start the magazine. She was turning forty soon. Today she wore a gray skirt suit and her stern Presbyterian face was adorned by a rare slash of lipstick, which served to make her more intimidating, not less. But when I told her about the living conditions at my relatives' house, she softened.

"I have no idea where, or even if, they shower," I said. "The other day my uncle put a pan full of water on the dining room table and washed his hair right there. I need to move out soon."

"Max might be able to help you. He's one of those Chinese people who doesn't have a cent to his name but has access to apartments all over the city."

I had no idea that such people existed. But I had noticed strange things about money here. In a supposedly Communist country where many were paid about ten dollars a month, the roads were filled with Mercedes-Benzes and the restaurants were bursting with fat men. Was this what my dad was talking about when he referred to corruption?

After work, I was supposed to go straight home because Bobo and Bomu didn't think it was safe for a young woman to be out alone in the city at night. I got on the subway at the northeast corner of the city and took a seat on an empty stretch of bench. The subway was eerily out of character for Beijing—the high ceilings and heavy stone of the stations made it as hushed as a mausoleum, and the cars were clean, efficient, and unpeopled, like a monorail at a theme park. The subway had only two lines, one that followed the old city wall and another just a straight line, so most people biked, cabbed, or took buses around the city.

At the next stop, an old woman got on, and instead of choosing the seat that was mathematically calculated to be the exact farthest away from me and everyone else as possible, as someone in New York would do, she sat right next to me, her leg touching mine. I recoiled as if her fist had punched through a glass wall separating us. Between the subway snugglers, chatty cabdrivers, and nosy relatives, the lack of privacy in China was both a lot to adjust to and all too familiar. I scooted over. After riding the loop line halfway around, I exited the subway and headed up a street lined with beeper shops for the short walk home.

The street was alive at this hour. Rush hour traffic in cheerful primary colors jammed the four-lane street: yellow breadbox vans, tiny red cabs, and navy-blue Volkswagens were all weaving madly, straddling two lanes, tailgating, lollygagging, rattling, and honking noisily. Hulking red-and-cream city buses wheezed slowly down the street and in their shadows darted lithe little turquoise-and-white minibuses that illegally plied the same routes, a ticket taker always hanging halfway out the door yelling the bus number and hustling people on and off the bus. In the bike lane filled with leisurely cyclists, a horde of androgynous teenagers in matching school tracksuits swooped through. As saccharine love songs blared from shop speakers, I jostled with grannies hocking loogies onto the sidewalk and paunchy men in thin pants clutching pleather man-purses and talking on big cellphones. I was instantly part of the mad flow without having to exchange a word or even a glance with anyone.

Today the city had opened itself to me, but with each step closer to home, I felt my family closing back in. After our altercation this morning, I knew the food on the dinner table would be laced with corrosive, gut-twisting guilt.

Just before turning the corner to the house, I saw a noodle shop and suddenly veered in. I took a table at the back, away from the big picture windows, and ordered a bowl of beef noodles. The beef was thinly sliced, the noodles jagged and yellow, and the broth salty and hot and swimming with scallions. I ate happily, savoring my privacy and the fact that no one in the world knew where I was right then. My only company were the two glassy-eyed waitresses next to me, listlessly watching a TV that hung in a corner; on it the two unsmiling anchors of the national news sat stiffly in their bouffant hairdos against a blue background. I watched people pass by the window in the distance. It was the first time I'd felt relaxed in days.

I thought back to the first time I'd met Bobo and Bomu, a year earlier, and how much had happened since then. Shortly after I'd moved to Tianjin, six of my relatives rented a van to come visit me and we went out for a big banquet lunch. I then proceeded to, as family legend has it, eat them all under the table while they looked on in shock that such a tiny woman could fit so much food in her stomach. A Chinese banquet host is required to load food onto a guest's plate, and while most know to leave a little bit on the plate, I thought the polite thing to do was finish everything, especially when it was so delicious, so they kept piling on more food, and I kept eating it all. My gluttony at this meal has passed into lore. I had already started falling in love with China before the lunch, but meeting them made me feel as though I truly had an anchor here. I began plotting my move to Beijing the next year.

The month after their visit, I took the three-hour train to Beijing and stayed with Bobo and Bomu in a large courtyard house, not the one they lived in now but a much bigger one down the street on Qianbaihu Hutong that they said was about to be demolished. Both houses were in Xidan, a quiet neighborhood of small hutongs, or alleyways, in the southwest corner of the old city a short walk from the Forbidden City.

Relatives came from all over the city to meet me. Some of them had evidently met me when they visited the States years ago. Bobo's sister I remembered, mostly because she had brought me a pair of dangly earrings. She told me she had lived in Great-Aunt Mabel's old apartment in New York for a year, the same apartment I lived in years later. Though she was a doctor in China, she had made a living in New York by wrapping dumplings for restaurants in Chinatown. She spoke no English, and when the phone in the apartment rang, she would pick it up and say her one English phrase, "You speak-a Chinese?" If the answer was no, she would hang up. My balding great-uncle with chipmunk cheeks I didn't remember. He pulled out a photo of us sitting together on a park bench somewhere in America. I examined it. That was him (same chipmunk cheeks, more hair, fewer liver spots) and that was me (cute, oddly self-possessed, legs too short to reach the ground), but the photo brought back no memories. I felt shocked, as if I had been leading a secret life with these strangers all these years and only now was my past coming to light.

In the center of the courtyard of the house stood an apple tree, taller than the house itself and loaded with fruit. From a bough of the tree hung a cage with two small yellow birds. Bobo brought out a rough-hewn wooden ladder and we all took turns climbing up and throwing the apples down to a bedsheet held below like a trapeze net. Standing in the spacious courtyard, I felt connected to the basic elements of life: Above was an open canopy of sky, below were solid gray stones, and on all four sides was the wooden house, dark and warped with age. Just being there gave me a thrill, like I was stepping right into one of Nainai's epic family dramas, the ones on videotape that she kept on constant rerun at home with the families fighting and scheming in their huge, pristine courtyard houses. This house was less than pristine, but to me it was beautiful, and when I told Bobo so, he looked pleased.

"My own small piece of heaven and earth," he said.

A traditional courtyard house, it had four wings: They lived in the tallest northern wing, cooked in the eastern, and let me stay in the entire western wing, Xiao Peng's old room. The southern wing was vacant and it was there that I took sponge baths with boiled water, just letting the bathwater soak into the concrete floor. I had to tie the door shut with a rag.

Xiao Peng and his wife, Xiao Lu, lived in a quarter of a small courtyard house ten minutes down the road, which they had to share with three other families.

After that first trip, I went back many times during the year I lived in Tianjin. Sometimes I would tell them I was coming to visit and cancel at the last minute, and they would call me a *xiao pianzi,* a little cheat.

Each successive time I visited them that year, more and more of their neighborhood had been demolished. They said the government was reclaiming the land to build an office building. People moved out of their houses and earthmovers came, their claws ripping through the quiet, old houses as if their walls were made of tissue paper. When I visited, Bobo and Bomu wouldn't let me stay out past ten o'clock at night because, they said, you never knew who could be lurking in the rubble of razed houses that surrounded their own.

But as the year went on, they still didn't move out and for some reason they wouldn't tell me why. Neither would they tell me where they would go when they did, only that they were debating between a courtyard house in the old city and an apartment in the suburbs. "No, we don't want to move," they said. "Because we're old people and old people like living in old houses." They had gone to see an apartment in a tower block on the outskirts of the city and Bomu had pronounced it "asymmetrical, lopsided, terrible, like a pigeon's cage." Bobo had said, "Too many stairs. Too few friends." They didn't seem to mind that the courtyard house didn't have a toilet or even an outhouse and that they had to use the public toilet out in the hutong.

I minded. The public toilet was a brick building surrounded by a moat of fecal odor so pungent it stopped me in my tracks at the door. I held my breath and forced myself into the dark chamber, where the smell kicked in the doors of my senses with a strong boot. The space was open and slats had been cut into a concrete floor. I squatted and added my contribution to the lot in the trench below. Once in the toilet I saw an old woman with sagging breasts wearing a T-shirt that read, I'M JUST HERE FOR THE BEER. The toilet *was* something of a party scene in the mornings, full of neighborhood grannies squatting and reading their newspapers at a leisurely pace, seemingly oblivious to being marinated in a foul miasma. As for me, I did my business as quickly as possible and fled before gagging or passing out. I always left with the sense that my delicate brain chemistry had been irrevocably altered.

Bomu apologized profusely for the inconvenience and dropped her voice to confide, "This house used to have a bathroom years ago."

"Why doesn't it now?"

"Long story."

I waited for her to tell it, but she didn't.

I visited one last time in the summer to look for a job, contacting Western newspapers as well as the two English-language magazines in town, *Beijing Scene* and *City Edition*. I gave the editors a story I'd written about a man in Tianjin who'd started a league for American-style football.

On that visit, Bobo and Bomu's house had been an island in a sea of deserted, half-demolished shells and piles of rubble. Bobo told me that they woke up one morning and found that someone had crawled over their wall at night and slept in the courtyard. It was during that last visit that I pried the truth out of them: The house didn't belong to them but to Great-Aunt Mabel, who now lived in Seattle. They had been living in and taking care of her house for almost fifty years and were stalling to give her lawyer son Johnny time to negotiate with the government for a new courtyard house. He could do so because Great-Aunt Mabel held an American passport.

When I moved to Beijing in the fall, I had expected to find Bobo and his family ensconced in Great-Aunt Mabel's new courtyard house with an entire wing set aside for me. Instead, they had moved to Xiao Peng's small courtyard house, somehow acquiring another quarter of it from one of the three families. No one had uttered a single word about what had happened to the old house.

Back in the restaurant, I finished the last of my noodles, paid, and left.

"Manzou," the waitress said automatically, as they all did when you left a restaurant. Take it easy.

Coming home, I wove around dark objects in the small courtyard. From the outside, the scene in the lit living room looked so peaceful: Bomu and Xiao Lu were clearing the dishes as Bobo sat in his easy chair watching the same news broadcast that had been on in the restaurant. Chillingly, it was the only show on TV. He looked older and more tired than my dad, as if life had been harder on him. After standing outside for a few minutes, I tiptoed in. My cousin Xiao Peng was nowhere to be seen. The room buzzed with tension.

"Where have you been?" Bobo demanded. His daughter-in-law Xiao Lu averted her eyes in embarrassment for me. A teacher of deaf children, she was quietly empathetic.

"I ate with people from work."

"You should have called."

"I know."

"You let two old people worry about you."

"Sorry."

"We told your Nainai we would take good care of you in Beijing," he said.

Taking care of me. I knew what that meant. Keeping me close to home for the opportunity to scrutinize and then mock me. My amusing behaviors supplied them with a constant stream of entertainment.

Did you see how much she ate at that first meal? We couldn't believe our eyes. Ha ha ha!

Did you see the big shoes with the hard toes in her room in Tianjin when we went to visit her there? We thought she was living with a boy. Ha ha ha!

Did you hear how much she paid for that coat? Ha ha ha!

The ties that bind, I thought. *And gag.*

Bobo narrowed his eyes, pursed his lips, and leaned back, and I knew a lecture was coming. His finger came up into the air. "And about this morning, you shouldn't be so irritable. My comment was just the kind of give-and-take that Chinese people engage in."

I felt frustrated. Being good made me dishonest but being honest made me insubordinate. It dawned on me: This was how family worked. These strangers, who would have otherwise elbowed me in the face to get on the bus ahead of me, instead picked me up at the airport, took me in, fed me, and gave me a cot to sleep on and a chamber pot to piss in at night. And in exchange, I had to behave. I apologized and sat down to watch TV with them. Bobo softened the blow of his lecture with a piece of flattery, saying he had recently told Nainai how quickly my Chinese was progressing.

The TV news gave way to one of the interminable soap operas they loved watching, this one featuring people in flowing clothing who swished slowly in and out of old houses and galloped around on horses and did pretty much what we do nowadays—feel anguished over betrayal and lost love, go on quests for obscure but valuable treasures, get angry and smash things. At least it wasn't one of the full-length, one-camera Peking Opera performances that Bobo got glued to for hours. Bobo then called Xiao Peng's cellphone and told him to come home immediately. I was gratified that someone else in the family was acting worse than I was.

A sooty white kitten tottered in from Xiao Peng's side of the house and I went over to pet it, happy to feel something warm, soft, and alive under my hand.

During a commercial break, I asked the question that had been on the tip of my tongue since returning to China. "Was the courtyard house at Qianbaihu demolished over the summer?"

Bobo and Bomu both looked up sharply. "Yes," he said. "Demolished."

"When?"

"About a month ago."

"It's just gone?"

"It's just gone." The sword had finally dropped. There was no sadness in the room, only a chill.

"That's sad."

"There's nothing to be done."

"So I guess Great-Aunt Mabel didn't get a new courtyard house, huh?"

"No, she did."

"She did? Where?"

"Near Dongsi."

"What's it like?"

"A beautiful, perfectly preserved house. Not like this house, falling apart and split among many families. You don't see many houses like that in Beijing anymore."

"And she didn't let you all live there?"

"No."

"Who lives there?"

"No one."

"Why?"

"No reason."

"Didn't you want to live there?"

Bobo didn't answer.

So many questions raced through my mind. Why didn't Great-Aunt Mabel let them live in the perfectly preserved courtyard house? Why did they live in only *half* of this house? Why did the old house no longer have a bathroom? Where was Nainai's old house? Why had Bobo's and Bomu's opinions of courtyard houses changed this year? Now it was *Old people don't have the energy for old houses. An apartment would be so warm, so convenient, no need to burn coal for heat, no coal dust everywhere.*

I glanced over at Bobo engrossed in the TV. He had such good posture and I wondered briefly if he was less than thrilled to be hosting his slouchy, moody, nosy American relative. I wished I could tell him that I sympathized with them more than they knew, having myself experienced Great-Aunt Mabel's slippery real estate tactics. I stopped asking questions.

Bobo and Bomu did not return the favor. I listed their odd queries in my journal. *Are we going to bother you with the TV on? Why do you have so much stuff? Do you want to sleep in the birdcage?*

Eventually we heard the outer door slam shut and saw Xiao Peng slink down the corridor to his quarter of the house. Bobo and Bomu sent waves of disapproval after him, combined with relief. I looked at my watch, my mom's old Gruen, which said it was just after nine o'clock. The watch that had linked her to America now linked my journey to hers. Bobo and Bomu finally shut off the TV and went to sleep.

A week after my altercation with Bobo, I came home to find him on the phone. When he hung up he told me he had just gotten off the phone with Great-Aunt Mabel in Seattle. Though she and Nainai had left China more than fifty years before, Bobo, ever the dutiful nephew, still kept in touch with them.

"She explained that your insubordinate behavior is normal for an American child and that American children naturally rebel against restrictions. She said the more restrictions you make, the more they rebel."

He looked befuddled by this logic.

"It's true!" I said. "Your rules are far too strict."

"Your Nainai will be very mad at us if something happens to you."

"I'll tell her it wasn't your fault. She knows what I'm like."

After the phone call they loosened their grip on me; I was permitted to come home late as long as I called so they could flip the small wooden flap on the inside of the front door of the courtyard that let the whole house know someone was coming home late and not to bolt the door from the inside.

Chapter Three

Like Extras Late for a Take

O n Saturday, Xiao Peng asked me if I wanted to ride bikes to Tiananmen Square. We'd been sitting around doing what Chinese families do so well together: absolutely nothing. He'd asked in an offhand way, as if half expecting me to say no. My ears perked up like a dog's at the jingle of a leash.

"I could," I said, trying to act nonchalant. His question surprised me. Xiao Peng and I had been watching each other since I moved in. He reminded me of a character from *Beijing Bastards*. As far as I could see, he didn't drink or swear or go to rock concerts, but there was something about him reminiscent of the hooligans in the film: the same untouchably bored air, the same monosyllabic responses dropped from the corner of his mouth, the same inability to find value in anything. Plus, though nobody in my family particularly looked like anyone else, he was the spitting image of my uncle who "did business" in Jakarta: wide face; porcine nose; skeptical, heavily lidded eyes. From what my parents said, Xiao Peng was starting to "do business" too, importing air conditioners or something, and even owned a car, a red Citroën. I instantly felt as if I knew him and sensed how hard he would be to impress. He played it cool; I followed suit. *Just because you're my cousin,* we each seemed to be saying, *doesn't mean I have to like you.*

I scrutinized the old framed family photos that leaned against the books in the bookshelf, searching the boy for clues to the man. Our dads had grown up together in Beijing but their fates had forked in 1949, and though Xiao Peng and I had ended up in different places, we were similar in certain ways. Xiao Peng was the baby of the family, like me, and was plopped front and center in the photos, looking slim with a wavy head of hair and a sweet face. He was now, as Bobo and Bomu did not hesitate to tell him, getting fat. His belly was pushing outward, his baby face ballooning, his eyes shrinking to beady dots. Plus how cool could you be if you were almost thirty and, though married, still lived with your parents who still called you "Little Peng" and still called your cellphone when you were out at night to tell you to come home?

His two older sisters had flown the coop for L.A. before I'd come to China. Bobo and Bomu spoke proudly of Sister Number One, who had gone boldly to America, helped Sister Number Two emigrate, and was on her way toward earning an accounting degree. At one point, they said, her visa had been about to expire, so she simply married an older Chinese man with a green card. "She's got a good head on her shoulders," Bomu said. I paged through a custom-made calendar she'd sent back: January was a group photo of the sisters with Great-Aunt Mabel, April was her posing windblown by the water somewhere (I noticed she had a good *and* beautiful head), and November was sad-looking singleton Sister Number Two dressed in autumnal colors sitting glumly with some ducks by a lake.

I wondered what Xiao Peng saw when he looked at me. Yet another American cousin, coming to teach English, learn Chinese, "find her roots," and then leave. There had been others in my family before me and I wanted to tell him that I was different. The whole point of moving far away from home was to leave my past behind and to do the things I somehow couldn't at home. Write. Make movies. Preferably a novel that would be an instant cult classic among the downtown cognoscenti and/or a gritty lo-fi documentary that would make me the darling of the indie film world. These were fragile, vaguely embarrassing dreams, never to be spoken aloud lest their spell be broken.

Xiao Peng biked swiftly through the hutongs and I wobbled along behind him. The traffic was chaotic: Bikes went the wrong way, swerved without notice, crossed in front of honking cars with inches to spare. Carts piled high with cabbages or pineapples careened by at full tilt. Nothing shielded me from the chaos around me. When I tested the brakes, they shuddered loudly but barely slowed the Flying Pigeon bicycle. Xiao Peng never hit the brakes and I scurried after him like a cat following a ball of yarn as it unraveled. If I lost him, the hutongs would collapse into short bits of string, all looking about the same, none leading anywhere.

Suddenly, we turned onto the Avenue of Eternal Peace. The avenue was as wide and flat as an airport runway and I felt ejected from my private world into the bright light of day. Xiao Peng and I rode side by side in the wide bike lane in a flotilla of other bikes, the air cool against our faces. Beijing was in the heart of its most beautiful season, autumn, when the city appears exactly as it does in my dreams: glowing with grainy golden light, crisp with the faint tang of coal soot in the air. The closer we got to the square, the more orderly the traffic became, as if we were entering the government's fantasy of how life in the country was supposed to run. Soldiers in olive uniforms stationed at intervals told us where to go and where not to.

Dusk was approaching and we arrived at the square just as it was emptying of people. Only a few lingered to pose and take pictures.

Tiananmen Square is one of the largest squares in the world and is flanked by immense buildings: the Great Hall of the People to the west, the Museum of the Chinese Revolution to the east, and Mao's mausoleum to the south. So much had happened here. I had seen the pictures. Mao waving from the rostrum of the Tiananmen Gate in 1949. Girls screaming and waving *Little Red Book*s during the Cultural Revolution. Student democracy protesters camping out in the square in 1989, dancing to music by China's first rock star, Cui Jian, in their shaggy, almost chic bowl cuts and huge glasses, never knowing what was coming to them. A place this big begged for grand, heroic, delusional gestures. Xiao Peng and I glided across the smooth surface and I felt a rush of pleasure. I was released from myself, reduced to a simple and happy character in a corny patriotic play. He told me it was illegal to ride bikes on the square. We were breaking the law together. I felt almost close to him.

We rode up to the flagpole at the north end of the square, where a crowd was pressing against the white railing that separated the square from the Avenue of Eternal Peace. Across the avenue was Tiananmen Gate hung with Mao's portrait. Traffic had been stopped in both directions on the broad avenue. The scene was hushed with expectation. We hurriedly joined the crowd like extras late for a take, and we waited.

"What are we waiting for?" I finally asked.

"Flag-lowering ceremony," said Xiao Peng. "Can you see?"

"Not really. There are too many people."

"These people are not Beijingers," said Xiao Peng, his eyes flicking languidly over the crowd. I got it. Beijingers were too cool to hang out on Tiananmen Square. These were mostly farmers from the countryside who had made the pilgrimage to the heart of China to bask in the greatness of their country.

I saw the red flag with the yellow stars going down and then the crowd straining to see. Xiao Peng held my bike steady and told me to stand on the frame and I realized then that he had brought me here especially to see the ceremony, which happened every day at sunset. I saw glimpses of olive-clad soldiers saluting and then goose-stepping their way across the avenue, their boots clacking in perfect unison. They marched the flag under Mao and into the Forbidden City to rest until sunrise the next day, when the ritual would happen in reverse. The crowd was still and silent, and I shared their sense of awe tinged with fear. Once the soldiers disappeared from view, the lights changed to green, and with a single crisp arm movement from the soldier on the traffic mound, cars began moving again and the crowd broke apart. The magic moment was over. We returned to our private concerns. Where to go next? What to eat for dinner?

Xiao Peng and I rode back down the avenue, returning home. We asked each other questions and tried to impress each other with the answers. I wanted to know what he did for a living, but because I sensed that no one in the family was very proud of him, I stuck to safe questions.

"Do we still have relatives in Anhui?" Though Nainai acted like a snobbish Beijinger, her family had actually migrated there several generations before. Now that I was in China, I figured I should find out more about my family.

"Yeah, we do. In Hefei City," he said with a sly smile. "Do you want to meet them?"

"I don't know," I said. It sounded like a trap. "Have you?"

"They came up to Beijing once," he said. "Asking for money."

His eyes narrowed to see my reaction and he added, "Do you still want to meet them? I can give you their number." He flashed his old mischievous smile, as if to say, *You have no idea what you're getting into.* For a moment, I glimpsed them out there: the Hefei relatives who had less than our Beijing relatives, who were hungry, badly clad, with leathery faces full of suffering, and, no doubt, these city relatives had poor relations in the countryside who came looking for them, asking for money. They unfolded before my eyes like paper flowers in water, thirsty and terrifying, the rural nightmare of the snobbish urbanite. Xiao Peng had gotten me. I could only laugh.

"No thanks," I said. He took a sudden turn into the alleyways. "Don't you ever get lost in these hutongs?"

"No, I know all of Beijing's hutongs by heart." He casually mentioned having been enrolled in Beijing Film Academy. My ears pricked up and I asked if he knew any young underground filmmakers. He nodded.

"Really? You know them?" I asked. I said their names like an incantation: "Zhang Yuan? Wu Wenguang? Shi Jian?" Was he actually one of them? Did he sell air conditioners just to make ends meet?

"Yes, they were my classmates at the film academy."

That made sense. They did all seem like versions of the same person, someone who had come of age in the heady 1980s, a time of idealism when China was opening to the world that came to a brutal end with the Tiananmen Square Massacre in 1989. That was when they'd all gotten so cynical. Now nobody in society talked politics anymore—everyone just wanted to make money.

"I really want to meet them," I said. "Can you introduce me?"

"Sure."

"I want to make a documentary about them," I blurted out.

"You want to make films?" he asked, looking surprised. I had surprised myself too by telling him.

"Yeah, that's what I want to do."

"You can stay here for a year or two and then go to film school in the States," he said enviously.

"Film school's expensive," I said. "I don't think my parents would pay for it."

Just as I'd planned, I could just document the filmmakers while I lived here. It seemed my cousin was going to lead me straight to them. Things were suddenly marvelous. I was biking through the hutongs with my cousin, talking about meeting underground filmmakers. We understood each other better than our parents ever could. Crucial puzzle pieces seemed to be falling effortlessly into place.

Xiao Peng owed me one. When I lived in Tianjin the year before, he had hatched an intricate plan with his friend to get visas to America by submitting a "business invitation" from one of Bobo's ex-students, a photocopy of my American passport, and, well, that was about it. Another

similarity between us was that the places where we had grown up somehow came to feel like prisons and the grass seemed greener on the other
side. The difference was that I was free to jump the fence while he wasn't.
So I'd lent him my passport despite reservations about getting mixed up
in the situation. In any case, I was sure that his two older sisters overstay-
ing their visas had doomed his application. My hunch was right but I
hoped that he remembered my favor because I was ready to call it in.

Over the next few weeks, I kept dropping hints that I wanted to go
meet his filmmaker friends. He was always evasive.

Chapter Four

Then There Is the Urination

I walked nervously up and down Sanlitun. Just as Sue had said, it was the kind of dinky bar street you'd find in a second-tier city like Baltimore or Omaha. Having lived in Beijing on and off for fifteen years, she could pin down the squirming, fluttering city with the most offhand comment. To me, the city still seemed enormous and elusive. Baltimore or Omaha. I'd never been to either city but I could imagine its bar streets looking like this: narrow, only a few blocks long, and lined with nearly identical cubbyholes, each as scantily decorated with strings of Bud Light pennants and blue-and-yellow sunflower tablecloths as the next. Under a sunless afternoon sky, skinny, black-clad boys were lazily putting out white plastic tables for the evening.

The bars had sprung up like mushrooms in the embassy district three years before. First came alcohol and moneyed expatriates, then alfresco dining, rich Chinese men, beautiful Chinese women, drunkenness, disorderly conduct, prostitution, taxis, live bands, Western pop music, pirated CD and DVD vendors, mutton kebab stands, outdoor clothing stalls, and street children selling red roses. The street stayed awake for hours after the rest of the city went to sleep. Sue told me the complaints of angry local residents had recently put an eleven o'clock curfew on the loud music and the outdoor tables. I was here because the bar street was on the brink of demolition. That was the rumor at least, the same one that reared its head every few months, Sue had said. The locals hated the bar street, and, more important, the government couldn't properly collect taxes from the cash-only bars; the street was doomed. This time it was for real. She had heard that the city government was going to demolish the bars and build a hulking complex called the Sanlitun Mansions. The demolition would devastate the social lives of thousands of expatriates. This was cover-story material.

The street may have been dinky, but friends who had been in Beijing since the early 1990s told me not to complain. Back then there hadn't even been a single restaurant open after nine o'clock at night. It was best not to get the old-timers started about Beijing's past. Veterans of the 1980s were even worse. Back then, Sue had had a sinecure as an English editor at a Chinese magazine and after work would bike furiously home to the Friendship Hotel and write her conspiracy novel (shelved long ago) and then go to the homes of her Peruvian friends and dance until late. Incontinent geriatrics could not have spoken with more nostalgia for the past than these people. I never imagined I would be sounding the same in a few years.

Sue had collected some facts—the strip generated almost five million U.S. dollars a year, etcetera—and my assignment was simple: Get the word on the street about the demolitions. Talk to both the bar owners and the disgruntled locals. See what they know and how they feel about it. My heart sank when I heard that. I had never done that kind of inter-view before, where I had to ask a complete stranger on the street to tell me intimate details of his or her life. *Hi, you don't know me, but have you heard that the government might demolish your livelihood? How do you feel about that?* I was a shy, fearful person who would rather get a tooth pulled without anesthesia than introduce myself to a stranger. Not to mention that it had to be done in Chinese. Why hadn't Sue called my bluff when I'd said that I was fluent in Chinese? *Chinese.* I wanted to shake my fist at it. The very thing I had resisted learning as a child was whipping around and delivering a roundhouse kick to my head. For the first time, my livelihood depended on understanding it.

I must have walked up and down the street ten times, looking for the perfect bar to ambush. The Boys & Girls Club? Easy Day? Side by Side? I was reluctant to break the thin membrane separating me from the city. The afternoon light on the sidewalk was so gentle and the bars looked so gloomy inside. I could see one or two people rinsing glasses or hunched over calculators or just sitting there. *Baltimore or Omaha,* I thought. *Baltimore or Omaha. I can take this town.* Seeing a bar deserted save for a woman punching rapidly into a calculator, I plunged in and spewed out some questions in rapid-fire Chinese.

She looked up from her calculator. "Excuse me?"

My skin prickled uncomfortably but I just smiled weakly and repeated my spiel more slowly.

"Your Chinese isn't very good, is it?" she said before shaking her head no and returning to her calculator.

I slunk out and went into several more bars. Most bar owners waved me away. Capitalists operating in a Communist country, they were understandably cautious. I wouldn't have talked to me either. Eventually a few reluctant bar owners agreed to be interviewed. We wheeled around each other like Greco-Roman wrestlers: me asking carefully practiced questions and them giving cool, evasive answers that I didn't understand very well. Or, rather, the meaning of the words I didn't understand very well. But the actual sound of Chinese flooding into my ears sprang open an ancient trapdoor in my head that had long been rusted shut. I felt myself lying on a cot in my parents' room at Christmas as the clicking of mah-jongg tiles and happy yelling in Chinese floated up louder and louder from downstairs until suddenly everything went blurry and then darkness. I concentrated on looking as professional as I could, nodding intelligently with my pen poised above my notebook, my face serious yet open, hoping they could not detect the faultiness of the vessel into which they were speaking.

"*Jumin baoyuan de ting lihai,*" one man said. Translation: *Jumin* vociferously *baoyuan*.

"*Ah, jumin baoyuan de ting lihai?*" I parroted back thoughtfully, fixing the line in my short-term memory before discharging the contents into my notebook in a desperate pidgin of Romanized sounds and words translated into English and the occasional Chinese character. I would look up the words later. (The local residents vociferously complained.) I asked his name but he demurred.

"One day they say they're not going to demolish, the next they say they are going to," he said with a shrug. "There's nothing you can do; you might as well let *mingyun* decide."

Mingyun is one of the many words for "fate" in Chinese, one of the more fatalistic versions, and while his statement at first sounded like weakness to American ears, somehow in this time and place it sounded like a pearl of the finest wisdom.

I headed back to the office. Peering into open office doors in our building gave me an enlightening glimpse into the inner workings of the state-run economy. A man read the newspaper while drinking tea. Women played ping-pong. Four people sat around a square table holding hands of playing cards, one with a fan of cards pinned to his forehead like a crown.

I shared a room with the art department and with Jade. I sat at a heavy, pale-gray plastic desk with a view of a tall ocher smokestack out the window. The industrial bookshelves that lined the wall behind me were all empty and the carpeting was thin and rough. The place had a stripped-down utilitarianism that said "newsroom" to me, like a place Lois Lane might work. The advertising saleswomen shared another room, and Sue and Max shared an office attached to a small conference room filled almost wall to wall by a huge glass table.

If I thought work would be a stabilizing force, it wasn't. I wanted to do my own stories but had no idea how to begin. The telephone is a journalist's best friend but not in China, which had no phone book. No way to find out someone's number unless you knew someone who knew them. And I didn't know anyone.

Max did though. He had started his career as a photographer, then opened a photo agency, MaxVision, that supplied Western journalists with photos, and now he was our boss, all without speaking much English. He was built like a bulldog, petite but tensely packed with muscle, and true to his name had a stable of high-octane personas each with its own complete outfit, like a Ken doll. Shutterbug Max had a many-pocketed khaki vest and a hat fit to hunt big game in. Sporty Max was poured into a casing of black spandex. Teutonic Max was in head-to-toe lederhosen. But underneath all Max's ready-made outfits, there was something unhewn about him. His head was as craggy as a granite statue, his nose bulbous, his few remaining teeth blackened and crooked. A man who had no money but did have apartments all over town (though none for me). A man with gonnegtions.

I'd heard that Max had access to photos that no one else could get, like those of a clandestine People's Liberation Army training facility that no one had even known existed. Max's photographs were all hard news photos, and he had even dated the CNN bureau chief for many years (though he insisted on referring to CNN and its ilk as "McNews," one of his few English words). He set Jade up with another part-time internship, this one at the AP with his good friend Steve, a photographer. Max had been impressed when she let slip that she had worked as a dominatrix during college, just to make a little extra spending money.

Jade and I could hear Max barking orders in the phone, as he strode from room to room of the office, telling whoever it was to recollect all the papers and bring them back to the office, immediately. He had a strange smirk on his face. Something was always happening with the distribution. Last issue, the papers had all disappeared from the bars on

Sanlitun the day after they were delivered. Max and Sue suspected foul play. Either *Beijing Scene* was scooping up our papers after they were delivered or they had planted a double agent right in our office.

Beijing Scene. Our mortal enemy. They were the original English-language rag in town, geared toward the wannabe bohemians who had decamped from dead-end lives in sterile, expensive Western cities in search of cheap rent and even cheaper beer in one of the final outposts of totalitarian chic in the world—where life had *meaning.* (Me, in other words.) They wrote exclusively about underground artists and Beijing street slang, all the things I wanted to write about. Getting shut down once by the government only added to their swagger.

No one would blink twice if our distributor, Lu, turned out to be a double agent. He looked the part almost too perfectly: skinny and ratlike with greasy hair and shifty eyes. And people's possessions had begun disappearing from the office in the few months since he had been working. Sorghum candy in my desk drawer began disappearing piece by piece, which I dismissed as the snacking of hungry coworkers, until the box was completely emptied. Others reported cash missing. And then a heavy pewter ashtray from Germany that Max was proudly displaying on his desk disappeared.

A woman often called for Distributor Lu on the office phone. "Oh. My wife," he'd say to no one in particular. Sue shook her head and said to me in English, "I went to his house once. It wasn't the house of a married man. It was so squalid with a narrow dirty bed in the corner." I thought Max and Sue were paranoid. That's what happened when you stayed in China too long.

When Max hung up the phone, the women in the office twittered around him like birds, begging to find out what had happened with the magazine. He grinned like a little boy.

"Someone slipped 'yellow' photos into our magazines."

"What are 'yellow' photos?"

Jade looked at me as if I were five years old. Her Chinese was much better than mine, especially where certain kinds of words were concerned.

"Dirty photos."

The girls continued. "What did they look like? Are they going to bring them back to the office? Was it *Beijing Scene* again? Tell us, Max!"

The next day I went back to Sanlitun to find some angry residents. This time I brought Jade, who had a boldness that I lacked. We walked to the park at the southern end of the street, a patch of dirt dotted with a few sickly trees and park benches, and prowled about. Elderly people stood in small groups, rocking babies in bamboo carriages and gossiping. Like a lioness preying on weak gazelles, I pounced on lone stragglers. Most fulminated about the noise and the disorder of the bar street, but when I said I was a reporter, they clammed up and walked away. I got only one woman, who lived nearby but refused to give her name, to complain on the record about the stench of urine in her yard that greeted her in the mornings.

Behind the bar street loomed brick apartment complexes. I popped into the yards of a few and rattled off, "I'm a reporter. Object to the bar street? No? Okay." After a few rejections, I was ready to call it a day. I figured one quote about piss might be enough. Jade goaded me into trying one more place and we ducked into a yard on the east side of the street. The narrow space abutted the backs of the low bars and I could see how cobbled together they were. Exhaust pipes jutted crookedly from their backs and the corrugated tin roofs were dented and dirty. Two women stood outside chatting.

"I'm a reporter. Object to the bar street?"

One of the women lit up. "Yes! The bars disturb us. People get drunk and *bang-bang* break bottles in the yard. There are lines on the sidewalk that mark out the areas that are supposed to be left clear. Foreigners aren't like Chinese people when they get drunk. They don't bother to follow the rules. They piss all over the place. People sit with their legs hanging over the line," she said, gathering steam. It was true. Though I didn't piss all over the place, I did feel like none of the rules—Chinese ones or the ones I'd left behind at home—applied to me here. She went on, "What am I supposed to do when I walk by? Kick their leg? I'm not going to do that. Chinese people have a long history of civility and politeness."

Civility and politeness? Was she referring to the spitting on the ground and the slurping of soup and the pushing ahead of people in line and the talking with one's mouth full and the telling people to their faces that they're fat and the dropping of gnawed-down bones straight onto the ground and the clipping of fingernails in restaurants and the stubbing out of cigarettes in the remains of one's meal that I had witnessed in China? Actually, those things were cultural differences, not rude at all, and they were what liberated me from feeling as though I had to follow the rules here.

"Plus these bars are built on three pipes. Do you know how dangerous that is?"

"Three pipes? What three pipes?"

"Steam heat, gas, and water. The bars are going to blow this place sky high! Wait—there is a woman in our building who got a petition signed by a thousand local residents. Let me find her."

A petition! Who in China dared to circulate a petition? Here was my story. She found another woman who nodded and told me to wait. I was passed from neighbor to neighbor like a hot potato until a plump, middle-aged woman introduced herself and, looking around with a suspicious glance, said that we shouldn't talk in the street. She led us upstairs to her top-floor apartment and sat us down on a butter-yellow couch covered in thick plastic. She gathered several other neighbors and they poured us tea and offered us snacks. She leaned in, pinioned me with her eyes, and, her voice rising two octaves, began reciting the litany of their complaints: The outdoor seating of the bars forced the cars normally parked on the sidewalk into the bike lane, which forced the bikes into the lanes of moving traffic, which made the whole street such a snarl that elderly people were afraid to cross it to get to the vegetable market on the other side.

"Last year a man, and not just any man but one who was deemed a model worker by his work unit, was hit crossing the street and now he has to walk with a cane! How can they treat the *laobaixing* this way? Is this just? Is it, Reporter Wang?"

I shook my head no as I scribbled furious notes. The *laobaixing*, or the "old hundred surnames," were everyday Chinese people who had a reputation for getting the short end of the stick. She sounded just like my relatives, and unlike with the bar owners I had no trouble understanding her.

"Is that all?" asked Jade.

"Then there is the urination. And the noise. There are bands playing and people yelling all night."

"Who *bang-bang* break bottles everywhere!" said the woman from outside.

"Schoolchildren are being kept awake at night and their grades are falling. We have to keep the windows closed in the sweltering weather or buy an air conditioner, and who can afford an air conditioner? And poor Teacher Ma with the heart trouble. She came home from heart surgery last summer and wanted to open the windows to air out her apartment but couldn't because of the noise. It was so hot in her apartment that she died of a heart attack!" She took a deep breath and went on. "You know what the locals call this place? A red-light district. There are prostitutes everywhere, and beggars and flower sellers. I really sympathize with the girls who are being hurt by this."

Her husband interjected. "Would a decent girl be out at dawn?"

"I tell you none of us are sleeping," she said. "The bar owners don't sleep because they're earning money. The local residents don't sleep because it's too noisy. The reporters don't sleep because they are investigating. The cadres in the local council, now they sleep well."

"Ah ya, why are you always repeating what you hear on the TV news?" asked her husband.

My head was spinning from the verbal ping-pong and the intensity of their emotions.

"So you wrote a petition?" I asked.

They pulled out a copy of the petition they had presented to the local management commission and the press. Signed by hundreds of residents, it detailed their grievances about the traffic, the neon lights, the noise, the lack of public bathrooms, the trash, and the shame of having little Chinese children running after foreigners for money and said that if Beijing hoped to become a "cultured and sanitary city," that Sanlitun was a blot on their reputation. If no action was taken, they threatened to form a delegation and visit the State Council. *The State Council would squash these grannies,* I thought.

"Aren't you afraid of being punished for speaking out?"

"If we don't say anything, no one will do anything," said a woman who had been sitting quietly. "That's the one drawback of Beijing people: We are afraid of rocking the boat. This is not the Cultural Revolution anymore." Nonetheless, she refused to let me use her name in the story, though the others were bolder.

This was the first time I had seen the Old Beijing at war with the new Beijing, and it seemed like a cultural revolution of sorts to me. Angry grannies were the ones rocking the boat while nouveau riche bar owners spouted ancient wisdom about fate. Beijing was topsy-turvy.

We stayed in the apartment for almost two hours listening to the same stories told over and over again, hostages to unstoppable windup toys. My limited Chinese skills did not include how to politely end a conversation; I always had to wait for others to initiate the elaborate ritual. But having gotten my story, all my tension melted away and I sat in a glowing haze that verged on the postcoital. I imagined tossing the petition onto Sue's desk with a casual "there's your story" élan. I wished someone would offer me a cigarette but instead they kept pouring tea, so we kept nodding until they dismissed us.

Chapter Five

Miss, You're Not a Beijinger, Are You?

a s I was checking the proofs of *City Edition* before it went to press, I saw a classified ad for a rental. ("One bedroom, furnished, great location. 2000 rmb/month. Call Constantine at 13-7555-3334.") I called immediately and a man with an Australian accent told me he was giving up his big dream of trying to sell bread makers to the Chinese people and moving back home. His landlords were nice and he wanted to find new tenants for them.

"Give it a few years," I reassured him. "They'll be clamoring for bread makers."

He told me the apartment was on a road just off of the East Third Ring Road. Beijing is laid out concentrically like an onion with the Forbidden City and Tiananmen Square in the center. Kublai Khan built the original walled city in the thirteenth century as an earthly mirror of the heavenly order, laying out the streets according to rules dictated in an ancient book of cosmological rules. The city was situated on a strict north-south axis with the imperial palace placed at the cross of the axes, symbolizing the contact point between heaven and earth. The east-west axis is now the Avenue of Eternal Peace, the palace the tourist destination known as the Forbidden City, and the streets around it the old city of hutongs and courtyard houses where my relatives lived. Chairman Mao had demolished the old city wall and made it into the Second Ring Road. Outside of that was modern Beijing. Then came the Third Ring Road. Then this apartment, which I went to go see.

The narrow road the building was on felt just beyond the edge of the universe. One of the shops just outside the gate was a sex shop. But the apartment had four walls, a ceiling and a floor, a flush toilet, and hot water. I paid Constantine for the newly installed metal security door as well as for the price of the classified ad (he was indignant that I'd nabbed the ad before it was published), and the apartment was mine. His bad fortune was my good fortune. It was the first sign that the city wanted me to stay.

When I told Bobo and Bomu that I was moving out, I could see they were relieved. It had been a long month for all of us.

"You're living alone?" asked Bobo.

"Yes."

"Don't you want a roommate?" asked Bomu.

"No."

"Be careful. If people know a woman is living alone, they'll wait for her to come home at night," said Bobo.

"And then?"

"I read it in the newspaper."

"How much are you paying?" asked Bomu. I hesitated, almost dividing the number in half as I routinely did when they asked their favorite question. But who cared anymore?

"Two thousand." About two hundred and fifty dollars.

"Two thousand! Out by the Third Ring Road? You're getting swindled because you're a foreigner," she said, her reproachful tone meant for both me and my landlords. People living in the old city still thought of that area as the countryside, which it had been just ten years before. There was also a touch of glee in her voice. "Why don't you pay us that much and you can live here?"

"Live here?" Was she joking?

"We'll even give you our bedroom," Bomu said. We laughed and I told her no thanks. Though our relationship had improved since Great-Aunt Mabel's intervention, we weren't really meant to live together. George Burns was right: Happiness was having a large, loving, caring, close-knit family in another city. And the old city and the area outside the Third Ring Road were as far apart as two cities.

A week before I was scheduled to move out of my family's house, Max came into my office to tell me he had a story for me. He was dressed that day as the Cosmopolitan Gentleman in an immaculately tailored Sun Yat-sen suit and black ankle boots that I had overheard him telling someone earlier were pure Italian leather.

I dreaded the hard news story he was going to fling my way, but today I was in for a pleasant surprise. He said a friend of his was at the end of filming a documentary about Li Yang, a Chinese entrepreneur who staged mass public events designed to teach people English, a program he called Crazy English. Max said Li Yang had made hundreds of People's Liberation Army soldiers march along the Great Wall screaming slogans like "I LOVE ENGLISH!" in unison. His friend had just called and told him Li Yang was having an event tonight, which he'd be filming. Max wanted me to go and write an article about Crazy English. To find out more, I should call his friend, Zhang Yuan.

"Zhang Yuan?" I said in disbelief.

"He's a filmmaker," said Max.

"The one who made *Beijing Bastards*?"

"Yes. He's an old friend of mine. So is Cui Jian, the rock star." Max wrote down Zhang Yuan's cellphone number for me. I stared at the ten random digits incredulously, as if I had just been handed the combination to an unbreakable safe.

I put off calling until Jade and I had finished lunch and I used the pay phone in the restaurant, dialing quickly before I chickened out. The low, rushed voice on the other end of the phone told me to meet him out front of Beijing Radio Station that night. Jade came with me to take photos.

Later that evening, our small red cab pulled through the tall metal gates and stopped in front of an imposing sand-colored building with lit red characters spelling out BEIJING RADIO STATION. The night air was still and the only people in sight were a small group of men standing next to large boxes of equipment. Zhang Yuan was tall and slightly squidgy with a short Afro topping his head. He turned to greet me, briefly but with warmth, his bright eyes taking me in. And just like that, I met Zhang Yuan.

We went into the building, and as he shot Li Yang taping a special radio program, I took notes. Li told listeners about his latest project to make a crowd of one hundred thousand students scream in unison, "Learning English is not mental brainwork! It is physical work, to make your tongue muscle international!" as they squiggled their hands in the air. When the radio show was over, we switched places. As I interviewed Li, Zhang Yuan shot me for his documentary.

Li looked like a classic nerd in rectangular wire-rimmed glasses and a trim pompadour. I listened as he told his story about growing up shy in Lanzhou and about the life-changing day when he went into an empty field to scream English vocabulary words at the top of his lungs. Phenomenal test scores and a career as an inspirational speaker followed. For him, inspiration starts with a dressing down. "I want kids today to feel ashamed, to feel pressure, to feel a crisis falling down on their heads. Chinese students are too shy. And China is too weak. The only way for them to learn English and for China to enter the world is to scream." He had a plan for world domination starting with one thousand model families that would master one thousand English sentences. Eventually tens of thousands of families would be using Crazy School Bag, drinking

Crazy Cola, Crazy Mineral Water, Crazy Beer. Li leaned in to say, "They will be studying on my Internet, buying the refrigerator I suggest. I will be their godfather."

I faced Li Yang, silently wondering how this nerdy man was going to achieve his megalomaniacal dreams, but I could feel the eye of Zhang Yuan's camera on me.

After the event, we all—Zhang Yuan, his crew, Li Yang, Jade, and I—squeezed into Li's Volkswagen Santana to go eat dinner. I was sandwiched in the backseat, almost sitting on Zhang Yuan's lap. As we drove through dark, unfamiliar streets, I told them about the past month of living with my relatives in a courtyard house without a shower.

"But you have nothing to worry about," I assured them. "I managed to get a shower yesterday."

"You just showered, Zhenluo!" Zhang Yuan said, using my personal name impudently stripped of my family name, a practice reserved for close friends. "No wonder you smell so fresh!" His voice was deep and warm and slightly nasal, and I could feel his breath on my cheek. I looked at his face, inches away. Was he mocking me? Flirting with me?

At dinner he sat next to me and continued in this jesting vein throughout the loud night of eating and drinking. To my surprise, he was nothing like the disaffected characters in his films and instead was the most charming and ebullient Chinese person I had ever met, with an ability to connect instantly with people, or at least with me. He seemed genuinely interested in hearing my stories about getting to know my long-lost relatives, but at the same time, his voice had a tease in it, like a line with a hook perpetually at the end of it, trying to reach me. The air at dinner was charged—Li Yang had the attention of a famous film director and a foreign journalist, Zhang Yuan and I had a good story on our hands and an oblique flirtation, and I was closing in on the future I'd dreamed of for so long. Talk zinged around the room like crazed bats and while Jade bantered easily, I struggled to keep up. I must have been easy to tease. Zhang Yuan said that he had a child on the way, and from that,

I presumed the existence of a wife. His inaccessibility only increased his appeal.

"I was interviewed the other day by this journalist, this sour woman with glasses . . . ," Li Yang started saying, then saw me and apologized in embarrassment. I suddenly felt like the ugly duckling. I thought there was some sex appeal in the gap between my front teeth, my androgyny, and my skinniness. Except that in China, all the women were skinnier than me, none had short hair, and anyone who could afford them wore contacts.

"I like women who wear glasses," Zhang Yuan said with a funny crook in his voice, before taking my number.

Later that night at home with my relatives, I told Xiao Peng that I had had dinner with his friend Zhang Yuan. He gave me an odd, unreadable look but said nothing.

There was one last thing I had to do before I moved out. I waited until Bobo and Bomu took their afternoon nap one Saturday and I set out for a walk. Though I knew what I would find, I went anyhow, the way you go to a funeral to confirm for your heart what your mind already knows.

I hustled through the hutongs, past low purplish-gray walls, which are the outer hides of the courtyard houses. Gray walls, then an open red door, a small shop hung with strips of tiny shampoo packets and stacked with cigarettes, broken bicycles leaning against walls, an old woman waddling at an unbelievably slow and steady pace, like a tortoise imbued with ancient knowledge withheld from us moderns. Most people in the old city were napping, it seemed, and the usual clang and push of the hutongs was gone. A flock of dark birds cut a swooping arc through the gray sky, the whistles attached to their legs emitting an eerie, inexplicable call like the wind wailing through an amplifier. The mournful sound seemed the very essence of Old Beijing.

People don't rush around like they do in America. You'll love it there. I wanted to trust Nainai—Beijing was her city and she did after all live in a place called Leisure World—but she obviously had a mistaken idea of who I really was. I actually liked rushing around, liked charging nervously down the hutong as if it were a street in New York, as if there were somewhere really important I had to be. I wore my only fall jacket: a puffy polyester Windbreaker in bright safety orange with wide shoulders and a tiny waist, sealed shut with a bold asymmetrical zipper and cheerfully festooned with three or four tiny zippered pockets of various sizes. A friend in New York had pressed the jacket on me, saying it made me look like the Bionic Woman, but I didn't feel very bionic in the gray hutongs of Beijing, only garish and out of place.

Bobo told me Nainai had been the *xiaohua'r,* the school beauty, and I imagined a young and beautiful version of the Nainai I knew strolling in this very hutong. These gray houses were the exact same houses she had gazed at, this air the same air she had breathed, albeit less noxiously polluted. It wasn't hard to imagine her here in the people I saw on the street: a baby in a big bamboo stroller, one of a herd of schoolgirls giggling over some secret thing, a young woman holding hands with a young man. Her presence was palpable in the hutong as if all the years between us had collapsed. Suddenly I felt my body crisscross straight through hers like one water drop passing through another. Her city, my city. Goose bumps stippled my arms.

I crossed Naoshikou Dajie and found myself walking through a clear, flat expanse of rubble that had been Bobo and Bomu's old neighborhood. When I'd lived there last year, no landmarks or street signs had remained and I'd navigated my way home through the bombed-out neighborhood solely by the curves the hutongs made on the ground. I retraced those familiar curves now, meeting no one along the way. Even the children who had played in the heaps of stones and wood were gone. I came to what had been their front door.

Poof! The house had vanished, leaving only a scattering of gray stones and the apple tree, its leafless arms lifted in a lonely and bewildered pose. The pain I came to experience stabbed me, clean as a knife between the ribs. The demolition had flayed off the walls of the house, laying bare our most intimate spaces for the whole world to see. Vaguely able to discern the outline of the walls, I rebuilt the house in my mind: Here was the courtyard that surrounded the apple tree, here the living room, the kitchen, the room I had stayed in when I visited. But the house was slowly fading into thin air with each moment that passed.

I was ready to cry, but I knew better than to make a scene in public, especially over a house I had lived in for only a week. How very Chinese-American of me to feel sappy about a past I had been told about in a fairy tale and, worse yet, to kind of enjoy the feeling. How did my relatives feel? They had lived here for more than fifty years.

I didn't linger long in the rubble. I walked north to the Avenue of Eternal Peace where the new office building had recently risen, all silvery and modern. It looked peculiar and out of place, not unlike myself, I suppose, and forced on me a nostalgia for what used to be here: a jagged row of one-story restaurants and shops, smells of buns steaming and oil frying, noisy, pushy crowds of shoppers, nothing special at the time. Now fewer people passed by and there were no sounds but the inane roar and beep of cars passing on the wide avenue. Bobo and Bomu's demolished neighborhood was hidden behind the building and the knife in my ribs twisted suddenly: The house was really gone. Within the year, the ruins would be cleared and paved over, the apple tree gone forever, and the land my family had lived on for so long would be a parking lot for this building. *A parking lot.* Could it be any more clichéd? I took out my journal and vindictively wrote down the name of the building: the Beijing International Financial Center.

I sat down by the entrance to an underpass and watched the fountains for the building being tested. Plumes bobbed up and down with frustrated jerks. I picked at a splitting seam on the sleeve of my orange jacket and pulled out some fluffy white ticking. As I let it fly away on the wind, I felt an unexpected stab of belonging to the house. Standing before this monstrous building with its vacant eyes, I wanted to tell the story of our houses. Who else would?

I thought of all the gossip about my family's courtyard houses I'd gathered in the past few weeks, mostly in the afternoons when Bobo napped and Bomu swept in circles, the air sparkling with dust motes. She told me that of course they had wanted to live in Great-Aunt Mabel's pristine new courtyard house, but when it didn't happen, they had acquired an apartment in the suburbs and traded it for another quarter of Xiao Peng's small house. He had had only a quarter of it because years ago Bobo's father had gambled away the other three-fourths of it. Not only had he been a gambler, but he'd also been a bigamist and there had been a lot of drama about which one of his two wives would inherit the remaining quarter of his house. The stories went on and on, full of betrayals and dashed hopes, our family ties bound and unbound through the houses.

I'd also found out more about Nainai's courtyard house. When Yeye and Nainai had fled in 1949, they'd entrusted the house to Nainai's only brother, Bobo's dad. The Communist government eventually took control of the house during the Cultural Revolution and started assigning families to live in the different rooms, ten in all. Even though the house had been legally returned to Yeye and Nainai, the families were still living there. Bobo had been taking care of the house since his father's death, and if Nainai got a new house, I was sure Bobo and Bomu wanted to move in. I imagined living there myself. I was a pawn in a game of musical chairs much larger and older than myself.

Several men in baggy suit jackets and mismatched pants stopped their bikes nearby, mesmerized too by the irregular bobbing of the fountains. Their faces were tanned and lined and their hair gray with dust; they had clearly come from the countryside to work on construction projects in the city. The clumsy slapstick of the plumes made me sad for what had been destroyed but I suddenly wondered if they saw the opposite: the extravagant promises of the future, majesty just practicing her steps. It was getting late and I looked at my wrist to find the time, forgetting that the day before I'd dropped my mom's old watch on the hard tile floor of the courtyard house and the hands had stopped. Nothing I did would make them start again. It was probably time to go home but I watched the fountains long after the workers left, partly to mourn the loss of Old Beijing and partly, truth be told, to avoid going back to the suffocating old courtyard house.

That weekend, I climbed into the passenger seat of a dinged-up yellow breadbox van, slammed the flimsy door shut, and told the cabbie, "To Maizidian!" I looked out the side window: My four relatives stood on the sidewalk like a family portrait, waving. I waved back as the van tut-tutted into action and we pulled away. I was free.

"Maizidian'r? The one outside of the Third Ring Road?" growled the cabbie in a voice straight out of a smoky gambling den. He had a flattop and the van smelled like a stale ashtray. He took a swig out of a brown-stained glass jar filled with tea that looked as if it had been steeping since the Qing Dynasty.

"Yes."

"Which way do you want to go?" he asked. We were heading east on Xinwenhua Lu, a busy two-lane artery slicing through the messy, capillary squiggle of the hutongs. People squatted on the sidewalk, watching life pass by.

"Can we go by the Square?" To soar down the wide Avenue of Eternal Peace with the red walls of the Forbidden City on the left and the expanse of Tiananmen Square on the right would be like shooting an arrow straight through the beating heart of the Middle Kingdom, a glorious way to exit the old city. Plus I didn't know any other way, and I didn't want to reveal my unfamiliarity with the city's geography.

"Sorry, miss. Can't take that road in the daytime."

"Well, you choose then."

The *miandi*, or breadbox van, can no longer be found on Beijing's roads but at the time it was ten kuai for ten kilometers, the cheapest cab on the road. Banned on certain roads at certain times, it resembled a motorcycle chassis with a yellow loaf of Wonder Bread stapled on top, with a motorcycle's legendary "feel" for the road. Every bump and jounce threatened to catapult me through the wide windshield about two inches in front of my face.

We veered into the hutongs and the familiar walls rose around us like a maze. The *miandi* barely fit down the narrow passageway and the cabbie honked noisily at the snarls of bikes and people in our way and swore steadily. Despite all the life that rattled between and behind its walls, the hutongs were deeply peaceful, like a place airlifted out of the past. I was going to miss living here.

"Miss, you're not a Beijinger, are you?"

"No, I'm not." I wondered if he were about to take me for a ride.

"I could tell from your terrible accent. Where are you from? Korea?"

"America."

"America?! You don't look American! You look Chinese."

"Well, I'm American."

"How is that possible?"

"Just is. I grew up there."

"So who were those people back there?"

"My relatives."

"I knew someone in your family had to be Chinese. So you're *meiji huaren.*" American-born Chinese.

"Sort of." This was the number one conversation people loved having with me in China. I wasn't in the mood to explain the subtle but crucial differences between *American-born Chinese* and *Chinese-American.*

"No 'sort of' about it. You are a *meiji huaren.* So you've come back to China to *xun gen.*" To search for your roots.

"No, I'm not coming *back* to China. I'm not from here. I'm American. And I'm not coming here to *xun gen.*" Couldn't he see that I was *fleeing* my roots with only the clothes on my back and my two suitcases? "I'm coming here to *xun* . . ." I racked my brains for the word I was looking for. *"Maoxian."* Adventure. I punched my fist triumphantly in the air for emphasis.

The cabbie laughed. "Miss, you're not half bad. You smoke?"

"Sure," I said, and he handed me a cigarette, lit it, then lit his own. We smoked in silence.

I read somewhere that Westerners typically cast themselves as the protagonists of their own memoirs, while Asians are usually bit players in theirs, one mere star in a great constellation. I had gone abroad intending to have swashbuckling foreign adventures and to get as far away as possible from turgid family psychodramas with Confucian overtones. As I told Yeye repeatedly years ago, I was American! But I had made one fatal mistake: I had set the story in China, where my family's past worked as an undertow, pulling me in directions I was powerless to fight.

We crossed over the Second Ring Road, which flowed under us like a river of cars, and turned onto a wide avenue clotted with vehicles of all sizes driving like maniacs and honking peevishly. But no one was actually going all that quickly, and the whole scene was at once manic and leisurely. Cranes floated high above us, wheeling slowly over the green-clad skeletons of half-built buildings. Pollution and exhaust hung heavily in the air and the avenue looked unpleasant to walk along. But people did. There were people everywhere, ambling along the sidewalks, stuffed into buses, biking shoulder to shoulder in the bike lane. Their faces looked gray and sad. Hatched from the protective cocoon of family, I could feel myself shrinking as a sea of strangers spread itself around me.

I thought of my two suitcases in the back and how little ballast they provided for my life. Back in the States, I had crammed them full, but hardly anything had fit. Just a few novels and mix tapes, a small album of photos, a year's worth of tampons and Wellbutrin, and a tiny but rugged wardrobe of clothing that could withstand the corrosive pollution and tiny washing machines of China. When I thought about the ugly clothing that I'd brought in lieu of my thrift-store treasures, the baggy Lee corduroys and misshapen sweaters I was stuck with now, my mind suddenly flashed back to the Sunday afternoons of my childhood, when I had worn my ugliest clothing reserved especially in a bottom drawer for that hated day's main event, Chinese School. Now every day was going to be like Sunday.

But tomorrow! Tomorrow I was having brunch with Zhang Yuan, the director of *Beijing Bastards*. Just yesterday he had called me at the office. "Zhenluo, I'd like to invite you out to brunch at the Kunlun Hotel; it's a five-star hotel." I'd protested, saying Max made us pick up the tabs when we did interviews and he'd kill me if I went somewhere so expensive. "Don't think of it as an interview then. It's my treat." It was true; I'd gotten all the information I needed from him at our first meeting. My life was now beginning for real.

The farther we drove, the wider the streets got. Soon we were barreling down an eight-lane highway that ran on a flyover above the city. The Third Ring Road. The meter clicked above ten and began ticking steadily upward. The city sprawled out on either side of the road. The Hot Spot Disco, marked with a giant bull's-eye. A single silvery skyscraper. A mausoleum laced with a filigree of unlit neon spelling out KTV: karaoke. In between were old Soviet-style concrete apartment blocks with rows of blackened balconies that seemed to trumpet a message of socialist realism: Comrades, life is suffering. The day was sunless and stern. Moving to Beijing suddenly seemed like the wrong idea. While the hutongs of the old city had been built to human scale, the wide roads we drove on now were meant to dwarf us lowly mortals. The scene was magnificent, squalid, and beautiful all at once.

"What's America like? Better than this, I bet."

"Better than this? No way. It's not like the streets there are paved with gold. People care only about money. It's meaningless. I prefer being here."

"People here are starting to just care about money too."

"Not everybody."

"No, but this place is changing."

We eased off the highway and made a right onto a narrow road lined with small shops and restaurants. Large trees arched above. The shops here were flimsier than in the old city, the air dustier, and the sidewalk appeared to be made of packed dirt like a frontier town. And people on the street looked even sadder. After living protected inside the old city, here I felt dangling and exposed.

"Miss, this is Maizidian'r. Let me know where to stop." I looked around and tried to remember. Large restaurant on right. Bathhouse on left. We were close. Smaller shops: hairdressers, skinny restaurants, a sex shop.

"Stop! It's here!" I said, gesturing to a five-story brick building behind a row of shops. The cabbie pulled up to a tall black metal gate. I opened it and he took a right into a narrow drive behind the building, which had twelve entryways. Just inside the gate was a small office from whose gloomy interior peered a granny wearing a red armband, mentally noting my arrival.

"Be careful coming home here at night, miss."

"Why?"

"There are men clubbing women over the head with *gunzi* this big," he said, holding his hands apart the length of a baby crocodile. "Then they're stealing their purses."

"Thanks for the advice." He sounded like my parents, in whose vision of the world everything was fraught with danger: Walking in a city at night could lead to mugging and rape, dating boys to pregnancy, driving a car to a deadly crash. But Beijing was quiet and peaceful at night, with none of the undercurrent of violence I expected from a big city.

We unloaded my two suitcases, I paid him, and the *miandi* backed out with a series of growls and rattles, leaving me all alone. I entered the dim concrete stairwell and lugged my suitcases one by one up to the fifth floor. I leaned against the wall in exhaustion as I unlocked the sturdy metal security door and then the inner wooden door. Ahhh . . .

But I wasn't alone! Someone was in the foyer, coming toward me. I jumped. She jumped. Then I realized that it was only me, reflected in a gigantic mirror that ran the length and height of the tiny, gloomy foyer. I pulled a string and a doughnut of light on the ceiling crackled on; the foyer was suddenly huge and lit like a school cafeteria. The light was not kind on my double's face: She looked so unsure and so serious dragging her luggage across the threshold into her new life. All the layers of her clothing were mismatched and the right arm of her pilly green sweater was dusted with fine white powder. Her posture was terrible. *Your mom is right*, I thought. *You do look like a bag lady.* I bared my teeth at her and she smiled back prettily. I turned off the light.

I walked the length of the apartment, from the snug bedroom on the left, down the hallway on the right, past the kitchen and bathroom, and into the large living room at the end, filled with an assortment of ugly furniture. Light filtered in through the dirty windows of the balcony. Out on the concrete floor of the balcony sat piles of my landlord's junk: boxes, paint rollers, a giant naked plastic baby doll. I sat down on the slippery blue couch. Fluorescent lights, cold tile floors, painted concrete walls. Objectively, the apartment was kind of depressing, but as I sat there, I recalled the hooligans in *Beijing Bastards* living in an apartment just like this. You could choose instead to see it as raw and true. Stripped to the essentials. Free of the smugness of courtyard houses and brownstones. I saw that there could be relief in living on the margins, outside of history. There could be a home for the outcast in me, right here.

And the magazine containing the apartment listing? It would hit the streets tomorrow.

Part Two

Chapter Six

The Original Beijing Bastard

I woke with confusion to find myself in a strange bed with sun coming
in through the window. I was in my new apartment. And I was having
brunch with Zhang Yuan in a half hour. I hurried to take a shower, my first
in a long time. My whole body itched, my face had broken out, my skin
was dry and cracked, my hair was matted—I couldn't wait to get clean. If
this meeting with Zhang Yuan wasn't an interview, I wondered, could it
be considered more of a date?

My new shower was a hose that dangled from a pipe in the bathroom. I shucked off my clothes and ran shivering into the kitchen and
turned on the water heater—*click, click, click*—until a blue flame came
on with a tiny roar. I rushed back into the bathroom, turned the metal
valve open, heard the water rush, and watched as the thin yellow hose
bucked upward—straight onto the bare lightbulb. Smash! Tiny shards of
glass rained all over me as the hose continued to whip madly around the
small, dark bathroom. I shut off the water and after checking for both of
my eyes (yes) and for blood (no), I stood silently for a minute getting
colder and colder. There was no time left to clean up the mess. I brushed

the shattered glass out of my hair, stepped around the shards on the floor, and got dressed, donning last my orange Bionic Woman jacket, which looked much better on the fringes of the city than in the center. I might not be clean but at least I looked good.

The hotel restaurant was quiet and spotless and bright, both deeply soothing and oddly jarring after the life I had been living at my relatives' house. Tall windows opened out onto a manicured garden. I felt cleansed by the mere proximity to cleanliness and light.

Zhang Yuan guided me to a table. The brunch was a buffet and I loaded my plate with bagels, eggs, and bacon and filled a thin white tea-cup full of coffee. The food was delicious. The caffeine, the light-filled room, and the sound of silverware clanking on plates made my head swim. *I am sitting here having brunch with Zhang Yuan.* He looked like a giant Muppet, tall and huggable with a frizzy shock of hair and shiny button eyes. I hung on his every word.

"China is a great place to be a writer because here is where the crazi-est stories in the world are. You won't find a guy like Crazy English in America. You could write a whole book about him. You have very valu-able 'international muscle,'" he said. "Do you know the secret to being a documentarian?"

"No," I said, leaning in to catch the holy words as they fell.

"To be *kuanrong* and to use *lixing.*"

"Oh, I see," I said. "Actually, I don't know what those things are." Since he didn't speak any English, he wrote the characters for me on a scrap of paper. Later, when I looked them up I learned they meant *toler-ant* and *rationality.*

He said that Crazy English had started out as just another documen-tary project but had become fraught as it forced him to confront his own inability to speak English and to ask uncomfortable questions about his own personal failings. Was it his shyness that was holding him back? Was the only way to overcome his weakness to yell, "I am strong!"? He said that when he was filming a huge rally in Hunan Province, Li Yang had called him to the stage and introduced him as a world-famous film director.

"I was completely tongue-tied with embarrassment. I couldn't say a word, even in Chinese. I was overcome with a feeling of *zibei*," he said, of inferiority. "Then I started to wonder: Is a fundamental part of being Chinese to feel inferior—to the people around you, to the rest of the world?"

All month at my relatives' house, I had felt swaddled in layers and layers of cotton, furiously trying to triangulate between what people said and what they meant. His words pierced through my confusion, showing me the possibility of speaking directly about China and about what was in one's heart. All the things that I hadn't said all month bubbled to the surface. *I couldn't stand living with my relatives but now that I've moved out, I feel all alone. I tried to shower this morning but the lightbulb shattered all over me. Everything seems so difficult. I miss home. I'm scared.* Zhang was a good listener, tolerant and rational. He told me to stop worrying.

"You have a home here now," he said. "Are you afraid of people in America forgetting you? You'll have your own life one day, have children."

"I don't want to get married!" I said wildly. The American women in the office, all in their thirties and married or engaged, had spent a half hour one day exchanging stories of their marriage proposals. I found it hard to believe that this was a viable topic of conversation for liberated modern women to be having and even harder to believe that one of them had gotten engaged on the steps of a church in Tuscany at dusk.

"You will one day," he said.

"It's hard here," I said. "I have no old friends here." Starting over was not liberating or glamorous. Sure, I had escaped the stale circle of New York, that ambitious gaggle of college graduates moving into lofts in Williamsburg or brownstones in Park Slope as if it were their fifth year of college and getting their starts in publishing or video production. I had struck out into a whole new world, but my own personal world was still as expectant as an empty shoebox.

"Sometimes new friends feel like old ones," he said.

"Almost," I said with exaggerated mournfulness.

We figured out that we had both lived in New York the same summer a few years before. We had both been lonely, both zigzagged aimlessly around the city, both watched a lot of films. Our slug trails had no doubt crossed. We agreed that New York was the best city in the world.

"If only we had known each other then," he said, the tease of his words lost on me. Taken seriously, the words were perfectly calibrated to touch the tender heart of a young woman. Something ephemeral and precious was passing between us like a current of electricity. A vision of the future was coming into focus.

I remembered my mom's warning about men on the hunt for a green card, and as I sat there, my relationship with Zhang Yuan progressed quickly and unexpectedly in my head. Ours would be a classic tale: American girl meets Chinese director, he divorces wife, marries her for a green card, they live turbulently ever after. It would be a deliciously ambiguous affair. Was he using her? In love with America? Or with youth? Was she using him for his stardom to realize her own artistic dreams? Would they fall in love or would it end in tears? Or both? Marriage proper was for squares, but marriage for a green card made me swoon.

"You're a very beautiful girl," he said.

I jolted out of my reverie, annoyed at his clumsiness. Beauty wasn't the point. Art was. We were artists. Equals. I was eccentric and messy, just like him. We were connected by something loftier than looks, I was sure of it.

"Hey, do you know my cousin Xiao Peng?" I asked.

"Who?"

"I mean Xu Peng," I said. *Xiao Peng* meant "Little Peng," a name only the family called him. "He took classes at the Film Academy."

"Oh . . . Xu Peng!"

"You know him, then."

"No, never heard of him."

I realized that Xiao Peng had probably met Zhang Yuan only a few times, if even that. By being American, I had leapfrogged him again. That odd look he had given me when I told him I'd met Zhang Yuan had probably been envy. But in a way I envied him. He had grown up in that old house in the old city. He knew all its hutongs by heart. The cookie-cutter suburbs where I had grown up were not a place you could really call home. The arbitrary curves of its streets were not worth memorizing or returning to. In a strange way, I had inherited my parents' condition: exiled from the motherland and searching for a place to call home. Even the middle-class American upbringing they had provided couldn't protect me from those questions, from that past.

"What's next for you?" I asked Zhang Yuan.

"I'm going to be shooting a feature film soon, a big one."

"About what?"

"A girl who goes to jail for seventeen years for killing her sister and then is released and comes home for New Year's. This is the first film I'm doing officially."

"What does that mean?"

"My script had to be cleared by the censors. It's already been approved."

"Did they cut much?"

"Not too much. We even have permission to shoot inside a women's prison."

"Where?"

"Tianjin."

"I lived in Tianjin last year!"

"Perfect then. You should come visit the set."

The next day I sat down at my computer in the office to write the Crazy English story. I stared out the window at the smokestack belching out lacy black puffs. The winter sky was a pallid industrial gray with only a bright smear where the sun should have been. *You have a home here now.* Meeting Zhang Yuan was further proof that the city wanted me to stay. *You're a very beautiful girl.* I couldn't get his words out of my mind.

I could see down into a schoolyard where elementary school students wearing identical tracksuits were standing in razor-straight rows doing synchronized calisthenics, their arms all outstretched like Christ. They were slowly and silently drawing tiny circles in the air in near unison as if underwater, or hypnotized. They were lead by their gym teacher Lao Li, the guy who doubled as our night watchman. Sue said she had come in early one day and caught him with a lady caller, who he claimed had come to "borrow a book."

Jade teetered in on platform shoes. "How was your date yesterday?" she asked with a suggestive lift of her neat, thin eyebrows.

"You mean my interview?" Something about Jade made me want to say or think the exact opposite of her.

"What-*ever*," she said. "Did anything interesting happen?"

"We talked about making films and New York and, you know, life."

"That's it? Did he pay, at least? You know my philosophy: I just think, '*What* can he do for *me*?'"

The next week, my phone at work rang. It was Zhang Yuan again. He invited me to a bar to make sure I had all the material I needed for my article. I couldn't bring myself to tell him I had already finished and that most of the parts involving him had been cut.

We met that night at the Pretty Bird Club, a former underground bomb shelter that had been converted into a fairy wonderland nightspot, complete with little wooden bridges, swings hung from the ceiling with rope, and hidden nooks shaped like tree trunks. When I arrived, I was surprised to find he was not alone.

He had brought his friend Xiao Ding, a film producer who spoke impeccable British English, to make sure there were no misunderstandings between us. It had the opposite effect. Xiao Ding was a proper-looking man with rimless glasses and thin hair pasted to his forehead. Instead of carrying a satchel made of leather or canvas, he toted around all his belongings in a plastic bag. I felt as if we were being chaperoned by Zhang Yuan's tax accountant.

We all chatted politely for several hours. At the end of the night I exchanged business cards with Xiao Ding and we all parted coolly. I felt confused—had I imagined all that had passed between Zhang Yuan and me during brunch? Was his interest in me all business?

In any case, we began talking on the phone every few days. My ideas about making a documentary were on hold; finding comfort and connection were much more urgent tasks, and he was the first person I'd found in Beijing whom I could really talk to. In return, he flung outrageous invitations my way: He would fly me out to a Crazy English shoot in Ürümqi in the far west of China, or out to Rome (which wasn't New York, he said, but wasn't too bad) where he would be doing postproduction on his next film, or would get his driver to bring me to Tianjin to visit the film set. The world was opening up in unforeseen ways. I fantasized madly about these trips, but any details beyond the setting—a desert hideaway, the Forum at dusk—were left fuzzy. They floated distantly on the horizon, where things always look better.

I kept my relationship with Zhang Yuan a careful secret from my relatives, who called occasionally to check up on me. If they had known what I was doing with a married man—whatever it was I was doing—they would have alerted my parents in the States, no doubt provoking an international incident of epic proportions.

When my phone rang at home on a Sunday evening, I knew right away who it was. My parents always called on Sunday mornings, their time, before my mom went to teach Chinese School and my dad to play tennis in the courts next to the school, as they had been doing since before I could remember. I instantly pictured the classrooms of Herbert Hoover

Junior High School and heard the droning sounds of Tang poems or ancient folktales being read in unison. Their calls were always filled with the latest gossip from their circle of friends, usually news about their children, who was going to what medical school, that type of thing.

"Hello?" A pregnant, international long-distance pause followed.

"Hi, Val!" said my mom, then my dad. They always got on the phone together. My stomach tightened at the sounds of their voices.

"Hi," I said. "How are you?"

"Everything is good at home. How are you?"

"Fine." I never confided my thoughts to them and I imagined their horror if I told them the truth about my life. The loneliness. The strange love affair. Even this apartment would even have upset them.

"How's your job?"

"Great! I'm starting to research this story about the government forcing American companies to take down their billboards on this avenue for the fiftieth anniversary—"

"Okay, okay," said my dad. Extremely frugal, they always cut me off once they had gotten the main gist of what I was saying. They seemed to call just to know that I was still alive.

"When are you coming back home?" asked my mom.

"I'm not really sure. I sort of like it here. There's a lot to write about and—"

"No, no, no," my dad cut in, with his favorite phrase. "Why don't you go to graduate school?"

"We can help you with the tuition."

"I'm not really sure what I would study. I'm kind of *doing* what I would only be studying about in the States and—"

"How about law school?"

"Mom!"

"Anyway, do you remember your elephant foot plant?" she asked.

"Of course I do." I had picked out the elephant foot plant almost twenty years before, when both it and I were only as high as my mom's knee. I had always wanted a little sister, or a pet, to lavish attention on, order around, and mold in my image. I had to settle for the plant. For years I had watered and cared for it and watched as it grew from a giant, squat bulb into a tall cascade of strappy, flowing leaves.

"It died."

"What do you mean it died?"

"The leaves turned brown. I tried to repot it but it didn't like the new soil."

"Were you watering it?"

"Yes."

"Are you sure?"

"Twenty years is a long time for a plant to live, Val."

"Oh, I can't believe it's gone. I loved that plant."

"You were too far away from home for too long."

"Are you *sure* you watered it? Plants don't just die, Mom."

"Okay, okay," said my dad. "We have to go."

"Well, bye then."

"Bye, love you."

"Love you too."

After we hung up, I sat thinking about my elephant foot plant, which had always seemed to have such a strong personality. It was a hardy, unruly plant whose narrow, sharp-edged leaves would cut you if you handled them wrong. But those same leaves tapered down to wisps at the end, making the whole plant look like a head of long green hair. I imagined my mom slowly depriving it of water and watching as the leaves turned brown and shriveled. But I didn't think she was capable of that. She was right. Twenty years was a long time for a plant to live, and everything has its time to go. I too had been repotted, and only time would tell if I would fare better than my plant.

I lay in bed staring out the window. My bedroom was a makeshift brick hovel with a tin roof, which was freezing in the winter and would be boiling hot in the summer, like a Parisian garret. My landlords had built it on the roof. The walls of the room were blotched with water stains, black and degenerate. Two huge windows formed one corner of the room and out of them I could see the cylindrical brown top of the Hotel Kunlun where Zhang Yuan and I had had brunch.

Any time I felt fear or despair over the life I was living, I just looked out the window at the hotel and the word *harbinger* popped into my mind—of good, of hope, of the future. Like a daffodil after a long winter. *I will make my own documentary*, I thought. *I will. I will work hard, save money for a camera, do what it takes.* The unspoken end of the thought went, *And then my parents will finally be proud of me.* I would never have spelled this out, nor would I have dared consider the consequences of not succeeding.

Chapter Seven

Harbinger, Harbinger, Harbinger

*M*ysterious sounds echoed into my apartment from the stairwell outside: a long metallic screech ended by an abrupt clang, low hissing, dull menacing thumps, a sound like a strand of beads breaking and spilling all over the floor. I sat alone in my apartment one Saturday night, the High Holy Day of Partying stretching out bleakly in front of me. And now a horde of angry ghosts was trying to break into my apartment. I tried to identify the sounds: security doors slamming shut, trash falling down the chute and hitting bottom, feet shuffling upstairs, giving a hard stomp on the landings, but the beads breaking—that one I couldn't figure out.

I heard someone climbing upstairs, stomping three or four times to activate the stubborn light sensor on the fourth floor. (The sensor on my landing was the exact opposite, set off by no more than a stealthy footfall.) I could picture the stairwell out there—dark and grim and full of things most sane people would have thrown out: birdcages with broken bars, toilet bowls blackened by dust, half-rusted bicycles. Then came loud voices on the landing, so I went to the peephole. It was like watching a tiny movie: I saw my neighbors—husband, wife, and teenage daughter—going into their apartment and shutting the door. Suddenly the light in the scene was snuffed out, my peephole plugged by the wide thumb of someone who was clearly a maniac. His hands would be around my throat next. I yelped and the sound activated the light again, making me realize I had been terrified by nothing more than the light timing itself out.

I called Zhang Yuan, but he didn't pick up. From the window onto the air shaft came a man's voice soaring in off-key karaoke grandeur into the final aria of the *Titanic* theme song.

In between the frightful and ridiculous sounds, there was something even worse: a silence more silent than anything I'd heard in my entire life. At home, I'd found the voices of my parents deafening. *You can be anything you want to be in life. We saved money since the day you were born to send you to college. You're spoiled. You've never eaten bitterness in your whole life. Do you know what we got for our birthdays growing up? One bowl of noodles. Life is suffering. You had a happy childhood, didn't you? Work harder!* The contradictory voices of my friends only confused me more. *Val, you work too hard. Just do what you want. What would happen if you just took their car and went out for a drive? Why do you keep your true self so hidden from the world?*

One reason I'd traveled so far away was to break out of everyone's orbit and to be able to say, *This is* my *life, this is* my *story, my toilet jury-rigged with dental floss by* me. I had no idea how vast and empty the world would seem. I sent my mind out as far as I could—into the dark city and the dark countryside rippling out to mind's end beyond that. It didn't touch anything familiar or comforting, just silence, fear, loneliness, as if all the love had been sucked out of the world. Sitting there felt hollowing and painful and mysterious—like some kind of meditation or fasting. Either I'd get stronger or just go crazy.

What did having a nervous breakdown even look like? From the name, I assumed it involved falling down on the floor and twitching like a bunny's whiskers until someone noticed and put you in a quiet rest home for weary women in the countryside, with beautiful manicured lawns and bars on the windows. But somehow I began to suspect that it might be something subtler, like your insides slowly melting into undifferentiated glop, the conversations you had with yourself becoming increasingly animated, and the food in the refrigerator rotting, as the world around you ticked obliviously along.

If I could have cried, I would have, but I never cried in China. Instead, I took a piece of white cardboard and began writing VALERIE all over it, again and again, each letter a shape with no meaning.

The next Saturday night, the phone rang.

"Hello? *Wei?*"

"Val! What are you doing right now?" asked Jade.

"Nothing."

"We're going out to the Den. Tonight is Eighties Nite. I cannot wait. Do you want to come?"

"I don't know. Eighties Nite?" It didn't make sense to me to come all the way to China to listen to '80s music from America. Plus, the darkness outside seemed so forbidding, as if the world simply dropped off beyond the walls of my apartment.

"You can't just stay home."

"I can't be bothered to get dressed and get myself into a cab."

"I'm in Steve's car. We'll come to pick you up."

"Well . . ."

"They'll buy us drinks."

"Who's 'they'?"

"Max is with us too."

"Okay." *No* was my normal social instinct—I am my father's daughter, after all—but new in town, it was time to say *yes* to everything. Jade was an excellent role model. Though raised by Chinese immigrant parents, she had not a shred of my self-abnegation.

"We'll be at your door in twenty minutes. Be ready."

The Den was dark, crowded, and smoky. Upstairs a DJ was spinning hits from the '80s. "My Sharona." "Take on Me." "Material Girl." Young Westerners danced in sweaty clusters. Now it was only the '90s—much too early to be nostalgic for that era. Standing awkwardly at the edge of the bar, my life didn't seem so different yet.

"What do you want to drink?" yelled Steve over the music. At least there was booze now.

"Long Island Iced Tea," Jade instantly said.

I waffled and Max cut in. "B-52s for both of us."

After Steve went to the bar, Max turned to Jade and said, "When I got you the internship with him, I didn't think you'd jump into bed with him!" His angry tone of voice was belied by a big grin.

Jade rolled her eyes. Steve was a ruggedly handsome New Zealander who had been working as a photographer in Beijing for almost ten years. After a few days of riding around in his jeep with him as he took pictures, what she wanted most was to hang out in his apartment in the diplomatic compound and watch cable TV.

"I just cannot be a photographer in this city without a car," she said. "Do you expect me to ride the bus everywhere?"

Steve came back with the drinks. He handed Jade hers and then gave Max and me shot glasses with blue flames shimmying above dark molten liquid. How did this work? Steve came back with a beer for himself and two tiny straws for us.

"Quickly," said Max. I watched as he slurped his shot down, then I did the same. I expected it to burn and tear on the way down but it was surprisingly sweet, and I could feel my head pop open a crack. I noticed that Max's pinkies were mere stumps. Jade took one sip of her drink and handed it back.

"*Tell* them to put some *liquor* in it."

"I'm sure it's fine," said Steve.

"Fine, I'll do it myself," she said, and made a beeline for the bar.

After a few more drinks, the air began to liquefy and I began to feel

a feathery connection to others in the room. In the dim corners of the
bar, strangers began groping one another. I danced. The past began to
seem further and further away.

On the way home, my cab was stopped around the corner from my
apartment by a man in a green army overcoat and red armband. A
Chinese-looking woman traveling alone at night in the neighborhood
aroused suspicion. I rolled down the window. He ordered me to get out.
I refused. I was suspicious of him too. Was he was really a police officer?
And would it be better if he were or if he weren't? Behind him was a
raucous crowd of men squatting and smoking and playing cards. He
opened the cab door and ordered me to show him my identity card. I
refused again, saying I didn't have one. I wasn't Chinese.

"Not Chinese? Where are you from?"

"I'm American."

"You can't be American. Americans all have blond hair and blue eyes."
Now was not the time for a history lesson about immigration. My hands
shook as I pulled a photocopy of my passport out of my wallet and thrust it
at him. Someone had advised me to keep it with me for occasions like this.

"Look at my American passport."

"This isn't a real American passport."

"No, it's a pho-to-co-py of a passport," I said with more arrogance
than I felt. I was bold with liquor and the tide turned swiftly. "And how
would you know? You've never seen an American passport before. I bet
you can't even read it. Can you read English?" Like a cornered animal, I
had become mean. He stood there, turning the paper over in his hands,
unsure of what to do next. He tried to order me out of the cab again. I
saw an opening, one that could even leave him some face.

"Besides, my Chinese is this terrible and you still think I'm Chinese!"
I said in my heaviest American accent and snatched the photocopy back,
while slamming the door and telling the cabbie to step on it. The cabbie
chuckled and muttered something about a narrow escape. I got to my
gate and ran inside.

That night, I awoke to hear a police helicopter pulsing noisily outside my window. I got out of bed and rushed to the peephole of my front door. Red pointer lights crisscrossed outside; a thin beam of red shone straight in and blinded me as a swarm of officers began to push the door down. The latch on the inner door kept coming loose and I kept slamming it shut. I was terrified for the small girl I was babysitting who was asleep in the bed. The police pushed at the door again, and this time I couldn't shut it. They flooded in. I yelled and woke myself up. I lay in the dark, shaking. Slowly, I raised up to look out the window, sure that the helicopter would be out there hacking the air to pieces, a policeman's murderous face mere feet from mine in the cockpit window. There was no helicopter there, only the dark cylinder of the Hotel Kunlun in the distance topped by a steadily blinking light. And no girl I was babysitting, aside from myself. *Harbinger, harbinger, harbinger,* I thought as I lay back in bed, trembling.

A few hours later, a rough banging at my door jarred me awake. This time I knew it had to be the police. Who else would be banging at my door at eight o'clock on a Sunday morning? My head was splitting and I pinched myself to make sure I was really awake. I lay still with my head and my heart pounding in unison, silently thanking Constantine for the security door, a heavy metal frame reinforced with thick grating. The inner door, of warped and ill-fitting wood, would have given way with one swift kick like in my dream.

My landlord's words—*you never know who it's going to be*—came back to me. The week before, Landlord Ma had come to collect my first month's rent—a thick stack of hundred-yuan notes. She was short and solid and full of suspicions about the country people invading the city. Her husband looked the same; they could have ribboned at a husband-and-wife look-alike contest.

"Do you have any friends like you who are also looking for an apartment?" she had asked. "We have another apartment just downstairs from yours. We own both, and both are legal to rent out."

"Legal to rent to *foreigners*?" I had responded. I wanted to clarify my own situation. Beijing supposedly had strict laws forbidding foreigners from living in Chinese housing but no one knew the exact rules. And no one knew what would happen if you were caught—a hefty fine, eviction, prison time, deportation? Fortunately, looking Chinese made it easier for me to avoid the police dragnet so by "like you" I took it she meant *Chinese face, Western purse strings.* She evaded my question and I feared that maybe I'd made her lose face, though she'd never tell me how or even let me know that I had.

"By the way, never open the door for anyone. You never know who it's going to be," she had said. Later that week, I came home one night to find a policeman in crisp olive from head to toe sitting outside the gate of my building. Just the sight of his lapel decorated with sadistically colorful pins started my heart thumping. I had read in the Western press about prison torture in China and had seen with my own eyes the rough and unsmiling way the police handled illegal touts. Not pretty. He stared at me as I walked in.

I lay in bed, hyperventilating quietly, while a hand tried the door, rattling the metal handle impatiently, then banging again, a low, hard thumping surrounded by a halo of loose metal sounds. After a pause, I heard the door across the stairwell unstick itself and open with a whoosh. I rose silently and tiptoed to the peephole. A plump woman with a jagged bowl cut whom I'd never seen before stood with her back to me. She wore a silky blue pajama set emblazoned with golden elephants and was exchanging something with my neighbor, a stocky woman. I couldn't hear my neighbor too clearly, but she seemed to know that I was a young woman living alone, that I looked Chinese but was foreign, and something about higher rent. I heard the woman with the bowl cut say, "Hong Kong."

"She comes home late," said my neighbor. "I wouldn't feel safe if my daughter were living alone."

She frowned, shook her head, gave a little smile, and shut the door. I crawled quietly back into bed.

I grouped all my neighbors in together with the nosy grannies wearing the red armbands stationed in the little office by the front gate; they observed everyone who came in and out and would report any suspicious activity back to the local police. I tried to spy on my neighbors too, peeking into their apartments when I passed by open doors. Often, three generations of a family were stuffed into the same space that I lived in alone. Televisions blared loudly and the stairwell often smelled of fresh cigarette smoke.

One winter morning, a key turned in the lock of my heavy security door as I stood inside lacing up my shoes, about to go to work. I froze in fear. The logical response was to run out to the balcony and hide quietly until whoever it was had looted from my apartment whatever they wanted and left. But fuck it. I was tired of freezing in fear, scampering, and hiding. This was *my* house! I took a deep breath, readied myself to bust some karate moves if necessary, and flung open the inner door just as the outer door swung open. I stood face-to-face with my neighbor sheepishly holding my keys in her hand.

"Who are you?" I demanded. "And why do you have my keys?"

She explained that she lived across the landing and that my landlord, her good friend, had given her the keys so she could come and close the *jie men'r* to get her heat fixed.

"*Jie men'r*? What's a *jie men'r*?" I asked.

"It's in your kitchen. It'll only take a second." She ushered in a scrawny worker who wore camouflage pants rolled up to the knee. He climbed up on a chair and slowly turned a small red wheel connected to some pipes that ran along the ceiling. Suddenly, the wheel broke off in his hands and boiling water began thundering down. He jumped off the chair. We froze, panicked. I began scurrying around clearing the floor and my neighbor ran to her apartment to get blankets and pails to soak up the water, the whole time whimpering, "*Daomeile! Daomeile! Daomeile!*" ("What a disaster! What a disaster! What a disaster!")

"Why don't you find a way to turn *off* the water instead!" I said.

"*Daomeile! Daomeile! Daomeile!*"

"*Bu* ben, *bu bu biao!*" I yelled over the roar of the water, stabbing my finger at the pipe spewing boiling water and hoping that this tongue-twisting chestnut of Chinese medicine wisdom ("Fix the *source,* not the symptom!") would get through to her, but she kept repeating her mournful refrain and running for more blankets. The worker stood unmoving in the growing fog. Water, an inch deep, was cascading over my tile floor, out my door, and down the concrete stairwell. Neighbors began coming up to investigate.

After a half hour, somehow the water was turned off. Word about the *jie men'r* spread quickly. My apartment filled up with curious neighbors, twenty or thirty of them. They were everywhere. Some were in the kitchen, offering advice about fixing the *jie men'r,* others lined the hallway and spilled into the living room. A few were in my bedroom fingering things on my desk. My papers were curled with the damp and the air was stiflingly close. I called Sue to tell her I would be late to work. No one owned a car, so the worker began a long bike ride out to a warehouse to get a new *jie men'r.*

My neighbor introduced me to the woman with the bowl cut, who lived in apartment 101. The woman said the ten apartments in our stairwell took turns checking the water and gas meters and collecting the money, and she had already come by a number of times, but I never answered the door. I lied and said I'd never heard anyone knocking. She then read the meter and issued me a tiny piece of foolscap with a number penned on it, the amount of which I promptly forked over to her.

Then a bulky policeman in olive showed up. I tried to shrink into the background and we played a deadly cat-and-mouse game around my apartment until he eventually cornered me and asked me where I was from. I cracked under his interrogation and admitted that I came from America. He fixed me with a look. Would I, possibly, be interested in teaching his kid English? I agreed but gave him my telephone number with two of the digits transposed.

Hours passed and the worker finally returned. He climbed up on the chair and held the new *jie men'r* up to the pipe. Too big. No one seemed surprised but me. This time, he measured the pipe first before leaving again for several hours. I called Sue and told her I wouldn't be making it in at all. Most of the neighbors dispersed, leaving their dirty footprints all over the wet tile floor. By five in the evening, the worker had returned, installed a new *jie men'r,* and my neighbor had finished mopping my entire floor. Everyone left; I took my shoes off and had a seat.

Chapter Eight

The Most Important Man in My Story

On Monday morning, the entire *City Edition* staff piled into the advertising department for our weekly meeting. Sue said the new cover story was about an underground drag show hosted by the French chef of the Parisian bistro Maxim's, provided it passed the censors, who'd been dragging their feet. If we had a story that Sue and Max judged sensitive, Max would take it to show our censors, whom I never met, and anywhere from a day to a week later, he would return with their yea-or-nay verdict.

Max strutted into the meeting. All eyes turned to him. Bad news, he said. He'd just met with the censors and they'd finally made a decision: It was a no-go. We'd have to come up with a new idea for a cover story soon.

A thought sprang to mind. Over the summer, I had seen *Inside Out: New Chinese Art,* a big show on Chinese contemporary art at PS1 in New York. Like the characters in *Beijing Bastards,* the artists had put their bad attitudes on flagrant display. Huge heads in pop colors laughed at jokes we couldn't hear. Chairman Mao's face was painted just as Warhol had done it years ago. In one gigantic photograph, a man sat naked in a public toilet coated in shiny honey and crawling with flies.

I dreaded opening *Beijing Scene* each week to find profiles of the latest artists, articles I'd wish I'd written.

"What if we did a cover story on underground artists?" I proposed. I didn't know any artists but I figured Max did. He shot me a scornful, pitying look.

"Chinese art is bullshit. I used to like art but then I decided it was a load of dog farts. Now I just have lunch every month with my friend Li Xianting, who runs the avant-garde art scene here, and he tells me who's hot and what's worthwhile. Everything else is shit. Do you want to know what is important?"

"Yes."

"News is important." He fixed me with a look to make sure his words had sunk in.

Max's cellphone rang. He looked at the number in annoyance before rejecting the call and I saw the saleswomen exchange sly glances. For the past few days, droves of women had been calling our office looking for Max. Whenever the phone rang my heart gave a little hop—was it Zhang Yuan? Once when I picked it up, it was an American woman on the other end, looking for "the Chinese man."

"Which Chinese man? Max?"

"I'm not sure," she said, sounding embarrassed. I told her she had the wrong number but she quoted Max's cellphone number. Sometimes he forwarded his cellphone calls to the office.

Max told us about a fortune-teller he'd been seeing recently. She knew things about his past that she had no business knowing as well as everything that would happen to him in the future, though she said there was one thing she wouldn't tell him: when and how he would die. Every single day he called her and she told him what was going to happen to him and what to watch out for. We all listened, rapt. This was typical: Max issued ridiculous pronouncements and my Chinese coworkers pampered his ego and doted on him, teasing and giggling. My natural tendency was to be sarcastic and emasculating but I was new here, he was my boss, and I needed his help. I tried to join in.

"What did she say today?" I asked.

"That my finances are not good, so I can't buy lunch for everyone today."

"But, Max, you are always so successful!" cooed another coworker.

"But my love life is supposed to go well. I am supposed to get together with a woman from another continent," he said, with a glance at our blond American art director. This made the women giggle and exchange more glances.

When his phone rang again, he stormed out of the meeting.

"Who are these women who are calling?" I asked Shannon, the graphic designer who shared a room with me. She had grown up in Beijing and still lived with her family in an apartment complex for army families manned by a military guard toting a machine gun. When I was still living with my relatives, Shannon and I had talked briefly about finding an apartment together but I was much more impatient than she to be on my own and I feared that she was like my relatives, a stranger to the concept of privacy.

"You didn't hear?" she asked, grabbing a copy of the latest magazine and turning to the personals, which were meant to connect Western companies and Chinese employees, Chinese nannies and Western babies, language tutors and eager students, and lovers of all stripes and sizes. "Ad sales were slow, so the ad department decided to put some fake ads in. Look in Lonely Hearts and see if you can figure out which one it is."

Most of the ads were Chinese women looking for Western men.

> Here lovely Chinese lady, early 30 years old, 160cm tall,
> can speak three foreign languages, now live and work in
> Beijing, looking for serious partner leading to marriage:
> European 175–180cm tall, 30–40 years old, white man,
> well educated, live and work in Beijing too.

Waiting for you. Chinese lady, well-educated, slim, curvy, long hair, starry eyes, sweet, good-looking, looking for her life partner here. You don't have to be rich to be my prince, as long as you are caring, responsible, athletic, well-educated, kind, understanding, extrovert, of course single, willing to spend the rest of your life with me, I would love to be in your arms for ever. By the way, you better be 30ys above, 170–180cm in height. Thanks! :)

Where are you ? I am 36-year-old Chinese female. I like swimming, music, film, and I like to write story. Looking for somebody has something same as me and become the most important man in my story?

Only one was a Chinese man looking for a Western woman.

I like the nightlife, I like to boogie!! I am a big strong Chinese man who speaks a little English and is looking to have fun, night and day. Ring me and I will rock your world! Call me at 13-9555-1977.

"You put in his real phone number!" I said.

"He has no idea because he doesn't read English and none of the women who call speak Chinese!" she said, and let out a wicked bark. I don't think they thought the ad would yield so many phone calls, that there were so many lonely Western women out there looking to have fun. Max didn't go out with any of the callers, but everyone in the office enjoyed seeing his feathers so ruffled for once. But secretly, I coveted Max's confidence. I found it hard to say anything with absolute certainty, a skill I suspected I had learned in college. What feeling or thought was to be trusted if everything and its opposite were also true? I wanted Max's macho swagger, wanted to dress up in corny outfits and have everyone hang on my most outlandish words.

Were those survival skills he had learned growing up in a prison? That was one of the rumors that swirled around Max. Beijing was a city that ran on rumors—no one in their right mind would trust any official news—and Max attracted more rumors than anyone else I knew. His parents had been jailed during the Cultural Revolution in the 1960s, the myth of his shadowy origins went, and the prison was where he was raised. He also had clandestine connections to the People's Liberation Army—how else would he have gotten those pictures of the PLA training grounds?

In each issue of the magazine we included how-to guides to help expats re-create the lives they'd left behind at home, and because it was almost Christmas, Sue told me to put together a shopping guide. And while I was taking cabs around the city, I was to gather quotes from cabbies about the traffic to help her with an article she was writing about the "Big Three" construction projects meant to ease the city's notorious gridlock.

I had no money and hence had never gone shopping in Beijing, but Jade knew the city better than I did, so she eagerly volunteered to come along and take photos. We'd been spending a lot of time together recently. She'd come to my neighborhood to have dinner, we'd gone together to Steve's apartment in the diplomatic compound to watch Clinton getting impeached on CNN and *Bride of Chucky* (her choice).

We stopped first at the office of a friend of her dad's to pick up money; then she dragged me to markets all over town, from the open-air Silk Market in the east to the three-story Pearl Market in the south to the warehouse-like Tianyi Market in the west to the traditional Qianmen market in the old city, each with rows and rows of tiny stalls crammed to the ceiling with goods and each manned by its own vendor who would grab our sleeves and say, *"Konnichiwa!"* Along with silk and pearls, we saw knock-off North Face jackets and Beanie Babies, chinoiserie, singing Mao lighters, fur coats with the claws still attached. Shopping was antithetical to my lifestyle, but Jade bought something at every stop: cream to keep her face pale and blemish-free, bright red dye for her hair, a long down coat, three-inch platform shoes, furry handbags. By the end of the day she was laden down with huge shopping bags. She had grown up on the Upper East Side of Manhattan and I guessed that her upbringing had given her elaborate grooming habits as well as confidence about what she wanted in life.

We spent a long time in traffic jams, the crawling, honking, smoggy, never-ending traffic jams for which Beijing was getting famous. Cabbies were only too willing to talk. They complained about the police who they said just stood in the middle of the road socializing instead of directing traffic, about pedestrians who didn't follow rules but whom you unfortunately couldn't just run over, and about the government that had reduced cab fares by 20 percent without reducing their fees.

At one point we drove down a rubble-strewn street that was more Beirut than Beijing. Courtyard houses on both sides of the narrow street lay in ruin and most of the roadbed had been dug up. As dust swirled up into the windshield, we navigated the crooked line of pavement that remained between tall construction barriers. This road was Numero Uno of the "Big Three" projects: Ping'an Dajie, parallel to the Avenue of Eternal Peace. The deadline for the project was the fiftieth anniversary of the People's Republic of China, less than a year away. The wheel of development that had crushed my relatives' courtyard house was rolling over other houses all around the city. This place that I was growing to love was disappearing right in front of my eyes.

Despite Max's attempts to dissuade me, I was still intrigued by the world of underground art. So when the *City Edition* fax machine spit out an invitation for an art exhibition that was being held in an apartment complex over the weekend, I decided to go. A crudely drawn pictograph resembling a cartoon treasure map indicated the location. Perhaps here I would find the underground artists at last.

I took a cab alone up to the North Fourth Ring Road. Out the window was a dusty wasteland dotted with apartment megablocks, low warehouses, and the occasional building crane. The desolation was overwhelming. I had the cab drop me off where I thought the map indicated and I circled around and around the huge and deserted apartment blocks with the map in hand, secretly hoping I wouldn't find it so I could turn around and go back home. Finally I saw a cluster of young people standing outside a doorway smoking. They nodded at me as I took the steps leading down into the basement.

I walked down a corridor over a series of gigantic lightboxes in which a man's face struggled underwater, his palms pressed against the glass, bubbles trailing out of his mouth. I walked from room to room in the dank and labyrinthine concrete bomb shelter. It was exactly what I'd hoped an underground art exhibition would be like. In one room, two eight-foot-tall beings constructed entirely of vegetables appeared to be locked in a distinctly carnivorous embrace. Body parts figured in many of the artworks. In one room a waxy torso floated upside down next to a pair of legs, which were next to aluminum pipes twisted like intestines, next to what looked like an actual intestine inflated with helium. Out of thin air phantom cellphones rang and people left messages, and the whole scene was harshly lit by a single lightbulb. In another room, a real fetus rested on a single bed made of a slab of ice. In another, an arm dangling from the ceiling gripped the end of a rope that reached down and snaked over the entire floor. A Chinese couple was standing on the pile of rope staring up at the arm.

"Is it real?"

"Looks real." It did too, all blackened and shriveled.

"*E xing,*" said the woman. Nauseating.

"*Ku,*" said the man. Cool.

I walked through almost twenty rooms. Cutting through the dank and sweetly rotten smell came a scent like french fries. I found my way to a room where many people were gathered. Two girls in tight dresses were standing behind a deep fryer from which they fished out things that they then gave to a fey creature with curly hair to line up on the floor. They were tanks. Was it a reference to the Tiananmen Square Massacre? What did it all mean?

The combined effect of all the pieces in the space did make me feel slightly sick to my stomach. Unlike the Political Pop and other high-minded, clean-looking art of the *Inside Out* exhibition, these pieces felt more visceral and more intimate, like alienation experienced truly from the inside out.

Most of those milling around were Chinese guys with hair of varying lengths and with cigarettes dangling from their mouths. A few young Westerners wandered through. I didn't know anyone and couldn't tell who the artists were but everyone there seemed to know one another. I passed the man whose drowning face I'd walked over before, but was too tongue-tied to say hi.

I finally saw someone I knew, a Chinese guy with a shaggy bowl cut and kindly eyes; I couldn't quite remember where I knew him from. I lunged at him eagerly but as he recoiled with a look of shock I realized who he was: Cui Jian. China's first rock star. Hero of *Beijing Bastards*. I almost blurted out that I was friends with Zhang Yuan and that the film they'd made together had lured me to Beijing, but at the last moment, I grabbed hold of myself and moved on.

Chapter Nine

The Redemptive Power of Family

*M*y phone rang early Christmas morning with an especially festive jingle. I knew who it would be. But it wasn't just my parents, but also my brother; Nainai; my aunt, uncle, and cousin; plus various other relatives, twelve total, all together on speakerphone yelling over one another. "Merry Christmas!" "We wish you were here!" "Do you have plans tonight?" "What is the weather like?" I tried to answer their questions but in the pause after I spoke others rushed in with more questions. Finally I gave up trying to speak and just let their words wash over me. I was happy to be so far away so I could avoid answering questions about what exactly I was doing with my life. I hung up and lay back down in bed.

Several months had passed since my brunch with Zhang Yuan and he became oddly elusive about setting exact dates for the trips to Ürümqi or Rome and began ignoring my phone calls, which only made me call more. I had a dream in which he spoke perfect English and I wondered if he had been pulling my leg the entire time. I decided it was time to visit the film set in Tianjin and called him to let him know I would be doing just that.

One Sunday right after the New Year, I took the three-hour train to Tianjin with Jade. Zhang Yuan met us at a hotel, looking harried and distracted. As his driver took us to the set, he turned around in the front seat and told us about the film. Called *Going Home for New Year's* (or *Seventeen Years* in English), it was the story of a woman returning home for New Year's after spending seventeen years in jail for killing her sister. He talked absentmindedly, as if reciting rote interview responses for a reporter.

"Going home for New Year's is an incredibly important ritual for families in China. So there is already so much tension there. Then add on the years they haven't seen each other and her killing her sister. You really don't know if her family will forgive her," he said. "It's a story that all of us who leave home live through. What do we find when we go back home for New Year's?"

"Mmmmm," I said. On another day I would have found him profound. Today he seemed infuriatingly mundane. I wasn't just an average reporter. What about Rome?

"Max says you got permission to shoot in a prison," said Jade, in her sauciest voice.

"Yes, the Ministry of Justice gave us permission to shoot in a women's prison."

"Can we go into the prison?"

"Sorry, we shot those scenes last week."

"Oh, too bad." Jade pouted. "I really wanted to go to prison."

We arrived at a brick apartment building and went into a ground-floor apartment with a hard concrete floor. The cast and crew were waiting for Zhang Yuan and he was quickly absorbed into the fray. The living room and kitchen were being used as the set, while the rest of the apartment was filled with cords and boxes. As the producers and technicians buzzed around the apartment, Jade and I sat on some big black boxes in the darkness of the balcony, waiting for the action to start. I felt moronic all of a sudden.

"I think he's hot for you," said Jade.

"Today he's actually being cold. Besides, he's married."

"So what? This is *China*. Everyone cheats on their wife here."

"I'm not into married men."

"Do you have the hots for him?"

"No, I don't think so. I think I want to *be* him."

"Don't lie. I think you want to be *with* him. Are you really attracted to him? You have *weird* taste. He looks like Eraserhead or something."

Zhang Yuan's fuzzy head loomed over everyone on the bright set and he looked so authoritative, pointing here and there. The actors wandered around, talking and laughing, one woman wearing a police uniform. We asked one of the crewmembers what they were filming today. He said they were about to shoot the last scene of the film: the reunion between the daughter and her parents.

Finally, Zhang Yuan called for silence and the actors took their places. Their faces suddenly became stoic and unemotional, just like a Chinese family's would be when something traumatic was about to happen. The daughter and the policewoman escorting her home entered and the reunion seethed with the tension of emotions felt but not expressed. Then suddenly the dam burst and the daughter collapsed into her father's lap, weeping and saying hysterically, "When I was in prison, I often missed my own father! But I couldn't remember what he looked like! In the end, I couldn't help thinking of you!" He forgave her in the most syrupy fashion possible like in those schlocky soap operas my relatives watched. They hugged.

I cringed. This wasn't the Zhang Yuan I knew. His films were understated, cynical, ironic. His films didn't have happy endings and they didn't celebrate the redemptive power of family. Family, for all its promises of unity, was supposed to be full of betrayal, like the mother who abandons her son in *Mama* or the father whose alcoholism breaks up his family in *Sons*. What was redemptive was Art. I blamed the censors.

At a break in the shooting, I told Zhang that I needed to go and asked if his driver would drive me back to Beijing as he had promised. It was late and I had to work the next morning. He was busy and barely gave me a glance.

"Actually, the driver's not going back tonight," he said. "He can drive you back early tomorrow."

"But I have to be there by nine o'clock. Max is bringing his friend from *The Wall Street Journal* to come critique our magazine. He said I absolutely have to be there." Sue was in the States for the holidays and I was the only editor in town.

"You'll be there. Just go sleep in my hotel room."

I scowled. "Sleep in your hotel room?"

"We're going to keep filming all night," he said. "It's fine."

So Jade and I went and slept in his room, each in a single bed. Very late that night, he came in and I woke up. He politely sat and read for a while as I peeked at him through half-closed eyes, then finally he crawled into bed with me. Ahhh. This was the Zhang Yuan that I knew secretly existed, less the esteemed film director and more of a bastard. I looked across the pillow but could barely make out his features in the dark. His face looked fleshy and tired. He flung a rubbery arm around me and slurred, "Zhenluo," and began whispering unintelligible nothings into my ear and stroking my head. What I wanted had finally zoomed up into my face, but up close, it didn't look so good. I wasn't a cheap film groupie who played mistress to someone else's fickle, doughy-faced husband who made corny films—not with my friend sleeping in the next bed over, anyhow. If Jade hadn't been there, I wonder how I would have felt and what might have happened. I rolled over and went back to sleep.

When I woke in the morning and looked out the window, all I saw was soft whiteness. A damp fog had descended on the city. Had last night all been a dream? Next to me was the bear-like, slumbering form of Zhang Yuan. Nope. I got out of bed, roused the sleepy Jade, and made

Zhang Yuan call his driver. As soon as he had, he fell back asleep. I shut the door softly behind us.

As we drove, the fog became thicker and thicker and as we were about to enter the highway, we saw that the taillights of the car in front of us glowed a faint rosy pink.

"We can't go any farther until the fog clears," the driver said, as he pulled off onto the shoulder. I looked at my watch: six thirty. I was barely going to make it as it was.

"But I have to get back!"

"Miss, look at this fog. There's nothing we can do."

"Okay, okay."

We sat quietly as the car was enveloped in a puffy whiteness. Needling through the fog was Max's voice telling me to find a way back to Beijing, to do whatever it took to get back. But something wicked in me told me to stay put and just be lost in the dream of last night. The bright lights of the set, the dark room, the arm around me, the words whispered in my ear. It was a relief to not have to try to see into the distance, calculating things and being rational. Because once I got back to Beijing, it would really be over with Zhang Yuan. And with it my idea to do a film about filmmakers.

We finally got back in the afternoon. Max was furious.

"Where the hell were you? There wasn't a single editor here when my friend from *The Wall Street Journal* was here. Do you know how embarrassing that was for me?"

"I'm sorry! We were in Tianjin last night and the fog was so thick we couldn't drive on the highway until after noon."

"Why didn't you take a train?"

I stood dumbfounded. "The fog . . ."

"What were you doing in Tianjin?"

"Visiting the set of Zhang Yuan's film."

"Zhang Yuan's film! You are unbelievable." Brought out into the light of day, the fluffy stuff of my dreams solidified, cracked, and crumbled to dust. He thrust the tape recording of the session at me and ordered me to listen to it, gave me a beeper with the admonition to carry it with me at all times, and stormed back to his office.

Our art director came over. "You didn't miss much. That guy's main piece of advice was: more sex," she said. "He was one of those white guys who comes to China and gets all excited about sex shops and prostitutes. I just thought, 'Well, go visit them yourself.'"

Chapter Ten

Seeks Trouble for Oneself

I looked in the mirror one morning and realized with a sinking feeling that it was time to get my hair cut. My artfully shapeless hair had become truly shapeless. Finding a hairdresser is hard in any city. You need someone who can prune away from your unruly bonsai anything that is not the essential you of that exact moment. There were many hairdressing salons on my street, all with the same basic look: a bare cube big enough for only one or two haircutting chairs, a tatty curtain hung at the back. One or two heavily made-up young women stared out in boredom. Most were empty during the day. Once I saw a man actually sitting in one of the chairs. *A real hole in the wall*, I couldn't help thinking. The ladies had skills, I was sure, but they weren't the ones I was looking for. Other shops lining the street catered to their needs, some selling skimpy, glittery clothing and fake eyelashes, others selling prophylactics and sex toys.

There was only one salon in my neighborhood that I was sure wasn't a brothel. It was a basement shop staffed by a handful of what looked through the fishbowl window to be diminutive glam rockers, men and women all identically clad in tight, shiny black clothing and all sporting puffy mullet cuts dyed different shades of dirty orange. Most of the haircuts I saw on the street looked so utilitarian: long straight falls pulled back into thin ponytails, shapeless bobs, stiff permanent waves. The best haircuts I saw were the crude pageboys on the ruddy farmer women who drove their donkey carts into the city. The mullets were a pretty radical look for Beijing circa 1999 and one that inspired slightly more confidence than the prostitutes. And so I went there.

The salon was big, with ten haircutting chairs, all empty. A TV hung in the corner of the salon, blasting Cantopop karaoke videos. The place smelled sour and burnt, but it was too late to turn back. The staff had already whirred lazily into action. One of the women led me to a chair, washed my hair, gave me a long head massage, then sat me down in one of the hairdressing chairs. I took off my glasses.

One of the men came over to pin on a bib and scrutinize my hair. The boss, who had been watching carefully, came and pushed him out of the way. He was tall, the only one of them taller than me, and had short, well-styled hair (still black) and a not-unhandsome face. He also had a disturbingly long pinky nail, which came in handy when it came time to part my hair. Make it look messy, was all I told him.

He began snipping cautiously, hair by hair. The other hairdressers sprawled out in the empty chairs and warbled along sporadically with the music in Cantonese, which was so cloying that my teeth felt as though they were rotting just listening to it. He cut so slowly that eventually the songs started to repeat themselves. I squirmed in impatience. When he finally finished, I put my glasses back on and looked in the mirror. Puffy on top, with a wispy frill of hair in the back like a lacy bed ruffle. I looked exactly like them.

"Oh."

"It's very feminine," he said.

"Not where I come from."

"And where is that?"

"America," I said, "and looking feminine is not what I want anyhow."

"Why don't I dye it for you?" he asked. I could see them kidnapping me, their perfect clone, and transporting me back to their home planet. No thank you. I had him hack off the fringe in the back, paid my twenty kuai, and left. At two dollars fifty, at least it wasn't an expensive disaster.

The salon was around the corner from my house, so I passed by often. Some days the boss would be outside tinkering on his big red-and-white motorcycle and he would rev the engine when I walked by and throw me saucy looks. I rolled my eyes. But after that first disastrous haircut, I went back a second time and a third and fourth. There was something I enjoyed about my monthly cameos. Everyone greeted me like an old friend and the boss always pushed his peons out of the way to cut my hair. They peppered me with questions. What was I doing in Beijing? Did I like it? And had I ever ridden on a motorcycle? I countered with questions of my own and found out that they were all from down south and had moved to Beijing together and all lived together in the same apartment. And all day long in the salon, they pickled in the saccharine brine of endless Cantopop together. What a life. Like a sitcom, the kind where everyone kind of looks alike, gets along, and talks about nothing all day long.

Each time, I came out with another bad haircut and I swore it was the last time, but I just wasn't ready for a messy breakup. In my neighborhood full of families, my young and single hairdressers who had come to the city from afar were the closest I had to kin.

My silent new apartment started growing on me. Even the mysterious sounds echoing through the air shaft off my kitchen had a routine of their own: Old men hocked phlegm in the mornings, chopsticks clickety-clacked together as they were washed after mealtimes, and almost constantly, a boy was caught in a screaming match with his grandmother. I dubbed them Screaming Granny and Horrible Boy. I even began recognizing them in the yard outside: Screaming Granny was a small and shrewish old woman and Horrible Boy was a child with a big head and a wispy tail of hair hanging down his back. Other neighbors started to take on distinct character too, such as the Perambulator, a bald, hulking old man with heavy-lidded eyes, who every day shuffled slowly, slowly around the neighborhood with a cane.

Our yard was always filled with middle-aged *xianren*—the loafers, idlers—who gathered at all hours of the day, playing badminton or mahjongg, walking their tiny white Pekinese dogs, watching everyone going in and out, as if they lived in a village where nothing much happened. They sat on old sofas that always stayed in the yard. My neighbor and the woman with the bowl cut, whom I nicknamed Bowl Cut, were often out there together. They had missed out on a proper education because of the Cultural Revolution and now they were being laid off from their state-run jobs. I thought of them as a lost generation. Bowl Cut, perpetually clad in her elephant-emblazoned pajama set, was one of the few who greeted me, even occasionally asking if I'd eaten or warning me not to go out too late at night. There was someone whacking women over the head with sticks, she said, robbing them and leaving them for dead. For some reason I chuckled. China's not so safe anymore, she said sternly.

After her turn to check the meters had passed, other neighbors took theirs, thus beginning a notorious monthly routine: first a light rapping like a snare drum on my locked security door, then an angry banging and rattling, and then finally the yell, "Open up! I know you're in there!" Was it the police? Or just a meter checker? I never opened up. Some learned to announce themselves, some left notes in my door, while others resorted to cornering me as I slunk in and out of the building. They would have a curious look around my apartment and ask me questions about what I was doing in China. I asked the same of them but none of us ever gave a straight answer.

My nightmares about the police persisted, but they took on an increasingly surreal cast. I dreamed one night that the police were going around to every apartment, banging on the doors and checking to see how much soybean milk each resident had drunk.

One day as I walked down the stairs of my apartment building, I saw the door of the apartment below mine close hastily, and so the next time I bumped into my neighbor across the landing I asked her if she knew of someone moving into 401.

"Someone said a girl who works in a karaoke bar down the street moved in last week," she answered.

"Karaoke bar?"

She shot me a look as if I didn't know what happened at a karaoke bar, aside from off-tune singing.

"Is she from Beijing?" I asked.

"Would a girl from Beijing be living here? I think she's from Sichuan," she said. I could almost hear her explaining what kinds of girls came from Sichuan to Beijing, the *capital* of China, to work in karaoke bars, but she just gave me a humored look. "You don't understand, do you?" She looked as if she'd said too much and shut the door. My neighborhood was a haven for the undocumented—not only Westerners but also Chinese people, particularly girls who came from places like Sichuan to work in places like karaoke bars.

Just outside of my gate was a young woman who tended stacks of small bamboo steamers, which sat on a large metal barrel filled with hot coals. Every morning on my way to work, I bought a steamerful of *baozi* from her. The woman's face was fresh and unlined but as she emptied ten tiny *baozi* into a wafer-thin plastic bag, I noticed her hands were as chapped and wrinkled as an old crone's. Winter in Beijing was gray and cold and the bag warmed my hands as I walked. I ate slowly, trying to make the *baozi* last the entire twenty-minute walk.

One morning I was suddenly struck by an image of my mom warming her hands with a hot bagel on a cold New York morning, a story she had told me many times. I knew my parents had emigrated to the States and worked hard so that I wouldn't end up back in China, warming my hands with pork buns. Our lives had a sick, sweet symmetry that they did not seem to appreciate.

As I walked into the office and popped into my mouth the last *baozi,* my coworker saw me and shot me a look of disgust.

"You eat those?" she asked. "Street food is filthy." She then took great pleasure in telling me that a few years ago they had caught a *baozi* seller from the countryside whose *baozi* had been stuffed with human flesh—right in the Xidan District where she and my relatives lived.

City Edition continued to be a shaky mast to lash my life to. While our art director worked alone in the office late one night with the goateed web designer Scott, he subjected her to a confession that he had participated in blood-drinking rituals in Florida years ago. He claimed blood didn't actually taste so bad. He was dismissed and a laptop disappeared with him. Soon thereafter I returned to the office one day to find Sue yelling at Distributor Lu and telling him to leave and never come back. He was the thief in the office and that wasn't the worst of it, she said. She may have been paranoid but Beijing seemed to confirm one's hallucinations.

Max decided to bring his fortune-teller into the office. "She's the real thing," he said. "From the countryside."

Everyone wanted a turn. Sue went in first, then other coworkers. Each came out seeming as though she'd looked a ghost in the eye. She was eerily accurate, they said. She knew the exact date someone's parents had gotten into a car accident. She knew someone else had had kidney surgery and she said it had happened without a knife because she'd probably never heard of laser surgery.

She spared no one.

"If you give birth to a boy, you'll die in childbirth."

"You will be a young widow."

"You had an affair," she said to the husband of a couple sitting before her and in the shocked silence that ensued she said, "But it's okay because so did she."

Everyone was reevaluating their lives in the light of what she had told them. She told Sue and Max that their company would never make money because the building had been built on the site of an old temple.

They had to move out of this building as soon as possible, but for a temporary fix, she skewed all the desks at weird angles.

When I went in for my session the next day and sat next to her on a couch, I saw she had the stocky build and ruddy complexion of a farmer, and the same impassive stare, as did a buddy she'd brought. The enormous glass table that had filled the small conference room was gone. Max shrugged when I asked about it. Bad feng shui, he said. She asked my birthday in the lunar calendar, slowly examined my palms, then looked me dead in the eye, as if seeing straight through to my soul or thinking deeply about what she was going to have for lunch. Her eyes lost focus and she began to speak cryptic rhymes as her hand tapped out a rhythm on the towel on her lap. When she came out of her trance, she and her handler interpreted what she'd seen on the other side.

She said I'd never be very rich but I'd never be very poor either. I'd stay in China for three to five years. After leaving, I'd have a constant desire to return, but I'd come back only once. When I was twenty-seven, I would meet my mate, who would be three years my senior and more successful than me. She told me I was doing the right thing, walking the road of culture, and that I should work at a TV or radio station. Most of what she said was vague because, she said, I was so young and my future so full of possibility. The Chinese idea of fate is less like a sneak preview of a movie already shot and more like a treatment for an as-yet-unmade one, especially near the beginning of life. It was up to me to make what I would of it. I confess to being disappointed.

However, she did say some clear and damning things about my personality—that I am very smart but afraid of everything, that I have a surly, inflexible personality, and that I *zixun fannao,* which I translated as "seeks trouble for oneself."

"Is there anything I can do about this?"

She shook her head no. I figured if I couldn't change it, I might as well make it the bedrock of my new idea of myself. *Seeks trouble for oneself.*

Then she started telling me about my past. She knew I wasn't born in China, that I had come one year before, that I had one older brother. Check, check, check.

"Someone in your family was in the government. Your father?"

"No."

"Your grandfather?"

"Yes."

"I see him very clearly. Well, he died disappointed."

I wasn't unduly impressed. Fish around in most families that had fled China and you'd find someone who had been in the government. And didn't everyone die disappointed?

The phone still rang each Sunday evening and my stomach would drop out as I prepared for the onslaught of self-doubt that my parents' calls would instigate. I was amazed that these feelings could be effortlessly transmitted halfway around the world on a thin metal filament. Now, not only was everyone's offspring going to medical school, but they were also getting married.

"We went to a wedding this weekend," my mom reported breathlessly. "My friend Janet, my oldest friend from Burma who lives in Philadelphia, remember her? Her oldest daughter, Lisa, the one named after me, got married. She's five two and her husband is six one. Can you imagine? Guess where they met? Emergency room. Emergency room doctors. All their friends at the wedding were doctors too. Boy, those doctors sure know how to party! All out on the dance floor until the wedding was over. I said, 'How do you do it?' And Lisa said, 'We work hard but we play hard too!'"

It wasn't enough that we had to excel at work, but we had to excel at getting married and partying too. Did it ever end? My best friend from childhood had gone to medical school but she had shocked everyone by marrying an East Village tattoo artist.

"Do you like him?" I asked my mom after the wedding.

"It's her life to ruin," she answered.

I wondered what my parents told their friends about me, or if they even spoke about me at all.

Then the conversation took an unexpected turn. "My friend Betty is organizing a tour group that is coming to China during the anniversary celebration in October," my mom said. "One week, eight cities. It comes to Beijing first."

"Are you joining it?"

"We're thinking about it," my mom said.

"No, no," my dad said. "No decision yet."

"Is it a tour for white people?" I asked. "That might be kind of weird for you guys."

"No, everyone on it is Chinese. All the tour guides will speak Chinese."

"I think you should do it. Bobo and Bomu and I can take you around Beijing."

"No decision yet," my dad repeated.

"Your sister can come for a week to take care of Nainai," my mom said to him. "You take care of her the rest of the year; Judy can do it for one week."

"Okay, okay," he said. "We have to go."

My parents in China: It was hard to imagine. As much as I associated them with this place, it was me who actually lived here.

For hours after I talked to them, I sat paralyzed on my couch, unable to reenter the fragile life I'd built for myself here.

Part Three

Chapter Eleven

It Stinks

City Edition moved to the Asia-Pacific Building, a ten-story yellow-brick building with red trim and a huge Bank of China billboard clapped to the roof. It was a step up from the Office of Defense Conversion, and to Max's delight, the building had been designed using feng shui principles dictating that none of the doors or windows could face a cardinal direction and so the whole building sat at an awkward angle to the road. (I laughed, but about a year after we moved into the building, Sue and Max sold the magazine for a sizeable amount of money.) The building was actually an apartment building and the new office was a three-bedroom. One bedroom held the editorial department, one the design department, and the third was Max's office complete with a "computer" that was merely a monitor and keyboard sitting in jaunty relationship to each other. The large living room was for advertising. In the kitchen, our driver regularly whipped up multicourse lunches for us. Max took an apartment upstairs and would drift lazily down to the office in a shorty robe emblazoned with the artist Xu Bing's fake Chinese characters. It was a homey arrangement.

But sitting with my desk facing Sue's all day was nerve-racking. She looked on impatiently as I labored over my articles, self-consciously doing interviews over the phone and polishing each sentence to a lapidary perfection. When I finally submitted them to her, she would crack them into pieces and rewrite them in her own voice, pooh-poohing my objections. "Why are you mad about my edit?" she said once. "That story was no good in the first place."

Most weekend nights found me drinking with Jade, Steve, and Max in a bar filled with other expats. I drank to forget the difficulties of my life: being lonely, struggling at my job, chasing a dream that seemed so out of reach. As winter deepened, so did the drinking. But no matter how much I drank, I never really felt better.

While I enjoyed spending time with Jade, there were so many ways in which we were mismatched. One Saturday afternoon we watched *Beijing Bastards* together in Steve's apartment; Jade had found a pirated VCD of it. "Val, *this* is the movie that brought you to China?" she said. "It stinks." And seeing it through her eyes, I realized it did stink. Plotless, inane, badly shot. Drained of all the secret meaning it had had for me. I saw the foundation of my dreams from a different angle, one that made it look flimsy and vaguely risible. I wished I hadn't rewatched it, especially with Jade.

So when a woman with a British accent called me at *City Edition* to tell me about an art exhibition of hers that she hoped I would promote in the arts listings, I jotted a note to myself to go. It seemed a promising place to meet some new friends. The woman introduced herself as Cookie Cousins and said she'd studied calligraphy at the Central Academy of Fine Arts the previous year and her work was all modern calligraphy, and that I should come along to the opening in a few weeks. There was something inviting in her voice, aside from the fact that she was inviting me to invite the whole city to her opening.

When the night came, Jade had no interest in going. I donned a new pair of boots, which were tall and black with three-inch high heels and two big silver buckles. In the store they had looked sexy and dangerous, but when I strapped them on, they looked gaudy and ridiculous. The more I looked, the less I could tell. I teetered down Sanlitun, buoyed by the rowdy laughter and yelling jangling out of the bars into the dark street.

The Dreamy Gallery was small, full of people and blindingly bright inside. I walked in mincing steps around the perimeter, looking at the art and trying not to topple over. The calligraphy barely looked like characters, more like abstract ink-drip paintings, wild and idiosyncratic. Tall paper lanterns painted in the same way glowed warmly on the floor. I looked around for Cookie. She was easy to spot, in an unabashedly loud thrift-store dress, messy spiky hair, and big clear-framed glasses, talking nonstop in a high-pitched, dotty British accent, surrounded by friends, some Western, some Chinese. *You should be my friend,* I thought as I stood blankly on the other side of room with the light glaring on my awful boots, *but I left my thrift-store clothes at home.* I went home without even saying hi.

The next Saturday night when my phone rang, it was Jade as usual. I dutifully headed out to meet her, Steve, and Max. While other parts of the city went quiet at night, my street was filled with a strange mix of people: dour and tired farmers who had come to the neighborhood to work on all-night construction projects, hairdressers who also worked all night, karaoke girls in tight floor-length outfits, men in suits driving black cars, young Westerners headed out to bars. I didn't blend in, but I didn't stick out either. My neighborhood was itself a nightlife destination, lined with pleasure palaces with English monikers: the Backingham Palace, a cylindrical bathhouse with gigantic copper columns; the Moon and Stars karaoke bar; and Maggie's 2, a brothel advertising itself with a huge photo of Arnold Schwarzenegger smoking a cigar. At the only intersection in the neighborhood sat the New Ark Hotel, a three-star affair that rented out what they called "o'clock rooms" that went for a much cheaper rate than a whole night. Being out on the street was like teetering on the edge of the world, but it felt safer than being in my apartment. At least I wasn't breaking any laws out there.

That night was like any other, save for the fact that one minute we were at the bar and the next Max was in my bed complaining about how uncomfortable it was. Max was not my type. Macho. Commanding. A bulldog. But this was Beijing, where the rules seemed to be the opposite of what they were at home.

His warm body was comforting. But his smoky breath was repulsive, as was the thought of the dark, rotting infinity where once his teeth had been. He wore bright red briefs, which I did not allow him to take off. He pulled me closer and I mimicked his desire. Our chests touching, the warmth of his back against my forearms, our legs beginning to entwine. I wanted it, then I didn't. It was warm, but it turned my stomach. Jade's voice popped into my head. *What* can he do for *me?* You had to know what you wanted. I did. I didn't. I didn't. My disgust coalesced finally into a hard kernel. I pushed him away and got up.

"I'm not really into this," I said, and then drove what I thought would be the final nail in the coffin. "I think I'm a lesbian. Sorry."

"If you're a lesbian, then we can snuggle and it will be no problem," he said, as if we were playing a game of logic.

"Go to sleep."

"I cuddle with my good friends all the time without any problem."

"We're not good friends. Go to sleep."

After that night, my relationship with Max slowly deteriorated until we barely talked to each other anymore. He no longer helped me with my articles and I stopped my clumsy attempts at pampering or doting. I was stunned and embarrassed. By getting involved with Zhang Yuan and Max, I had alienated the two men who were going to help me reach my filmmaking dreams and help me make it as a journalist. Everything I'd come here for seemed to be slipping out of my hands.

I told no one at the office but Jade and I told her the story mostly for comic effect, about his clumsy kisses and the red briefs and about my lesbian confession.

"I guess I'll be buying my own drinks from now on."

"Lesbian?" she said in a naughty tone of voice. "Really?"

"Maybe," I said. "Probably not. All I know is I don't like Max. And I don't need him."

And I realized it was true. If I wanted to be these men, why didn't I just be them, instead of idolizing them, depending on them, ending up in bed with them, and waking up in the morning even more empty-handed than when I went to sleep?

Chapter Twelve
Yijia's Grand Opening

One Saturday morning, Bobo called me to tell me that Xiao Peng was driving the family to IKEA—Beijing's first—up on the North Fourth Ring Road and to ask if I wanted to meet them there. I said yes, welcoming the chance to spend time with them out of the house. I was so thankful not to be living together anymore and so glad they knew nothing about the messiness of my life. IKEA was the newest tourist destination for locals in Beijing—I even brought along my camera.

The store was packed. A sign in the bedroom department invited shoppers to try out the beds for at least a few moments, but there was no need for such an invitation. Entire families bounced up and down together on the beds. People sat on all the sofas and picked up and examined every utensil in the model kitchens, as if encountering the relics of a futuristic civilization. We joined in.

After a walk through the store, Bobo and Bomu sank down into two recliners. They looked slightly ill at ease and seeing them there reminded me of my very last visit to their big courtyard house, the one that had been demolished the summer before. I had returned to that house one day to find a pert single bed sitting in a corner of the living room, which had been completely cleared of the sagging couches and worn side tables. The bed had been covered with a fresh pink bedspread, and the two cracked walls of the corner it sat in had been plastered with flowery wallpaper. *This is unexpected,* I thought, but no one acted as if anything were different.

I finally asked, "This bed—why is it here?"

"We've thrown out the old furniture and bought new furniture," Bomu said. "We got this bed just for you. You should sleep here from now on." They all turned to me and smiled, and when I smiled confusedly in return, they all roared with laughter. I stood helplessly, cursing them. Xiao Lu finally took pity on me and told me that a TV series was renting out the courtyard house to use as a set and paying my relatives four thousand yuan—almost five hundred dollars—for a few days' inconvenience. Our house was going to be in one of those cheesy soap operas that they were always watching! Bobo and Bomu were giddy like children the night before a circus comes to town. "My" bedroom was to be the boudoir of a pop singer, a girl with sophisticated Western tastes. I imagined the camera framing the immaculate corner and cropping out the threadbare reality of my relatives' lives.

The crew descended on the house the next morning. I heard them arrive as I was taking my sponge bath in the room with a rag for a knob; moments later a crew member burst in on me. We both yelled in surprise and the door quickly shut. They unleashed chaos in the house. Actors got made up in the living room, directors called for silence during takes, and camera operators clambered over the roof like monkeys. Bomu's mother, a squat, bowlegged granny with no teeth, flirted mercilessly with the handsomest of the young actors. The crew set up a washing machine (clearly a fiction) in the middle of the rundown courtyard and took and retook a scene of an utterly ordinary middle-aged woman—a *very* famous actress, my relatives whispered to me—uttering a plaintive monologue that I didn't fully understand, her voice going high and wheedling over something (the licentious pop singer girl? the world gone awry?). We were riveted. The house was full of laughter and I saw, for the first time, my relatives smiling and looking happy. The crew admired the old courtyard house; my relatives beamed and demurred.

"It's so run-down," they said.

"But it's so rare for one family to have their own courtyard house these days," said the crew, and my relatives had to agree. Most houses were now divided among many families. No one mentioned the fact that the house would be demolished soon.

Bobo pulled out *Quadrangles of Beijing*, a glossy bilingual book about courtyard houses, to show me. The houses in it were not like the rustic shanty we were sitting in now—the courtyards were all palatial in size, emptied of bicycles, laundry lines, and stacks of coal, and perfectly restored. They looked exactly how I had imagined courtyard houses to look before I actually came to China, like miniature Forbidden Cities. In fact, each courtyard house was designed using the same cosmological rules as the Forbidden City, and Confucian hierarchy was embedded right into its architecture; the tallest northern room always housed the eldest family members while the lower rooms housed younger generations. The book said the house was originally designed to be a symbol of stability in an eternally fluctuating world, and the empty space of the courtyard—with its piece of sky, its fruit tree, its caged bird—was meant to cultivate family harmony. The photos staged picturesque scenes: an old couple playing chess and drinking tea, or three generations of a family sitting together making dumplings.

But Bobo and his family never sat in the courtyard of their house. They never set out a table to eat or drink, never played chess or stargazed. The skies in the day were milk white with pollution and the night sky too obscured to see stars.

The TV series injected the courtyard house with one last burst of life right before its destruction and I learned the fun way what my family had been learning the hard way all these years (the second time is a farce, after all): that life could be shuffled around as easily as sets in a play and we, its unwilling actors, would be forced to play along. If Bobo and Bomu suffered any sadness about the impending destruction, they did it inside, silently.

For those few days, fact and fiction were melded together, but after the house was demolished, the fiction peeled away like wallpaper. It was all that remained.

Back in IKEA, Bobo and Bomu had settled into their chairs. Had there been a TV on, we could have stayed all afternoon. It was a strange, cozy scene, so I took out my camera and told them to smile; they assumed stern, beatific expressions and I snapped a photo, setting off a bright flash. A salesman in a blue oxford rushed over.

"Please stop taking photos."

"What's the big deal?"

"Store policy is no photos. Please put your camera away."

Xiao Peng stood on the side, smirking. "People are taking pictures of the furniture and getting it copied cheaper elsewhere, you know."

"I know," I lied.

On the way out, I noticed that most shoppers left empty-handed. By the checkout counter was a row of waist-high cardboard bins filled with loose and inexpensive items: shrink-wrapped stacks of six colored plastic cups or five concentric containers for leftovers, bags of one hundred tea lights. Shoppers clustered around the bins and seemed to buy the items as souvenirs of their visit, or consolation prizes. We left without touching a thing.

Chapter Thirteen
Peking Man

a giant coffin held aloft by several men in long gowns bobbles merrily down a narrow hutong and arrives at the door of a courtyard house, where the men try to collect the payment for the thirty new layers of lacquer recently added to it. The lady of the house instructs her servant to turn them away. The coffin is her father-in-law's pride and joy, which the Old Master has spent the family fortune lacquering up year after year.

Xiao Ding stopped the tape and rewound to the beginning, apologizing for the low production value of the made-for-TV movie. Several days before, he had called me, reminded me of who he was (Zhang Yuan's "translator" friend from the Pretty Bird Club), and asked if I'd be interesting in a job helping him polish some English subtitles. China Central Television had hired him to subtitle a movie adapted from an old stage play that was airing on their English-language channel. The movie wasn't so great, he said, but he remembered me saying that I wanted to make a documentary and this job would be good practice if I wanted to go on to subtitle independent films later, which was a good way to meet other filmmakers and start making my own documentary.

And so I found myself in Xiao Ding's apartment on a Sunday afternoon. The apartment was alarmingly stripped down; the walls and floors were bare concrete and the fixtures protruded abruptly out of the walls, as if the builders had abandoned the place halfway through construction. He said the movie was based on a play from 1940 called *Peking Man*. The playwright, Cao Yu, was one of China's first Western-style playwrights and had studied Eugene O'Neill and Aeschylus in college. The play was about the Zengs, an ancient fossil of a Beijing family in the 1930s who are educated, mannered, snobbish, and completely out of step with modern times. They are deeply in debt to their neighbors, a nouveau riche textile manufacturing family, and the Old Master is thinking of handing over either their decrepit courtyard house or his coffin to settle the debt. Xiao Ding was prim and fussy with the subtitling, dictating exactly how many characters could fit on a line and pressing me to make each line sound like real conversational English. We sat close together, debating every line of the movie.

The story focused on the worst few days of the Zengs' lives. At the end, right before the family is forced to hand the coffin over to their neighbors, the Old Master delivers a speech in which he calls all his children "stupid, lazy, and unfilial." The playwright could have taken the words right out of my Yeye's mouth. It was eerie to see him fictionalized this way, years before he became who he was. The playwright had been about the same age as him and in fact the play had been published in the year of my dad's birth. Amazing also was the fact that this play could still have so much meaning sixty years later, that traditional families would still be struggling to adapt to modern times.

When we finally finished subtitling, I was exhausted. I looked around Xiao Ding's apartment and saw photos of his wife and daughter, who was almost a teenager. He told me that during the week they lived with his wife's parents in a courtyard house in the old city, where their daughter went to school, and they came back to the apartment on the weekends. They were out for a few hours to give us privacy.

"How old is she?"

"Twelve. I got married very young," he said. He was in his thirties. "My daughter is really growing up. Every week I bike her home—she sits on the crossbar of my bike and we talk. It's one of my favorite parts of the week but she's getting a bit too big for it. It's awkward."

"Why don't you let her ride her own bike?"

"She wants to but I don't think it's safe."

"You've got to let her grow up."

"I know, but it's hard."

After subtitling *Peking Man*, Xiao Ding and I began to talk often on the phone and to have dinner occasionally, always during the week. This time I could get direction for my wayward life with none of the moony stuff or the bombast or the pesky element of sex. Xiao Ding was so practical.

"Well, you have to decide if you want to shoot a documentary about the city or the country."

"The city, of course."

"Well, then you've made your first decision. That's good. Now you just need a topic."

"I'm working on it."

Then one day Xiao Ding told me he had another job he needed help with and asked if I wanted to split the work and money with him again. The job: subtitling *Crazy English*. Months had gone by since I'd last talked to Zhang Yuan, and after all that happened between us, I couldn't believe I was saying yes. But the reflected glory, the money—those were all things I couldn't refuse. We sat in my apartment watching *Crazy English* as we translated. Zhang Yuan and his crew themselves appeared in the first scene of the film, tramping down a snowy street filming Li Yang, all of them yelling in unison, "Crazy! Crazy! Crazy! Crazy!" Zhang Yuan's cheeks were rosy and he looked so pleased with himself. Was he finally triumphing over his shyness? As if echoing my earlier thoughts, Xiao Ding said he couldn't believe he was helping Zhang Yuan with the subtitles. I was surprised—I'd thought they were friends.

"We are friends but he takes advantage of me."

"He does? How?"

"He doesn't speak any English, so he takes me abroad to translate for him at film festivals but then he doesn't pay me anything to be there. Nothing."

"Why do you go with him, then?"

"I can't resist the chance to go abroad. I won't make it there by myself. And he's my friend and I want to help him. I know what my job in life is: to help other people."

It was a noble character trait but I couldn't help but find it kind of pitiful.

"Once we were in Berlin together and he had gone off to talk to some people and I didn't even have any money for food. I was starving and I had to wait for him to return to eat," he said, his voice sour with humiliation. "He treated me like his *puren.*"

Puren? After he had gone home, I looked it up in the dictionary. Servant.

"He uses people. If you're a member of the press, he'll befriend you, especially if you're a beautiful young woman."

"Oh."

The footage of me interviewing Li Yang hadn't made the final cut of *Crazy English.* Instead Zhang Yuan had used footage of an interview by a reporter from *Time,* a pretty, bright-eyed Caucasian woman.

Xiao Ding was a good listener and I took advantage of it, barraging him with my complaints. That day I complained about how hard it was to make friends, especially Chinese friends. I told him, "I look Chinese. I speak Chinese. But I just don't feel close to most Chinese people."

"Chinese people feel the same way," he said. "People have trouble trusting one another here. And you have to understand Chinese society. The key to Chinese society is relationships and Chinese relationships exist as a series of concentric circles. At the middle is your family, then come friends, then acquaintances, then strangers. Sometimes, friends become so close that you treat them like family. But that takes a long time."

After we finished, we went to get foot massages at a place I'd been frequenting recently, a neon-lit parlor off of the Second Ring Road that was open around the clock. Inside was a hive of cubicles filled with throne-like recliners. We lay back and soaked our feet in a medicinal brown brew; I could feel my troubles streaming out the soles of my feet. Eventually the masseurs came, a man for me and a woman for him and began their methodical journey of pain across the terrain of our nerve endings.

"Ow!" The pain was intense and direct.

"That's your number 10," he said as he handed me a tote bag printed with a map of the foot. Number 10 was my head.

"You don't sleep very well." He pressed down extra hard.

"Owwww!" Sometimes it scared me that the masseurs knew what was going on inside of me better than I did. I started in on my usual litany of peeves to Xiao Ding. I complained about how frustrating my job was, how bad my Chinese was, how I was never going to be able afford a video camera.

"Why do you complain so much?" asked Xiao Ding. "Your life is pretty good, pretty easy. Where I grew up, we lived in a simple house and in the winter one night as I was sleeping, a rat ran over my face. I'll never forget the feeling of that. At least there are no rats running over your face while you sleep. Buck up. Study Chinese."

He sounded just like my parents. *You're spoiled. Your days just pass so pleasantly. When I was in boarding school we had to shower with cold water, which we had to carry by ourselves in buckets.* I realized that part of my reason for coming to China must have been to experience some fraction of what they had experienced, partly so I could understand them and partly so they couldn't hold it over me anymore. I wanted to prove that I could eat bitterness with the best of them.

"How is your documentary coming along?" he asked.

"I still don't have a topic. But I meet so many people through work—I should be able to find something."

"You will."

Xiao Ding began speaking in English, in his clipped British accent. "Some days I feel like I am too ancient. I only live for other people. I am too scared to offend anyone," he said. "You can't be like this in the modern world. But I am too scared to be modern."

"I feel old-fashioned too, some days. Like having integrity and being honest don't get me anywhere."

"But my problem is that I'm dishonest. I help people because I worry about what they think about me, not because I really want to help them."

"Well, what do you really want?" I asked, while thinking back guiltily to all his help I'd accepted without giving anything in return.

"I don't know. Some days, I want to produce my own films instead of just feeling like I am only helping other people with theirs," he said. "But other days, I just want to kill myself."

I didn't know what to say. "No, that's not the right thing to do. And your daughter . . ."

"Yes, she's the only one I don't mind living for. She's the best thing that came out of my marriage," he said, and added bitterly, "I got married too young and it is impossible to undo what I've done."

"Have you thought about divorce?" I was twenty-three and anything seemed possible. Every mistake seemed fixable. He didn't answer and we sat in silence as the masseurs bore down firmly on our most vulnerable spots one by one, causing excruciating pain. At the end of the massage, I felt alert and relaxed, as if I had just swum a mile and then cried my eyes out. The masseurs dried and moisturized our feet and handed us thin ankle stockings to put on, nude for me, black for him. I took mine but Xiao Ding refused his.

"Why?" I asked. I had never seen a Chinese person refuse something free before.

"Lao po?" asked the masseur, who had obviously been watching our interactions. Your old lady?

Xiao Ding nodded sheepishly. I guess no wife would want to find evidence that her husband had gone to a massage parlor with a twenty-three-year-old American girl, however innocent it was. Oh my god—it was innocent, wasn't it? He noticed my surprised look.

"Did you know that Zhang Yuan calls you my girlfriend? My squeeze? My mistress?"

"No."

"Well, he does."

Outwardly I shrugged, but inwardly, I was furious—at myself for not seeing it coming and at all men for having only one thing on their minds. Though I depended on Xiao Ding's friendship, after that day we rarely saw each other.

Chapter Fourteen

To Fill In the Blanks

That spring, huge news stories broke in Beijing. In April, some ten thousand Falun Gong practitioners sat silently outside of Zhongnan-hai, the leadership compound, to seek official recognition, which eventually triggered a government crackdown. A few weeks later an American jet bombed the Chinese embassy in Belgrade, accidentally they said, killing three. Riots ensued outside the American embassy in Beijing. But because we were officially registered as a Chinese newspaper, *City Edition* couldn't do any real reporting that deviated from the party line. Max wanted to run a huge blank photograph to signal our gagged state but even that he thought was too risky. So, frustratingly, our work went on as usual, as if nothing was wrong.

Then *Beijing Scene* did a cover story on Zhang Yuan as he was finishing up his latest film, and as he stared puckishly at me from the cover, I decided, *That's it. I'm going to do stories about artists, Max or no Max.* Sue would have liked me to do more hard-hitting stories to set us apart from *Beijing Scene* but when she saw how determined I was, she didn't stand in my way.

A young writer with the pen name of Gezi wrote a novel about a friendship that veers into lesbianism, which was touted as the first lesbian novel in China. I wanted to track her down. Though China had no phone book, I'd discovered that you could call 114 and ask for the phone number of any company, and so I phoned her publisher and they helped connect us.

Gezi had a stern little bob framing a round face with close-set eyes, and her life story was similar to her protagonist's: At nineteen, she'd left home against her parents' wishes, moving from Beijing to southern China to attend college. But unlike her protagonist, there was no getting involved with an older woman after graduating. She obediently returned to Beijing, moved back in with her parents, and got a job. But about a year before, she'd quit her job and rented a small studio where she went during the day to write. The catch was that her parents had no idea that she'd quit her job and no idea that she wrote. They thought she still went off to work every day.

"It's strange, isn't it?" she said. "We get along but they'd rather I have a stable job and profession. They say that I had the right upbringing to get a well-paying job. I oppose them but not directly. This is my way of separating from them in a harmonious way." She laughed, her childlike eyes crinkling up.

I couldn't believe what I was hearing. Keeping things from my parents seemed so natural to me but coming from someone else's mouth, it sounded shocking.

"They don't suspect anything?"

"People have called my house asking for Gezi and I just tell them it's a transliteration of my English name."

"Is it '*Gezi*' for 'Pigeon'?"

"No. Do you know the term '*pa gezi*'? It means 'to fill in the blanks,' and it's what writers call writing, as a joke. It's the 'blanks' meaning of '*gezi*.'"

"Are you ever going to tell them?"

"Women here, before they're married at least, have so little independence. We're watched over by our families. In a few years, when I'm married and perhaps more successful with my writing, have kids, then I won't mind if they know."

I had much more independence than her, on the surface, but inside I felt just the same. And married? Kids? I surmised that Gezi wasn't a lesbian. However, she did know a few lesbians who were having a get-together on the weekend. Did I want to go? My journalistic curiosity prompted me to say yes, as did plain human curiosity. Maybe what I'd said to ward off Max had more than a grain of truth to it.

The meeting was in someone's cramped, fluorescent-lit apartment. About fifteen women were there and I scanned the crowd. Gezi was there, as was one glum-looking American woman in a plaid shirt. She's just arrived from San Francisco, the leader of the group said proudly. Gretchen said she was in Beijing on a Fulbright to study contemporary Chinese art. She was unfriendly to me, as if rebuffing an unwanted advance, and I was unfriendly in response. Two Americans are never supposed to be nice to each other when meeting in a foreign country. The whole get-together felt more like a meeting than a party and at the end of the night I lay on a bed having a polite, boring conversation with a Chinese woman. I have no recollection of what we talked about, probably where we were from and how we had found our way there. I concluded I probably wasn't a lesbian after all.

Beijing Scene also jumped on the Gezi story and our stories came out at about the same time—theirs was given prime real estate in their magazine, while mine was relegated to the back pages of the Entertainment Guide.

My next story was about the new contemporary art galleries springing up in Beijing that were nurturing undiscovered artists as well as giving artists who exhibited abroad a place to show their work at home. I first interviewed expats who ran contemporary art galleries like the Courtyard Gallery and the Red Gate Gallery, and they put me in touch with Chinese gallerists like Ai Weiwei, who had recently returned to Beijing after twelve years in New York and teamed up with a Dutch collector to open a gallery in a warehouse south of Beijing inspired by the cavernous dimensions of galleries in SoHo. Almost impossible to locate, the gallery was intended only for art insiders. But it wasn't very hard to get inside the small and welcoming community, especially as a Western journalist. Ai Weiwei said he was impressed by how much newer artists were "looking inward to get something out, not just looking around to find a good way to sell their work." I also met the independent Chinese curators who had organized the exhibit in the bomb shelter I'd been to, which had become a legend in itself. They said they'd closed it after two days because everyone who was expected to come had come and the fresh produce had started to rot, not even to speak of the corpses. A Texan art collector who had started a website about Chinese contemporary art told me with delight that after a writer had described the exhibition, many people wrote in with outraged responses. "They said something like, 'Such barbarism is a thing of the past.'"

Shock value was in the DNA of Chinese contemporary art. The era had started with an ill-fated group exhibition in February 1989 called *China/Avant-Garde* that showed at the official National Art Museum of China. It was the culmination of the 1980s, a decade of unprecedented political and cultural openness, and the government had laid down just three rules: nothing political, no pornography, and no performance art. So of course one artist set up an installation consisting of two phone booths with a mirror in between them and came one day, stepped into one of the phone booths, and fired a gun into the mirror. The government shut down the exhibition, and avant-garde art, like avant-garde film, went underground and overseas. The Tiananmen Square Massacre happened four months later. News of underground exhibitions in Beijing now spread only by word of mouth.

When a record nineteen Chinese artists made it into the Venice Biennale this year, 1999, the appetite of the international art market was truly whet for Chinese art. As more galleries and curators came from the West to pluck artists out of obscurity, more and more artists poured into Beijing from the provinces. The artists and the curators were trying to get the market to move past art that was recognizably "Chinese." The god-father of the avant-garde, curator Li Xianting, once asked in an essay whether Chinese art was merely "an eggroll at an international art ban-quet" and an outraged collector wrote back saying, "Are we looking for an eggroll? We're more sophisticated than that."

But were they?

I interviewed the assistant at the Red Gate Gallery, a young guy named Anthony, who said in a dashing accent I took to be British, "There was a big kick-up last year about a *New York Times* write-up of the *Inside Out* show in New York. It was very much still talking about Mao and the Great Leap Forward and the Cultural Revolution. Chinese artists got really angry. They're insisting on giving their own interpretations of the work rather than simply conceding to what Western audiences have to say about them."

I nodded, thinking how nice his voice sounded and how dark his eyes and hair were. Then he used the words *soiree, hoi polloi,* and *anarchy* in the same sentence, and so I took his number.

The article made it onto our cover and I began getting invitations to new exhibitions and gallery openings. I liked being around artists and seeing China and the world through their eyes.

It was around this time that my parents confirmed that they had booked spots on the group tour. They were coming.

Chapter Fifteen

Young Woman, Old Men

Do-DOO-do, do-DOO-do, do-DOO-do!

I fished my small black beeper out of my bag and called the unknown number, asking the man who answered if he'd beeped 16386. I was impatient, as the magazine had to be put to bed that night. I was sitting in the design department finishing the layout of the Entertainment Guide.

"Wang Zhenluo." The voice was deep and loud and jagged, as if the man's windpipe had been removed and replaced with an industrial-grade rock polisher.

"Wu Wenguang! How are you?"

"Still alive," he said. Wu Wenguang was another one of the Sixth Generation documentary filmmakers I'd read about long ago and hoped to meet. Xiao Ding had introduced us, and Wu called me occasionally to get help with translations or just to check up on me. He seemed to like me because I was young and idealistic and wanted to write and make documentaries that told the unvarnished truth about China, once I fig-

ured out what that was. If he had more in mind than that, I never found
out. "What are you doing right now?"

"I'm at work," I said, cringing slightly, knowing what was coming
next.

"You're still at that job? Why are you wasting your time with a full-
time job? How do you expect to make a documentary if you spend all day
nailed to an office working on someone else's project?" he growled. I could
picture him on the other end of the line: small glasses, bony angular face,
wispy facial hair, looking exactly the part of an old wise man who has
retreated to a mountain to regard society from afar. He was only in his
forties, but I was young and to me he seemed ancient and full of wisdom.
I swore I could smell cigarette smoke drifting through the phone line.

"I need the money," I said, not wanting to say more in front of my
coworkers, who despite their appearance of quiet diligence surely had
their ears flapping madly. I wished I'd never told him I wanted to shoot
a documentary.

"You need to go *freelance*." Wu Wenguang said this last word in
English with the stress on the second syllable. His English was a ragtag
affair that he claimed to have picked up "on the street."

"I'm not ready to quit my job." I had no savings, no way to get a visa,
no safety net. I was already living in a gray zone—now he wanted me to
work in one too? I imagined telling my parents when they came that I
had quit my job and was shooting a documentary.

"You're staying in that job for the sake of security. That's bullshit.
You're young. You need your freedom."

I laughed. Freedom. He said the word *ziyou* with a desperate rever-
ence that made me laugh. Wu was an ideological hard-liner, not for
Marxist-Leninism but for other pure ideals: Freedom, Truth, Art.

I laughed when he said I needed my freedom but something about it
stuck in my craw. It was an inner state that we all sought, no matter what
system we lived in. This was the voice I'd been waiting for, someone who
would tell me to let go of other people's ideas for me and to follow my

own, not just about making a documentary but about everything. I needed someone to say that I could be anything I wanted to be in life, and mean it.

"Have you gotten yours yet?" he asked.

"My what?" He had been blathering on about something, his words tumbling out in his Yunnanese accent that wobbled higgledy-piggledy with the stress on all the wrong characters like a chair with a bum leg. My mom's family was from Yunnan too and I found the difficulty of his accent familiar and comforting.

"*DV* camera," he said, saying the letters in English.

"No."

"You should get a *DV* camera. *DV* is a revolution."

"I'm broke, I told you," I said. How on earth did Wu make ends meet? He had long since quit his job in state-run TV and seemed to spend most of this time making rambling, overgrown documentaries that screened exclusively at international film festivals.

"Plus the longer I'm here, the less things seem to make sense," I said. "I'm not really a Flying Pigeon anymore but I'm not a Forever either." Those were the two popular brands of bicycles in China and were how a Chinese woman categorized foreigners in a book I had read: The foreigners either fly away or they stay forever. I didn't want to be shallow and fleeting, but I also didn't want to be trapped here for the rest of my life.

"Don't make it out to be so complicated. You've been in China long enough and met enough people to be able to say something meaningful about China. I have this Italian friend who was just like you, here for years and always wanting to make a documentary. Finally he took a car trip with a Chinese friend and made a documentary about it. It was simple but deep. You could do the same thing."

"Do you really think so?" Like Dumbo, I was desperate for my magic feather.

"*DV* cameras are not that expensive. Save some money and get one. Don't you want to join the revolution?"

Wu Wenguang was right. My job was becoming tedious and repeti-
tive, and I had become slipshod and unreliable. I wanted to write more
articles but I spent all my time calling up aquariums and shooting ranges,
many of which wouldn't send me their information because they said
they'd already sent it to *Beijing Scene,* and I was running out of steam to
write entertainment blurbs. ("Remember the Rainbow Bar? We didn't
think so.") All that redeemed the job was the soap opera that constantly
unfolded in front of my eyes. Someone had recently spotted our klepto-
maniac ex-distributor Lu downstairs at our building sans front teeth and
Sue had found out that our blood-slurping former web designer Scott had
"assumed someone else's identity" in Texas years ago.

"What are you working on?" I asked Wu, hoping to draw fire away
from me.

"I just finished traveling around the countryside shooting a documentary called *Jiang Hu: Life on the Road,*" he said. "I shot a group of
traveling opera performers who live a *jianghu* lifestyle. *Jianghu* includes
anyone outside of society who travels around, including thieves, prostitutes, and, long ago, martial artists. The tradition is almost dead and I
wanted to document it, so I traveled with the troupe for months, shooting
hundreds of hours of footage. I wanted them to forget I was shooting, so
I held my camera at chest level. I never once looked through the viewfinder. The picture is not pretty but my technique captured the essential
spirit of the people."

I laughed to myself, imagining Wu Wenguang lopping off heads like
a bloodthirsty revolutionary in his zeal to record on his tape nothing less
than the spirits of his subjects.

"Do the performers in the troupe have interesting stories?"

"Interesting stories? People's stories aren't interesting," he growled.
"What is interesting is people's *knowledge,* their *relationships,* their *attitudes.* Stories are shallow. Those things are deep."

Deep. That word again. So high school. And yet . . . so true.

"Actually, that's why I called you today," he said. "I'm doing the sub-

titles and I need your help translating one of the folk songs. It's an excep-
tionally dirty song and my translator is a nice Chinese girl who is too
much of a prude to translate properly. Plus to make everything harder,
the government has censored many of the dirtiest characters from the
dictionary and I have to make them by hand on my computer. These
country people have such a rich vocabulary of dirty words and the government wants to choke it to death. They want to control how we think
and feel. Can you believe how disgusting they are?"

I mm-hmmed, fiddling with the magazine layout on the computer.
"I can help you translate it. Just fax the song to me."

"Actually, that won't work. It's in a local dialect and I'll have to explain it to you, plus it has to go out to a festival tomorrow. Do you have
time to translate it right now?"

"Why not?" This was not a country of people who planned ahead.

"And you're not a prude, are you? It is *crucial* that I get a really dirty
translation. If you're not comfortable doing this, just say so." I looked
over at my coworkers tapping away on their computers.

"No, I'm not a prude."

Translating was a painstaking process. He read the song to me line
by line, first in their local dialect with the obscure slang, then translated
it into Mandarin obscured by his thick accent. He explained the dirty
parts and repeated it slowly to make sure I had understood him. I then
repeated the lines aloud in Chinese. Saying dirty words in Chinese was
like saying any other words to me, but the sound of them made my coworkers look up in alarm. I then read Wu back my English translations.

"Roll over and stick it in," I whispered, suddenly shy.

"What was that last part?"

I cupped my hand over the mouthpiece and scrunched down behind
my computer screen, glancing nervously at my coworkers, who were now
as oblivious to the dirty English as I had been to the Chinese. I enunci-
ated loudly and carefully, "Stick it in!"

"What?"

"Stick. It. In," I said, blushing. "*S-t-i-c-k!* It! In!"

"Are you *sure* it's dirty enough?" he asked.

"How about 'Roll over and stick your dick in. Your. Dick. *D-i-c-k.*"

"That's better."

"Okay, read me back what you have."

"Roll over and stick your dick in."

"Deep. Add 'deep' at the end. *D-e-e-p.*"

During my first year in China I taught myself how to read Chinese with a textbook published by a state-run publishing house. I saw in the table of contents that there was one chapter on film and I turned to it eagerly. Aside from teaching me some useful vocabulary words, it taught me all I needed to know about the state of Chinese film under the Communists.

movie
film
documentary film
scene
parade
peasant
People's Liberation Army (PLA)
mouth
to shout
slogan
to hold up
placard
leader
to wave
to found
activity
gala party
youth

firecrackers
happy

"Ha ha, how useless!" I chortled to myself. "When will I ever use the words *documentary film* and *People's Liberation Army* in the same sentence?" But China always had a way of surprising me.

Wu Wenguang called again a few weeks later.

"Wu Wenguang! How are you?" I said.

"Good, good. I just saw a fantastic new documentary film, called *Old Men,* about a group of old men who live in the neighborhood of the young woman who shot it. It is the best documentary I've seen in a long time."

"Is it 'deep'?"

"Very deep," said Wu, not noticing my sarcasm. "It's amazing that this young woman made it. You would never guess by her appearance that she had this documentary in her—she's actually a dancer in the People's Liberation Army dance troupe."

"What? Are you kidding?" The People's Liberation Army is the largest standing army in the world, ready at a moment's notice to crush all enemies of the workers' paradise. I had no idea they had a dance troupe.

"No, no. Talent really blooms in the most unexpected places," he said. "Yang Lina asked me to help her find someone to polish the English subtitles. I thought of you first. Are you interested?"

"Of course I am."

"Tonight?"

"Tonight is fine."

"Have you quit your job yet?"

"Soon, soon."

I went downstairs after work and looked around. The only person standing outside was a woman I thought far too attractive to be a documentary maker. I was expecting someone serious and maybe a little sour, like a female version of Wu Wenguang. This woman was cartoonishly beautiful: Her eyes were big and bright, her lips rosy, and her cheeks as full as apples. I gave her a quizzical look.

"Wang Zhenluo?" she asked. She smiled to reveal crooked front teeth.

"Yang Lina?" With those ruddy cheeks and her curvy physique, she did look like a robust revolutionary heroine. I could easily imagine her performing a ballet with a gun in her hand, playing a peasant girl who had thrown off the shackles of oppression and joined the Red Army. Underneath the soft appearance of those heroines always lurked a steely core.

"Thank you so much for helping me. I just realized today that I need this done in three days to submit to a film festival, and someone told me the English translation I got is just terrible but I don't read a single word of English. It won't take long to fix, just a few hours. Wu Wenguang said you are the best translator in Beijing," she said, her words rushing at me like a waterfall. "I don't know what I would do without you. You are saving my life. You really are my rescuer. Really."

She dished up a long-lashed look of gratitude. I expected nothing more than a gruff—if deeply felt—thank-you from most people in Beijing, and the limpid pools of her eyes rendered me utterly defenseless.

"Oh no, don't thank me. I'm just happy to be able to help you," I said, and began walking.

"Really, I am completely helpless without you," she said, shifting into a breathy tone that caught me in midstride.

"Stop, stop. Let's go," I said, angling toward the road to catch a cab. She stopped me and pointed at a white Volkswagen Santana sitting in my office building's small parking lot.

"I have a car."

These were magic words I rarely heard in Beijing. I clambered eagerly into the passenger seat and we started the long drive out to her apartment on the western edge of the city. She was a terrible driver, absentmindedly swerving all over the road, speeding, tailgating, turning to scrutinize me in busy traffic. She said she knew my boss Max from years ago, that she used to date one of his friends who lived in his dormitory.

"What was he like then?"

"He used to keep a monkey in his room and when he came home drunk, which was often, he would beat it."

"He hasn't changed much," I said with a roll of my eyes. I felt instinctively that if I told her about what I'd been through with Max, she'd understand.

"Wu Wenguang said you want to make documentaries," she said sweetly.

"I do!" I said, not mentioning that I'd originally wanted to make a documentary about filmmakers like her. "But I don't have a topic yet and I don't have any equipment. It's just a dream right now."

She turned to me again with an unexpectedly stern look on her face, her brows knit, and said firmly, "You can't stop dreaming. I have a camera and an editing machine." My ears perked up. "You can use them whenever you'd like."

I had another one of those moments when the sky seemed to crack open and blind me with the unbearably brilliant light of my future. You'd think I'd have learned to mistrust the grandiose promises of the universe by now.

"Really?"

"Really. I know you can make a documentary and I'll do anything I can to help you." She wove erratically through the erratically weaving traffic. I trusted her words more than any man's. She turned to look at me as she accelerated toward a line of cars stopped at a red light, and as I braced myself for a bone-shattering crash, she declared emphatically, "I like you."

"I like you too," I said. I liked her recklessness, her generosity, the messy thrill of being with her. In my heart, I felt an instant bond between us—a rare feeling in Beijing or anywhere really. I'd never had an older sister, and I'd always imagined it would be something like this: She would do the things I wanted to do a few years before I did and then steer me in the right direction. Though as I clutched the door handle and jammed on the invisible brake with my foot, I felt like the stodgiest of older sisters.

Her neighborhood, Qingta, felt more anonymous than mine, the buildings higher and blockier, and more stained with age, with no shops nearby. We climbed the concrete stairwell and paused before her door as she rummaged in her bag for her house keys. A magenta sign with four gold characters brightened up the dark wall and I sounded it out slowly: *a mi to fo*. Her two-bedroom apartment was similar to mine, its clinical rooms softened by girlish disorder. Papers and bags were scattered everywhere. Photos were taped directly onto the wall. A big off-yellow teddy bear lay on his side on a pink leatherette couch.

Off of the living room were two rooms, on the left her bedroom and on the right a narrow room filled almost entirely by the metallic bulk of an editing machine. With two monitors like heads perched on two tape decks like gaping mouths, it looked as majestic and dumb as an idol in the wilderness. To find such a thing in an apartment on the edge of Beijing in 1999 was nothing short of a miracle.

Yang Lina brought the machine to life and sat at the controls as I read along with the translation. It documented a year in the life of a group of old men who gathered in the same spot every day in her neighborhood, squatting on low stools, gossiping, not doing much. The documentary followed them through four seasons, starting in the summer when they searched for shade to sit in and swatted flies from one another's heads. They were salty old fellows in Mao suits who complained about everything: being nagged by their wives, neglected by their families, forgotten by the Communist Party and about how worthless they felt, fit only for the trash heap. (When one of their wives complained that he doesn't love her, the old man responded, "If I didn't love you, I would have strangled you long ago.") The only thing they enjoyed was one another's company.

The documentary moved as slowly as the old men, as did our subtitling, which had to be completely redone. She had already distilled each long line of dialogue into its basic meaning in Chinese and I had to translate it into something that sounded like spoken English and would be short enough to fit on the screen. Xiao Ding's training was coming in handy.

By two in the morning, we hadn't even gotten through autumn. Everything in China took longer than I thought it would. She drove me home all the way across the dark and sleeping city.

She picked me up again the next evening after work and as we drove past the exact place where her documentary had been shot, a chill shot through me. The documentary had consecrated a completely nondescript spot on the sidewalk, though the old men were no longer there. Through her film I was seeing a side of the rapidly changing city that was hidden in plain sight. It offered me one of the deepest understandings I had of the city yet.

She picked me up for two more days until the subtitling was finished. At the end of the documentary, one of the old men doesn't show up for the daily meeting and the others go around to his house, only to find out that he has died.

The credits rolled and I saw that she worked under another name, Yang Tian-yi, which she said was her Buddhist name. She had put only one reference to herself in the movie, an old man saying that she was the staunchest comrade of them all, arriving each morning before they did.

"You went every day?" I asked.

"Almost every day."

"For how long?"

"Two years total."

"How did you start doing it?"

"At the beginning, I saw the old men in the neighborhood and something about them really moved me. I had an instinct about it, so I borrowed cameras from people and started shooting them. You always have to follow your instincts."

"Didn't you have to go to work?"

"Our work unit doesn't meet very often, only when we have to perform."

The rest of the old men, she said, were now too frail to make their daily meeting and so stayed home alone. Though I was glad to be done with the subtitles, I was sad to leave their slow world. Wu Wenguang had been right—it was strange that this steady documentary about old men had come out of such an erratic flibbertigibbet who had never had big dreams about filmmaking and had never even watched many films. She had simply seen something that moved her and picked up a camera.

"How much does a machine like this cost?" I asked, running my finger around the plastic shuttling knob of her editing machine. I was turning Chinese, asking the price of everything.

"Twenty *wan*," she said. Two hundred thousand yuan. I did some quick math in my head. With my salary, about eight thousand yuan a month, it would take more than two years to earn enough to buy that machine, if I lived in a cardboard box on the side of the road and ate only grubs and leaves. Yang Lina was a dancer in the People's Liberation Army troupe. It didn't add up.

"How did you afford it?"

"Oh, I didn't buy it! My boyfriend bought it for me."

"You said, 'I want an editing machine,' and he just went out and bought it?"

"Well, I started editing in those places you rent by the hour, but he didn't like to see me doing that. When he saw I was really doing this movie, he just bought it for me, and my camera as well."

"And the car too?" China was supposed to be a Communist country, but some people seemed to be rolling in it.

"Yes."

"What does he do?"

"He's in finance."

"How did you meet him?" I felt embarrassed to be prying, but she spoke completely matter-of-factly about him. She bustled around the apartment doing a version of cleaning that I was familiar with, just moving things from one place to another.

"He came to the troupe one day and he picked me out of a lineup of dancers," she said, giving a naughty squeal and looking away, as if replaying the scene in her head. I imagined a back hallway of their theater, all bare and Communist-looking with heavy industrial fittings running along the ceiling, and the soft, beautiful heroines standing in a line as a man with a black pleather man-purse clutched under his armpit walked up and down, pinching their arms before making his selection. "We're all from the provinces and we all moved to Beijing alone, so we look out for one another. Whenever one of us meets a *dakuan,* we'll introduce him to whoever needs one."

I acted cool, as if pimping for your friends was a completely common occurrence in my world too. The *dakuan* were the Mr. Big Bucks who zipped around town at night in their expensive black cars, talking loudly on their clunky cellphones, eating big dinners, always accessorized with a young, slim creature on their arm. I imagined the dancers sitting on silk pillows and eating bon-bons during the day, beautiful Communist heroines basking in the spoils of capitalism.

"Many of the dancers have married their *dakuan.*"

"Are you going to marry your boyfriend?" I noticed that she didn't call him her *dakuan,* so I didn't either.

"I really don't know," she said with sudden solemnity. "He's very good to me. I'm always losing my house and car keys, so he made me ten copies of my keys so I'd always have extra. I'm always leaving my cellphone in cabs or restaurants and he always buys me new ones of those too," she said, shaking her head at her own hopelessness. She was such a *xiaojie,* the all-purpose Chinese word that meant *young woman, waitress,* and *prostitute.* I followed her into her kitchen and found it dusty and empty save for one small pot. She said the only thing she knew how to make was instant noodles. Then she dropped her voice to a whisper as if

letting me in on a big secret. "The men in my life have been very important and influential to me."

I looked around at her apartment, which he no doubt paid for as well.
No one in China seemed to marry for love.

I went over to her wall of photos. Taped up were close-ups of the tanned,
leathery faces of the old men and a group photo of them at Tiananmen
Square, where she had taken them on a field trip when she had owned a
small breadbox van. Attached to their lapels were tiny butterfly pins with
flapping wings that she had bought for them. There were also many photos
of her family but no complete family photos, only duos and trios, with her
younger brother. Many were of herself and I recognized the set of feminine
poses I'd seen her strike already that day, like a deck of queens. The pin-up
with flirty eyes. The displeased mother with mock knit brow. The theatrical
nun with wide solemn eyes. She sighed and pointed to one photo.

"This was me at my most beautiful age, twenty-five," she said. She
stood with her back to the camera posing outside near some spring blos-
soms, wearing a long, sleeveless magenta dress that luridly hugged her
curves. A thick braid hung down her back and she looked over her shoulder at the camera, smoldering with virginal chastity. She looked like she
came straight out of the countryside, though I would never have said
that. I was a good leftist with none of my dad's ugly bourgeois derision
about recent Chinese immigrants he found too rustic.

"I don't really like this photo," I said. "You look too—"

"Rustic?"

"Yes. I was embarrassed to say that," I said. Now, at twenty-seven, her
hair was chopped to her shoulder and the look in her eye had become
much more knowing.

"Don't be," she said. "You're twenty-five now. You're at your most
beautiful. I forgot to ask you earlier: Are you looking for a boyfriend?"

"No." I was actually twenty-three, and I wasn't the type to go looking
for love like a sad beachcomber sweeping the sands with a metal detector.
If love wanted to find me, I was right here.

"Because I have an ex-boyfriend I think might suit you. He's a good man and he has a good job at Motorola. He lives out in Tongxian but don't worry—he has a car. Do you want to meet him?"

"No thanks," I said. I was American, a liberated woman who was going to make it on my own, even if I had neither of the two things I had learned from Yang Lina that one needed in order to make a documentary: time and money. I just had to find those, choose a topic, hone my abilities to be *kuanrong* and to use *lixing,* and I was most of the way there. "But can I really borrow your camera one day?"

"Yes," she said, picking it up. It was an expensive three-chip camera. "My axe."

"And your editing machine?"

"Of course."

Chapter Sixteen
The Evening Swan

The city was full of manic energy in the months leading up to the fiftieth-anniversary celebration of the founding of the People's Republic of China, which had happened on October 1, 1949. Periodically the newspapers and TVs would announce a *jieyan* and the police would seal off the Second Ring Road, barring anyone from going in or out of the area for a few hours as they did a dry run for the great military parade. Gigantic empty floats would roll down the Avenue of Eternal Peace bound for Tiananmen Square. Fighter jets flew in perfect formation past my office window.

The year 1999 was also the tenth anniversary of the Tiananmen Square Massacre and well before June 4 the square was completely shrouded in construction scaffolding and closed to the public.

The city began cleaning up my neighborhood of Maizidian'r. They leveled the dirt sidewalks and set down intricately patterned concrete tile. They demolished some of the hairdressing salons that lined the street, along with some small restaurants and convenience stores, pirated CD shops, and boutiques catering to girls with cheap tastes. I came out of my building one morning to find the police swarming around the *baozi* seller. Her barrel was lying on its side, the coals spilling out onto the sidewalk. The police were yelling at her and she looked scared, a few tears streaked down her face. I never saw her again.

An inexpensive Italian restaurant called Peter Pan took over the shop fronts where she had been. Unlike most of the restaurants on my street that were dim and grimy and whose doors were hung with dirty plastic flaps, Peter Pan was bright and clean with big windows. I wrote a scathing review of the restaurant for the magazine ("Instead of being a symphony of starch and cheese and grease and tomato sauce, the pizza tastes like a pizza muffin made cautiously on a saltine") but every day when I came home, people I knew would be inside the lit fishbowl eating like starved guppies.

Moral pollution had to be cleaned up too. The police began crawling around the neighborhood like olive-skinned cockroaches, checking identity cards at gates and systematically going door to door to *saohuang,* to sweep out decadent elements like prostitutes and foreigners. Everything took on a suspicious look. A white van with police license plates slowly cruised the street with its door provocatively slid open. A small swarm of young policemen on bikes pedaled up and down the street. A traffic light went up at the intersection by the New Ark Hotel and at night a red-armbanded officer wielding a red light saber would be posted there trying unsuccessfully to stop people and check their identity cards.

The construction of the Fourth Ring Road neared completion, pushing the edge of the city outward.

I started dating Anthony, the dark-haired man from the art gallery, whose accent turned out to be, in his words, "overeducated Australian." He had earned a law degree but had forsaken a proper career at home to come to Beijing and work at an art gallery run by a fellow Australian. He lived nearby, also in a questionably legal apartment, and he said his parents were also planning to visit during the fiftieth-anniversary celebration.

I began to go along with him to help him translate as he interviewed

Chinese artists for magazine articles. His Chinese was terrible. He tried to take lessons, even got a tutor who he heard was a semifamous but washed-up writer from the 1980s whose books had been translated into French and who had fathered a child who now lived in Paris with his *maman*. Anthony enjoyed being tutored by a fading literary luminary, but for reasons I can't remember—did Xu Xing come to lessons drunk? did he talk about sex too much? did Anthony lack entirely the gift of learning languages?—he wasn't learning much and fired him. Anthony's lack of language skills embarrassed me and I wondered why I was merely doing the translating instead of publishing articles myself, but he was charming and kind and would sing to me as we walked around the city together at night. And after being alone for so long, it was a relief to have someone to eat dinner with, to accompany me to buy a bike, to wake up next to.

One night I grudgingly went to dinner at Peter Pan with Anthony and two of his British friends. One of them was Cookie Cousins, the calligrapher whose show I had gone to months ago. I couldn't believe I was meeting her at last. We ate on the roof, from which we could see down into the yard of my building. I was surprised to hear Cookie say that she worked at an international news agency, translating stories from Chinese newspapers into English. Mostly about coal mine accidents, she said. Her dad was a journalist too and had helped her get the job. She said she had grown up all over the world—she had been born in Tanzania, then lived in Pakistan, then Thailand. Her parents were in India now. She had been named after an American whom her parents had met on a train.

"But Cookie is really an artist," said Rachel, who had moved to Beijing recently from Hong Kong to start a new contemporary art gallery in a courtyard house. "A calligrapher." Cookie said she was experimenting with spray paint now. I looked at her hands. She was tall, but she had tiny hands.

I was also surprised to find out they lived in my neighborhood, in a big compound next to a deserted lot, accessible only through a narrow dirt lane that wound past a row of hair salons and a hospital specializing in treatment for sexually transmitted diseases.

"Today my washing machine broke with all the clothing in it, and I had to go see Big Sister Bao to get it fixed," said Rachel.

"That's the good thing about having no washing machine," said Cookie. "Xiao Pan, our male *ayi*, does it all by hand. He has to scrub the cream off my knickers by hand." *Ayi* was the all-purpose word for everything from *housecleaner* to *nanny* to *auntie*.

"Cookie!" said Rachel. "Anyhow, she told me, 'Big Sister Bao will take care of you.' She actually said that!"

"Who is this Big Sister Bao?" I asked.

"She's this woman resembling a small ferret who brokers all of the deals in our compound," said Cookie. "She finds apartments for people like us, collects rent, pays off the police, repossesses furniture when people leave, all of it. She's a nosy bugger—she knows who lives where and how much we pay and what we do for a living."

"Every month, to pay rent I take a fat wad of cash over to her apartment and she asks lots of questions."

"I can't tell her who I work for, so I say I'm teaching English," said Cookie.

"No doubt she skims a bit off the top," said Rachel. "Her nest must be pretty well-feathered."

"Why don't you just pay your landlord directly?"

"I've never met them," said Rachel. "She says they've moved down south of the city into cheaper apartments—they just basically live off of the rent we pay, like twenty-five hundred kuai a month." Most people in Beijing made around one thousand a month.

"What a great scam for all of us," said Cookie.

"Sometimes I wish I didn't know my landlords," I said. "I came home last week and found them there running a load through my washing machine. They said they thought I'd be out. Then a few days later I dreamed I found a Discovery Channel camera crew in my living room that my landlord had let in, thinking I was out at work. I told them to get the hell out and then a helicopter flew right by the window."

The night air was sweet and cool. People in my building had finished dinner and were coming out with their yappy Pekinese dogs to take in the night. The Perambulator was out perambulating and I pointed him out to my new friends. I told them about Bowl Cut and Screaming Granny and Horrible Boy. They told me about the characters in their yard, and my ears filled with the narcotic sound of British accents that would ring in my head until I fell asleep.

Yang Lina had looked close to home to find a subject for her documentary and I realized that my neighborhood was a veritable treasure trove of topics. I could make a documentary about hairdressing salons and call it *Salon.* Or one about the small shops and call it *Boutique.*

I went by one day to see my hairdressers but they were gone. I peered into the darkened salon; everything was still intact inside. *They probably just migrated back south for a spell,* I thought. I walked by every day, expecting to see them inside busy doing nothing, but a sad, creeping feeling grew. I was never, ever going to tear down the avenues of Beijing on the back of the boss's crotch rocket with the wind whipping through my mullet. Within weeks another set of hairdressers appeared who looked pretty much exactly like my old ones, as if someone had ordered up another six-pack of Cantonese Glam-Rock Hairdressers. Though nearly identical, they were complete strangers. *Tres bizarro,* I thought. It was time to find a new documentary topic, and new hairdressers.

A friend who was in her thirties and who somehow maintained glowing skin and sleek hair in Beijing's dry and polluted sandstorm climate recommended a salon across from the Indian embassy.

"Ask for Li Bin," she said. "He's a genius."

I slid open the door and walked into an oasis of quiet. No Cantopop here. Sitting in the waiting area was a young Chinese woman with perfect nails and hair as long and smooth as water who did not look in need of a haircut. I, on the other hand, looked like a yeti at the tail end of winter. To complete the look, my teeth had recently gone mysteriously black.

"Is it possible to get my hair cut by Li Bin?" I asked the receptionist with my frostiest smile. She looked at me in amusement.

"Today?"

"Yes, today."

"No. You need an appointment for him."

I sat down and assumed my most aloof look, pursing my lips and floating my eyebrows upward as if to say to no one in particular, "Oh, really?" Li Bin came over to the reception area. It was obviously him—the leonine hairdo, the Rico Suave manner—and my waiting area companion glided out of her seat for an air kiss. He led her away.

I took a look at the salon. The circular room was frosty white and minimalist. Haircutting chairs orbited a hair-washing throne, which was partitioned off by a translucent curtain and was exuding the delicate scent of aromatherapeutic shampoos. Beijing had a lot of smells, many odors and miasmas, but scents were rare, and the salon felt as if it were floating high above the city in a bubble of luxury and calm. *Places like this are dangerous,* I thought. The world outside became even harder to live in afterward.

In a few minutes the receptionist introduced me to Xiao Cai, a slight man with glasses, more a mortician than a stylist. After a hair washing, he led me to a chair. I asked for a short and messy haircut. I moved my hands wildly as to evoke a thunderstorm, a gazelle in flight, anarchy. He nodded. I took off my glasses and closed my eyes prayerfully. When I opened them and put my glasses back on, I saw a big wave of hair sweeping imperially across my forehead. I had aged ten years in the chair. I looked like the Empress Dowager.

"It's called the Evening Swan," he said. Maybe I could grow into it, I thought. Grow up a little. Make fancier friends. Go to dinner parties. Who was I kidding? The whole reason I was in Beijing was to prolong my adolescence, or to finally have the one I never actually had. To live heedlessly. Avoid respectable, full-time work. Drink too much in dirty bars. That was not a job for the Evening Swan.

Beijing had many bars but the fashionable crowd was big enough to keep only one bar at a time packed full. For a while it was Half Dream, a bar run by Jin Xing, China's most famous transsexual, a globetrotting modern dancer and choreographer whose M-to-F surgery had been video-taped from start to finish by Zhang Yuan. Decorated in burnt sienna hues and filled with oblique statuary, Half Dream had the seedy, highfalutin atmosphere of a Roman bath. Then came Vogue, a dark cavern of white frosted glass that personified the L.A. of my nightmares, and the Loft, a carbon copy. That summer it was the Havana Cafe, a Cuban bar built on an empty patch of cement north of the Workers' Stadium and run by a French-Algerian DJ who had told me before it opened that one successful Latin dance party he had thrown full of "crooowds and crooowds of people" had inspired him to open the bar.

I met Jade there. We picked our way around huge sacks of dirt out-side, on which slept exhausted construction workers, through the bar whose walls were covered with lurid murals of Havana at sunset, and onto the patio. There were indeed crowds and crowds of people here, expat and Chinese, standing shoulder to shoulder and all trying to get the attention of the harried waiters so they could yell the one magic word: *mojito!* Sud-denly, my beeper went off. I pushed my way to a phone and called the unknown number. It was Cookie.

"Where are you right now?" she asked.

"At the Havana Cafe."

"Smashing. I'm coming over to hang out."

She showed up soon afterward in a pair of calf-length knickerbock-ers in a loud fuchsia-and-green phoenix print with her peroxided hair spiking every which way; it looked less like bedhead than the result of a fork stuck violently into an outlet. She was an exotic cockatoo in the company of gray pigeons, and people stared at her as she walked in. The room seemed to grow brighter when she was in it. She downed a mojito and we talked about how we'd both made our way to Beijing. She said she had studied Chinese in college and loved all things Chinese, especially Chinese men.

"Really?" I asked.

"I think they're sexy!" she said.

Jade and I wrinkled our noses.

"Why?"

"They're hairless and sleek. Like dolphins. I dated this one artist. He was married. Actually he was about to get a divorce. The first night he took off his pants and underneath he had on bright orange long underwear." She laughed uproariously. I thought back to Max's red briefs, and knew we would be friends. We count this night as the beginning of our friendship.

I came back very late that night, and tipsy. My building was hushed. All the lights were out in the windows and the yard looked peaceful without its screaming children and little white dogs. A cat ran out into the light and then back again. The defensive mental armor I donned every time I'd gone out at night in New York was completely unnecessary here. Without it, the nights felt light and carefree. The few people who did come out were completely different than those who went out in the day, and as long as they weren't the police, I wasn't scared of them. I often saw two blade-slim women with identical haircuts and handbags walking slowly past, like two vampires. That night I walked in at the same time as two young Asian men with guitars strapped to their backs. One came right up to me.

"What's your name?" he whispered in English.

"Val. And you?"

"Marco." He must have been in one of the ubiquitous Filipino bands that played Eagles and Beatles covers in the lounges of the city's hotels.

"Hi."

"Hi."

We nodded covertly and went our separate ways.

I climbed up the stairs as quietly as I could. Stacks of cabbage, enough to last the winter, were piled up in the stairway and someone had started raising a baby chick in a Styrofoam box.

I began spending more time with Cookie and Rachel. It felt strange coming all the way to China to hang out with white Westerners but I had more in common with them than with most Chinese people I knew. I also envied them. Even though they stuck out like sore thumbs, there was a lightness to their existence in Beijing. While I tried to live as they did, a heavy weight inside always seemed to be pulling me down.

Chapter Seventeen
Peking Opera & Sons

Feeling bloodied and bruised from jostling with *Beijing Scene* to stay atop the cutting edge, I decided to write an article for *City Edition* about the most uncool topic I could think of: Peking Opera. In opera's heyday, from the 1920s through the 1940s, opera stars were the pop stars of the day. Today the only people who watched were the older generation, people like Bobo.

I was interested only in traditional Peking Opera, not in the model operas with revolutionary themes sung during the Cultural Revolution when traditional opera had been banned. The born-again leftist in me could not overpower the idea that I had inherited from my family: that Chairman Mao and Communism had destroyed China. I saw traditional Peking Opera performers as the keepers of an old order, from a time when my family had thrived in China; my parents' imminent arrival no doubt exerted a subconscious influence on this choice of stories. After interviewing an opera performer named Mr. Yang who had quit the state-run troupe to pursue the slightly humiliating but ultimately lucrative work of singing for money at a restaurant, I asked if he knew a traditional Peking Opera family I could interview.

"The Zhang family is perfect for you," Mr. Yang said. "Their entire existence revolves around Peking Opera."

So on an unusually warm September day a few days before my parents were set to arrive, I met Mr. Yang at the Feng Ze Yuan Restaurant near Tiananmen Square so he could take me to Teacher Zhang's house. He said I'd never find the house on my own. The restaurant was a big, gaudy affair at the foot of a modest street, onto which we turned. Meishi Jie looked like dozens of others in the old city, lined with cube after cube of tiny shops and restaurants and swarming with sights and sounds that screamed Old Beijing: weather-beaten shoe repairmen hunching in the shadows of buildings, white-smocked women steaming dumplings in huge baskets on the street, the *ring-ting-ting* of bells as bicyclists glided past in slow motion. *You are about to find what you are looking for,* the sweltering buzz of the street seemed to be saying. *The real China.*

"During Peking Opera's golden years in the 1930s, Teacher Zhang trained under So-and-So, the legendary performer," Mr. Yang explained in hushed tones as we walked. "He then trained his sons and grandson in the ancient art. China has gone through its ups and downs—you know about those, don't you?—but this family has persisted in practicing and performing traditional Peking Opera. To make ends meet, they now run a home-cooking restaurant in the bottom floor of the house that they've lived in since the 1940s."

He veered into a restaurant only two tables wide. I followed. The restaurant was empty save for two men dipping their chopsticks into steaming plates of food and lazily waving away flies. The air was garlicky and humid. Mr. Yang made a beeline for the back and barged into the dim and cramped heat of the kitchen, past the stares of the cooks, and up a set of uneven wooden stairs soggy with years of rising heat and cooking oil. He knocked on the door at the top of the stairs and, without waiting for an answer, pushed it open and threaded his way through a maze of small, lightless rooms. Each room seemed to have less fresh air than the last. He pushed open one final door and we emerged into a large room that was cluttered and dusty and full of people.

There on a platform bed at the far end of the room lay the unmoving body of an old man. His torso and head were bloated and bare, and a sheet covered him from the waist down. Gnarled hands rested near his face like a child's. His eyes, peering out from their puffy casings, looked in my direction. I felt a shiver of terror.

"This is the great Teacher Zhang Mingyu, who was once a talented and famous opera star," said Mr. Yang with a deferent sweep of his hand. "Go ahead and talk to him."

I accepted a stool by the bed and introduced myself. He made no response. "I'm here to interview you. About Peking Opera." Was he conscious? I nervously mumbled my questions all in a row: How had Peking Opera changed over the years, how had their family adapted, what about the restaurant downstairs? He gave a slow smile with a mouth full of jack-o'-lantern teeth. His wife, a diminutive woman with a short graying haircut, had been buzzing around the room, first putting the kettle on to boil, then squatting down to scrub clothes. She came over and plugged in his hearing aid.

"You're going to have to speak louder," she said to me in a grainy voice. To him, she yelled, "She's a reporter writing a story about Peking Opera!"

I took a deep breath and repeated the questions in my loudest voice, grimacing at the sound of my flat American accent. His wife yelled into his hearing aid, simply, "She wants to know about Peking Opera in the glorious days before the Communists took power!"

His voice came out in a wheezy, growly puff, its forcefulness taking me by surprise: "So, you're interested in Peking Opera!" One of his middle-aged sons poured me some tea.

After many repeated yellings of questions and answers, I teased out the bare bones of his story. He had started as an apprentice when he was seven and had grown up to perform in Tibet and Russia. As he spoke, his wife took out yellowed programs to show me and tapped the glass on the nightstand by the bed, under which were trapped photos of a young and virile Grandfather Zhang posing in his opera outfits, here with a spear in his hands, there with his leg high in the air. His pale face, painted white with full mascara and lipstick, looked furious.

"And when did . . . ?"

"Teacher Zhang was a performer of martial operas," explained Mr. Yang. I imagined his supple body, enrobed in a heavily brocaded costume, doing backflips across a stage. "He fell during a performance in 1963 and was paralyzed." He had lain in this bed since then. The bed was pushed against the wall, leaving a large practice space on the floor. From this position, he had trained his sons and grandson in Peking Opera, barking out commands as they practiced in the room.

His two sons, Zhang Laisheng and Zhang Laichun, ricocheted around the room like Tweedledee and Tweedledum, cleaning up, doing stretches, refilling my tea. Both were performers in the state-run Beijing Opera Troupe and were in their forties. Both were short, blockily sculpted like gymnasts, and inexplicably tanned. They listened closely to my interview.

The high-ceilinged room was insulated from the hutong outside by a balcony crammed with birdcages and old boxes, and only the sliest light could find its way through the dusty windowpanes. The room was warm and stuffy with the musk of stagnant flesh and urine and I began to feel dizzy. Teacher Zhang's wife spoon-fed him rice porridge and tea, wiping his mouth with a cloth when most of it dribbled out.

I imagined him lying in this bed for more than thirty-five years while the world outside the window changed and changed again. Cultural Revolution. Reform and Opening Up. Tiananmen Square Massacre. Capitalism. He'd missed it all. Even his language seemed to be frozen in time. Arcane words wheezed out of his mouth and fell to earth before reaching my ears. He seemed pleased to have a captive audience who had never heard his stories before and he talked endlessly. Nodding occasionally, I began to slip into an interview coma. I took a deep breath that succeeded only at filling me with sadness. I let out a noisy sigh.

"Do you understand what I'm saying?" he roared at me.

I glanced in fear at the pale face of fury trapped under the glass. "Most of it," I said. "If I don't, I'll ask."

The family started asking me questions that began with the usual *You're not a Chinese person, are you?* that so many people always asked, as if I had somehow stitched together an intricate disguise from the skins of real Chinese people. Usually I responded in my snippiest tone that I was American, but I wanted the family to like me, so I said I was a *meiji hua-ren,* an American-born Chinese. The grandmother led the interrogation.

"Do you miss home?" By *home* they meant my family.

"Not really," I said. Seeing the horrified looks on their faces, I hastened to add, "But some days I do."

"Don't your parents worry about you?"

"Not really," I lied. "They've come to expect the unexpected from me." I thought they would smile, but they only looked troubled.

"How old are you?" one of the brothers asked. "You look very young."

"I'm twenty-four," I said indignantly. "I can take care of myself. We do that in America after we're eighteen."

"That's true," chimed in the other brother. "She is independent of her family."

"Are they supporting you?" asked the grandmother.

"I have a job," I said. "I'm a reporter."

It was time to regain control of the interview and get out of the house. I turned back to the grandfather and shot off another awkward volley of questions. *Why aren't people going to see opera anymore? How much are your sons paid in the troupe? When did you open the restaurant?*

The grandfather didn't answer any of them. He launched into a monologue that was, as far as I could tell, about the crucial importance of the genealogy of Peking Opera stories and the influences of regional opera styles on Peking Opera, among other topics. I made chicken scratchings on my pad, pretending to take notes. Did I already have enough for an article? I had no idea. The sons had been watching my efforts with pity and one volunteered that they had opened the restaurant in 1984.

1984. I wrote that down.

"Life is easier now but singing opera is still hard," he said. A quotable line! Finally someone understood what I needed for my article. I wrote it down and the son took the cue. He started complaining that of the thousands of operas that existed—most dramatizing historical folktales, ghost stories, and classical novels—only thirty or forty were still being performed now. The brothers' state-run troupe made its money by performing for foreign tourists the most blood-racing fight scenes culled from these operas, calibrated to inject a quick and painless dose of Chinese culture into the tourists' packed schedules.

"They perform only a fraction of the original operas nowadays. What good is that?" said the grandmother with sudden acrimony. "Who can perform the original operas anymore? Who's cultured enough to appreciate them?" She saw me scribbling in my notebook and hastily added, "Don't quote me. I don't know anything about opera."

"Did you understand what I said?" roared the grandfather again.

"I did," I said.

"Explain what I said to you!"

A constellation of family members constantly came in and out of the room, all revolving around the body on the huge bed, all interjecting their opinions about Peking Opera, correcting and censoring one another. I wrote down what I could understand. I wondered which of them actually lived there, as several single beds were scattered around the room. Like most Chinese families I knew, they seemed loath to throw anything out and the room was crusted over with the detritus of decades. The walls were covered with brush paintings from calendars of years past and faded New Year's decorations that had once been shiny red and gold. Molded

Buddha statues in many colors held court in glass-fronted hutches. Plastic soda bottles containing mystery liquids were scattered around on different surfaces. This was the real thing, all right, and I couldn't wait to leave.

I spent two hours there that first day. Eventually, the family members gathered around the grandfather and flipped him over, which I took to signal the end of the interview. My head was spinning. The grandmother welcomed me back anytime.

Picking up my notes the next day, I found them completely illegible— a smattering of Chinese characters, English words, and crude Romanizations of sounds I thought I'd heard. I had no story. With dread I made the long trip back to their house a few days later for a re-interview. Forget conversing this time. I was a journalist. I needed cold, hard information. Names and numbers.

The house was a beehive of family activity again. The grandmother was there, the middle-aged brothers were there, as were a few teenagers. The grandmother eyed me warily as she escorted me to the stool by the grandfather's bed. I sat down like a heavy weight. His eyes lit up and he said he had never seen a young person so dedicated to Peking Opera. *Surgical strike,* I thought. *Surgical strike.*

"I have just a few more questions," I said in my loudest and firmest voice. "I want to know about *one* opera that has survived through the years. Why did it survive? What parts are performed nowadays? What is the basic story behind it?"

The grandmother yelled into his hearing aid, "She wants to know about one opera that has survived through the years." She looked at me and asked, "Is this your meaning?" I nodded and she repeated the question several times into his ear.

He launched into a story about when the family had staged a one-night performance of an opera that hadn't been performed since 1949. *1949.* I wrote that down. The year the Communists took over China. His story might not be so off the mark. As he spoke, I took furious notes. He described training his fourteen-year-old grandson for three years in the technically complex opera, which involved twirling poles and rings on his arms and legs. He had trained seven other performers, rented a theater for a night, which cost more than a month's wages for his sons, printed programs, and performed the opera.

"The title?" I asked. They wrote down the characters: 乾坤圈. Later, I found it meant *The Ring of Heaven and Earth*. The grandmother pointed to a teenager sitting in the corner, the grandson who'd performed the piece. I smiled at him, but his expression—imperious with eyes that bore into me like drills—did not register any change. She then showed me a video of the performance. The old opera hall was only half filled with an audience of friends and family. This family was perfectly tragic. Or was that tragically perfect? I couldn't have scripted their lives better.

"Today's Peking Opera performers would never have the skill to perform the opera," snorted Grandfather Zhang. "They treat Peking Opera as a job, not an art. A fourteen-year-old can perform better than they can. Look at my grandson. Look at how poised he is." The grandson certainly was unnerving. In fact, all the family members who performed opera seemed wound like coiled springs. I would not have been surprised if they had started doing backflips across the large room. The house set me on edge.

The family had another grandchild, a girl, who was not in the least interested in Peking Opera. She sat lazily on the couch eating Dasbro brand potato chips, which came piled high in a bright tube just like Pringles. Zhang Laisheng's and Zhang Laichun's wives, if they had any, were not present.

I pressed on with my interrogation. I found out the sons each made a base salary of two hundred ninety-nine yuan per month in the state-run troupe, plus twenty to thirty yuan per performance. The combination of a bloated troupe and dwindling audiences meant that each month they performed at most ten times. In a good month, they would barely make eighty U.S. dollars. Satisfied with the details, I shut my notebook.

"You are getting only the skin and bones of opera, not the meat," the grandfather roared at me.

"But I'm only writing a newspaper article," I said.

"She's only writing a newspaper article, not a book," yelled the grandmother. "She doesn't need to understand all of Peking Opera. She's just writing one story."

"Even if I talked to you every day for ten years, you still wouldn't know anything about Peking Opera," he said.

"Oh?"

"Are you willing?"

It seemed rude to reject such hospitality. I imagined years of rigorous physical training in Peking Opera singing and acrobatics, or hours of listening to arcane Peking Opera stories over cups of tepid tea. I agreed limply, but I suspected that we would never see each other again.

As I put my notebook in my bag, the invitations came from all sides. One son said fervently, "We're good friends now. A Swedish journalist also came to interview us, but we like you much more. You didn't come to interview us. You came as a friend." The grandmother casually murmured to me that I was welcome to come again to visit.

"We're always home," she said.

"Thank you very much. I will if I have time," I said insincerely. Chinese people are incredibly hospitable; I had met people on trains who had invited me to their homes for Chinese New Year after only a fifteen-minute conversation. But such warm hospitality also set off alarm bells in my head.

Part Four

Chapter Eighteen

Fifty Years Later

*M*y parents looked wordlessly around their hotel room, taking in the sagging beds and peeling paint. They had arrived a week before their group tour started, on the day of the fiftieth-anniversary celebration on October 1, 1999. The Chinese government called the Communist takeover "Liberation," and preparations for the celebrations had reached a fevered pitch. Right before my parents' arrival, the government had shut down the city's most polluting factories and the sky changed from its usual mealy gray to a brilliant blue. But beneath that beautiful facade lurked our side of the story: The date also marked the anniversary of my parents' exile from the country and the moment their lives had veered off course. If they hadn't left China, my dad would have stayed in the north, my mom in the south, and they would never have met in New York—and I wouldn't exist. The accident of my own existence seemed worth celebrating.

Bobo and our extended family had just left the hotel. We had all gone to the airport together to pick up my parents, per Chinese tradition, and thanks to Xiao Peng's friend had even bypassed security to wait at the arrivals gate to catch my parents right as they got off the plane. Droves of strangers walked out first. When they finally emerged, we hugged and I felt relief, as if they were unaccompanied minors who might have missed their connections in Chicago or Tokyo.

"Hey, you put on a little bit of weight" were the first words out of my mom's mouth, then seeing the video camera in my hand quickly added, "Good," as if she had meant it as a compliment all along. I had borrowed Anthony's video camera to record this momentous occasion and kept it running for most of their visit. I hoped it would force everyone to be on their best behavior, myself included. My parents hugged Bobo and Bomu and the moment brimmed with many years of unspoken emotion. My dad hadn't seen his cousin since he was eight.

"You didn't have to come to get us," he said. "She could have come alone."

"No," said Bobo. "We had to come."

"I told you twice not to come. I told her to tell you."

"She did. Xiao Peng has a car; it's no problem."

They each performed their half of the polite ritual flawlessly and I could see it put them at ease. They walked ahead of my mom and me and talked in a familiar way despite all the years they hadn't seen each other.

"We'll just come over to see you tomorrow. It's late now," said my dad.

"Yes, tonight just go to your hotel to rest."

"I meant, you didn't have to come tonight to pick us up."

"No, no."

My mom took another close look at me. "Do you floss your teeth?"

"Don't look at them, please."

"Do you floss it?"

"Yes."

"Why are they black?"

"It's the water. There's no fluoride. My teeth are embarrassingly disgusting."

"Yes," she said. "Need to bleach it."

I was excited for their visit, but nervous too. I had spent the last year in Beijing setting up a whole life away from their prying eyes and now it would be exposed to their scrutiny. Deliberately disconnected parts of my life were about to be set side by side. The police had recently caught Anthony just as he was returning home one night and kicked him out of his apartment. He had moved in with me, but I didn't say anything about him or our living situation to my parents. Every time we spoke on the phone, they still asked me when I was moving home.

I had booked them a room in a charming little hotel in an old courtyard house, with windows onto a communal courtyard. The lobby was very Chinese-y, decorated with lanterns and large paintings of peonies and furnished with wooden chairs and benches lavishly carved with flowers and mythical beasts. But all of a sudden their room looked run-down and decrepit, and I knew it would reinforce all their negative ideas about China being backward and dirty, a step down. I could see my dad silently shaking his head, regretting that he had ever left home. My mom, the more adventurous of the two, was trying to be upbeat and carefree. I couldn't imagine what it felt like to flee your homeland forever as a child, and then come back as an adult tourist, and I felt the complicated swirl of the moment. My teenaged anger at them dissipated; I felt protective instead. I wanted them to enjoy China, to feel connected to it, and to see what a hopeful place it was and how exciting it was for me to live here. We had somehow switched places—I was the one pushing the old country on some picky Americans. It was night and I hoped the courtyard would reveal its beauty in the morning.

They filled me in on some of the changes they had made to the house in Maryland: They'd replaced the old refrigerator, bought their first microwave oven, and bought a new front door that, even on the hottest days, would be cool to the touch. They'd replaced the kitchen table and the couch. They were planning to get the hardwood floors buffed and to replace the beige aluminum siding. I nodded absentmindedly, not wanting to think about the faraway house.

Anthony's parents were also visiting and he had booked them into the same hotel. They had arrived from Australia at roughly the same time as my parents, and in fact, I could see them in their lit room across the dark courtyard, getting settled as we were. I said nothing.

The next day I met my parents for lunch before taking them to Bobo and Bomu's courtyard house. My dad complained about the water pressure of the shower and on the way over assured me, "I have the antidiarrhea drug, plus the napkin."

Bomu poured tea and put out fresh dates as my parents distributed the presents they'd brought: vitamins, echinacea, earrings, Mauna Loa macadamia nuts, a Washington Redskins sweatshirt, a red envelope. They'd also brought a stack of family photos, mostly of groups of people standing in stiff rows.

"This is last year, the one-year anniversary of my dad's passing," said my dad. "My little brother came from Singapore to be there."

"He rushed over," said my mom, who was eagerly crunching her way through the dates.

"In the background is the Lincoln Memorial. This one was last year in June when Chris just got his law school diploma—"

"And he said, 'I'll take it to show Yeye. It'll give him comfort,'" said my mom. I leaned in for a peek. My brother stood flanked by Nainai and my dad behind our family gravestone with WANG emblazoned across it in English and Chinese, holding up his diploma. I seriously doubted that he had come up with the idea himself. Sounded more like something my dad would have cooked up, the filial son that he is. Or my mom, who has a performative streak.

My parents and relatives segregated by gender. Bobo sat in his easy chair and my dad on the couch next to him and they talked about our family's courtyard houses: who had lived in which house when, what year their children had immigrated to the United States or Australia. Of the

house we sat in now, Bobo explained which parts had been sold off and
how it had been laid out originally.

My dad had trouble recalling the house as it had been then. "I remember coming to this house just once."

"Oh, no. You came many times."

Bobo's real aim was to talk with my dad about Nainai's house. When
the government began returning confiscated houses to their owners after
the Cultural Revolution ended in 1976, Bobo wrote Yeye and Nainai
and they mailed him a photocopy of the old Nationalist-era deed and a
letter authorizing him to be their legal proxy. Bobo navigated the bureaucracy office by office to get the house back. He said he was becoming
anxious because the demolitions were creeping closer and closer to the
house and they had to decide what to do if it was next. He was happy to
finally rope someone with an American passport into the process and he
talked through all the technicalities as my dad took notes in a little notebook. He laid out the options: My dad could try to go to court and get
another courtyard house like Uncle Johnny had for Great-Aunt Mabel or
he could take cash. Bobo told him about Great-Aunt Mabel's new house:
It had sixteen rooms and the courtyard was so big you could drive a car
around in it. It was empty right now, awaiting renovations.

"Xiao Peng and Xiao Lu can live there," said my dad.

Bobo laughed heartily as if my dad had told a good joke, then turned
to me to ask half in jest if I knew anyone who might want to rent it. I
laughed too, but then asked how much rent would be. Around two thousand U.S. dollars, he said. At almost ten times my current rent, it seemed
like a fortune.

Bobo said the big problem with Nainai's house was the tenants. The
house was a *zayuan'r,* literally a "mixed house," which more than ten
families occupied. Some of the families actually lived there and others
just squatted in the hopes that they would be compensated when it was
demolished. Bobo collected—and kept, I think—the nominal rent from

them and fielded their irate phone calls asking for repairs that no one had the money to pay for. How would we get them out? Who was responsible for remunerating them if the house got demolished—the government or Nainai?

Bobo said that to help grease the wheels, he had set up a banquet with the Xicheng District party secretary of the All-China Federation of Returned Overseas Chinese, who had helped Uncle Johnny secure his new house.

"I'll introduce you as a Nationalist—"

"The descendant of one," my dad clarified.

"I'll tell Party Secretary Li your dad was secretary-general in Chiang Kai-shek's Nationalist Party." I assumed this would be a strike against my dad, not for, but I figured Bobo knew what he was doing. "At dinner, you just bring up one request," said Bobo, before feeding Dad the script for the evening. " 'We very much thank the government for returning the house to us after the Cultural Revolution. I hear from my cousin that there's a document in the Beijing archives and I'd like to ask your help in arranging to see this document.' "

Bobo explained that the document, which I began to think of as *The Document,* stipulated that if Nainai returned and established residency, the government was required to return the house to her empty. "If they let you see The Document, you say to them, 'May I photocopy it for my mother to see?' " Here Bobo let out a nervous laugh. "If they don't let you, it's okay. Take down the filing number. It will come in handy when it comes time to demolish the house."

My dad looked miserable. I remembered the warning he'd given me about people doing favors for you and expecting favors in return. In dealing with the house, he wanted to follow carefully in Uncle Johnny's footsteps but Uncle Johnny was an immigration lawyer. What did my dad, a midlevel manager at IBM, have to offer?

Bobo took out the old title encased in a shiny red folder and we handed it around.

The women—Mom, Bomu, and Xiao Lu—sat to the side talking about an assortment of safe topics, like the impossibility of losing weight. Mom is a talented ink-wash painter whose work adorns the rooms of the house I grew up in, and she explained how the artist had done the calligraphy hanging up on Bomu's walls—with a slow preparation and a fast execution. She also trotted out some of her favorite stories, like the time when my journalism teacher in high school had asked if the editor in chief two years before me who shared my surname was my brother (he was) and I'd said, "No, I don't have a brother. How could you think someone so ugly was my brother?" She still found my effort to step out from my brother's shadow hilarious. Mom was also still nonstop eating dates. "I haven't eaten fresh dates since I was a child," she said. "I was four when I left but I still remember the taste."

In an aside to me, she said, "I'm so glad we made it to China. I didn't think Dad was going to be able to leave Nainai." Since Yeye's death two years before, things had changed at home. I was gone, for one, and my brother had moved back to D.C. after law school to work. My parents had begun spending Saturdays with Nainai and my dad's conscience made it difficult to leave her even if his sister came to fill in. "Every single Saturday, we cook for her and we clean. I drag my whole vacuum cleaner over there. It's okay to leave her for two weeks."

"How is she?" I asked. "Is she okay without Yeye?"

My mom dropped her voice. "They say some women have a second life when their husbands die. She plays mah-jongg every week with her friends in the building. Actually, she couldn't be happier."

My dad had immigrated to the States with his entire family and lived with them until he got married and is filial in a way that would make Confucius proud. But I suddenly realized that my mom enjoyed sacrificing her own freedom for her elders as little as I did. And actually my parents were not the unified two-headed beast they had merged into when I was in high school, but in fact were quite opposite: my dad pessimistic and reticent, my mom optimistic and ebullient. Though one trait they do share as the eldest siblings in their respective families is the conviction that they are always right.

Xiao Peng asked my parents, "So what do you think of Beijing?"

"I've found that drivers on the road don't really follow the laws here," my dad said sternly, causing Bobo, Xiao Peng, and me to burst into laughter.

That night when I dropped them off at the hotel, my dad told me he had avoided the outhouse the entire time we had been at their house. I tried to convince him it wasn't so bad, but he said it was no problem so long as you drank nothing.

We returned to Bobo's house every day. Just like during my first visit to Beijing, relatives swarmed in from all over the city to see my parents. They gossiped about all the relatives not present. There was so much talking, so many banquets. Everyone made the usual jokes about how much I had eaten at that first meal years ago, and like they had to me years ago, they piled food onto my dad's plate, even against his protestations.

The night of the banquet with Party Secretary Li came. We arrived first and were led to a private dining room garlanded with rainbow tinsel. As I took a seat at the one circular table filling the room, my dad said, "Valerie, you can't sit there. The head seat is the one facing the door."

Bobo assured him it didn't matter but after a look from my dad, I muttered, "Gotta follow the rules," and ceded the seat to Bobo, who had invited everyone and was picking up the tab.

"American tables are always rectangular," my dad said, before launching into a lesson about American seating hierarchies.

When Party Secretary Li arrived, we all leapt to our feet and they fought over who would sit where, until finally she took a seat between my dad and Bobo. She was a smiling, round-faced woman with a cylindrical coxcomb of bangs perched atop her head. She wore a seafoam green suit jacket and had a bright, precise voice.

During the dinner, punctuated by numerous toasts, Dad became

charming and full of jokes and Chairman Mao quotations but I could see
that underneath he was profoundly uncomfortable. Chumming up with
the Chinese bureaucracy was not his idea of fun and he did it only to
fulfill his obligation to Nainai. He asked his scripted questions as ordered
and Party Secretary Li promised to do what she could.

She told him that China had changed since he'd left and as the son
of a Nationalist he had nothing to worry about. She said the government
no longer "puts hats on people and whacks them with sticks"—old code
words for labeling people politically and punishing them. "Policies are
looser now."

"If I were afraid, I wouldn't have come back," he said.

The next order of business was to visit the cemetery where our ancestors
are buried. Nine of us went together. Wan'an Cemetery was far outside
of the city, near Fragrant Mountain in the northwest. We bought flowers
from a man selling them out of a van and signed in at the front gate; you
had to know someone inside to get in.

As we waited in the rain for the gates to be opened, my dad asked
Bobo in a hesitant manner I'd never seen before, "So, do you think yesterday went well?"

"Very well, very well," Bobo said in a schoolmasterish tone that made
us all laugh, even my dad.

"Are you the director or the leading actor of this drama? I can't tell,"
said my dad, who must have been feeling like a bit player. I knew the
feeling.

"Party Secretary Li, didn't she promise she'd get this done for you?
I'll call her tonight. Once it's all arranged, we'll go see The Document
tomorrow morning."

Water dripped out of the many trees in the lush and overgrown cemetery. Birds squeaked loudly all around us, and the world felt damp and
heavy. The burial plots stood shoulder to shoulder, a city of the dead, and
most were family tombs, some guarded by fierce marble lions, others just

simple stones. As we walked through, Bobo pointed out the graves of relatives they knew and they traded gossip about them as if they were still alive. He pointed out the graves of famous people too, like the large ocher slab flanked by flower vases that marked the final resting place of Cao Yu, the playwright who had written *Peking Man,* the movie version of which I'd subtitled. Seeing his grave felt as meaningful as seeing my own relatives' graves; here was someone who had made stories out of the lives of the families buried around him, stories that would outlive us all.

Bobo said that our family grave had been defaced during the Cultural Revolution and Nainai and Great-Aunt Mabel had sent money to restore it. But Bomu muttered that after Nainai's brother passed away she had stopped sending money to the family. I never knew she'd even been sending money but it didn't surprise me. This story about the graves was one of the many stories I never heard until I came to China, most having to do with the Cultural Revolution: Our ancestors' graves had been defaced, our courtyard houses had been confiscated by the government, Bobo's youngest sister had committed suicide. No one wanted to talk about the past.

We finally arrived at the grave. The plot itself was as big as half a tennis court. At the back of the plot was a large gray tablet as tall as I was, engraved with Nainai's surname and the names of people running down it. The names at the center of the tablet were Nainai's father, a Qing Dynasty military general, and her mother. In front of the tablet were two carved plinths under which they lay and in front of that a simple concrete bench. Xiao Peng swept it and set down offerings: a plate holding a small pyramid of apples, another of peaches, another of Oreos. It being Mid-Autumn Festival, he also set out a plate of mooncakes. Dad set down the flowers.

Bobo's sister traced her finger down the family tree, through Nainai's generation, down to her own, stopping on her own name, carved already into stone. It gave me goose bumps. Nainai's name was also carved next to her brother's, and I thought of our family headstone in Maryland that also had her name carved onto it, above her birth year with a hyphen dangling off of it. Talk about being divided—half in China and half in America, half in this life and half in the next already. The tree continued down to Xiao Peng's generation; his name was there, as was that of his older sister in L.A., but the younger sister's wasn't; Bobo's sister didn't say why. I was thankful not to see my own name staring out at me.

Bobo said that due to space considerations the government had decreed that no more graves were to be dug in the cemetery. Even the people whose names were on the tombstones would have to be cremated. If they wanted to, they could sell off the unused sides of the plots to another family to bury their dead. The real estate of the dead was as much in demand as that of the living.

After a bit of *you go first, no you go* jostling, Bobo got down on his knees in front of the offerings. With his palms on the ground, he inclined his torso all the way down, his forehead touching the ground, then up, three times in a kowtow. Then rising stiffly he bowed three times from the waist. He stepped to the side and my dad came up. Bobo mimed the movements for him. We took turns in order of seniority, with me last. I found it difficult. At the moment my head went down, I sensed the amount of humility it would take to do this fully, and my neck strained upward, not wanting to submit. I saw that while my mom performed with theatrical solemnity, she too had the same problem.

I hoped they weren't going to make us talk to our dead ancestors, as they had made me talk to Yeye two years before as he lay in a coma in a brightly lit intensive care ward. I thought back to what the fortune-teller had said about Yeye. Had he really died disappointed? I knew he was disappointed in his three ungrateful grandchildren, none of whom had earned a Ph.D. as he had or spoke much Chinese. I never felt as though I lived up to his expectations.

But something odd had happened at his last Christmas dinner, during my senior year in college. He was uncharacteristically quiet and as I looked across the holly-festooned tablecloth at his stooped form, I saw something I could barely believe: There was actually a soft look in his eye, and I swore I saw something ineffable pass over the table from him to me. It felt a lot like the gesture of approval I had been waiting my whole life for from him. I wasn't sure of what I'd seen, but when he became sick the next month, it made sense that he had known the end was near and had finally shown his hand. Not wanting to interrupt my studies, my parents forbade me from coming home to visit him in the hospital until Spring Break, after everyone else in the family had already visited. When I got home, we drove straight to the hospital. "Just talk to him," said my mom as we stood over his bed. "He can't hear us," I'd said. I'd been tongue-tied and embarrassed and had mumbled a few things. My mother had stepped in and told him in a clear, chipper voice that Val was standing here and that she was about to graduate from college and was going to China in the fall. I'd nodded mutely. Shortly after we got home that night, the hospital called to say that he had passed away. The last words he heard on this earth were that I was going to China. Unless he didn't hear it at all.

According to the traditional Chinese custom of ancestor worship, when your elder dies, the cycle of obligations that constitutes your relationship to him or her doesn't end—it just kicks into a higher gear. You care for their graves, and in return, they bring you prosperity and good fortune, and your success glorifies them. But if you neglect them, they become vengeful "hungry ghosts" bent on your destruction, and your failure then reflects back on them, bringing shame and disappointment. It is a vicious, never-ending cycle.

I wasn't sure how much my family still believed in these ideas after all that they had gone through, all that China had gone through. All I knew was that we went to bow before my ancestors' graves and that I felt Yeye's presence in my life every day. I felt watched and judged but I also felt part of something strong, something that had survived.

Yeye's death had an unexpected effect on my family—all my closest relatives suddenly seemed like complete strangers who had no connection to me whatsoever. I realized we had all related to one another through him, and when that nucleus disappeared, we flew apart like errant electrons. Whenever an old person exits or a new person enters a family, everything changes.

Now that I was in Beijing, I suddenly had so many questions for him about what the city had been like in his day, what his life had been like. I had lost my chance. And I had no way of telling him what it was like now or that my Chinese had improved a lot, thanks to all of the "eaah training" I'd undergone at home. My only consolation is that he knows my news already or had even played a part in me going to China.

As we were cleaning up to go, Xiao Peng asked if I was hungry and offered me one of the apples. I was disgusted. Wasn't that like eating the bodies of our relatives? Like the wafer and the wine? He laughed and said it wasn't like that at all, as he took a big bite of the apple.

The next morning, instead of going to see The Document, we went to visit Great-Aunt Mabel's new courtyard house. The hutong was thick with the call of food vendors and Bobo had to shove out of the way two tricycles and two bicycles blocking the doorway so we could enter. The courtyard was like a jungle inside, with vines hanging from the eaves and from a lopsided trellis, semidead trees languishing in pots, weeds straggling up from between the bricks on the ground. One big tree loomed over it all. The house itself was in good shape, and when we went inside the rooms, we saw they were big and high-ceilinged. We walked through all sixteen empty rooms, our voices bouncing loudly off the concrete floors and dusty plaster walls. Bobo said Nainai's house had twenty-two rooms, and if she exchanged it for a different one, it would be even bigger than this one.

As I stood between my mom and Xiao Peng, she said to him, "Two or three years of living here is enough for Val," hoping for his corroboration.

Xiao Peng smirked and said, "But China's so big, there are so many places you haven't gone to visit yet."

On the drive home, Bobo said that he'd gotten a call from Party

Secretary Li that morning. She had corroborated the existence of The Document but said it was in a repository that only someone from a *danwei*, or work unit, someone like her, had access to. But seeing it would be no easy feat even for her—she would need explicit written permission from the head of the Xicheng District Housing Management Bureau. Bobo counseled holding off on seeing it until there was an impending demolition.

My dad asked in a hesitant voice, "What does The Document say again?"

"That if the titleholder ever returns to China and establishes residency, the whole house will be returned to you, empty. Why are there tenants there now? Because you haven't established residency."

"If I want to do that, does it mean I have to live here, long-term . . . ?"

"No, you don't have to move here. But when it gets demolished, and you're negotiating with them, you put The Document right in front of them and say, 'Here! You must give me an empty courtyard house. And you take care of the tenants. I'm not taking care of the tenants!' " Bobo gave a big smile, and slapped "The Document" into his open palm with triumph. I never understood how, if it was so hard to see The Document, Bobo knew its contents so well. "Do you understand?"

Dad nodded grimly, then smiled with his mouth only. "I understand. I understand perfectly." He paused. "So I don't have to establish residency here."

"No, no."

"But if I don't, there's no way to chase out the tenants unless it gets demolished."

"Right." Bobo thought it would happen in the next five to ten years. "The most important thing is that when it comes time to demolish this house, they know that the owner is an overseas Chinese and that they won't be able to dismiss you so easily."

I wondered what Nainai would want to do. I suspected that she didn't want the connection with Beijing anymore. She was never coming back, and even if she did, she would no longer recognize the city she grew up in. I suspected she would probably take the cash.

Bobo, of course, didn't mention his own wishes for the house. Did my parents suspect Bobo's hope to live in the new house? Did he even have that hope, after what had happened with Great-Aunt Mabel's house?

I took my parents to the *City Edition* office, introduced them to my co-workers, and showed them the magazine, pointing out the masthead with my name on it. My mom looked proud but a little puzzled to see the desk and computer where I spent most of my days, far away from her. My dad didn't look unduly impressed but he did seem reassured to meet Sue and to see that another sane, intelligent American had made the same decision I had to move halfway around the world from her family to work on a two-bit magazine. Sue asked about the Peking Opera story, which was scheduled to be the cover story of the upcoming issue, and I told her that due to the re-interview I needed more time to finish it and we should probably push it to the next issue. She disguised her annoyance as best she could.

I organized a lunch for my parents to meet my friends. We went to Jin Ding, a raucous dim sum palace, and sat around a lazy Susan covered with tiny plates. Anthony was there, as were Jade, Cookie, Rachel, Yang Lina, and a few others. We went around in a circle and each of us solemnly stated how many years we'd been in China. When we were done, my dad chuckled and said, "You all sound like you're talking about your prison sentences!"

My mom chimed in, "Val's always complaining about the pollution here—it's really not so bad!"

I had instructed everyone to keep mum about Anthony but halfway through lunch, Rachel forgot and dropped an allusion to my boyfriend. Everyone froze, silent.

"What was that?" my mom asked.

I shook my head slowly at Rachel.

She warbled something unintelligible in a British accent and I quickly changed the subject. There were still limits to what I would show my parents of my life and what they were willing to see.

I gently refused to let them visit my apartment, saying that it was too far away and not worth the time. Not only would the local sex shops, prostitute neighbors, and bomb-shelter décor of the apartment have upset them, but also I would have had to systematically efface all signs of Anthony's presence there, just like that character in Ang Lee's *The Wedding Banquet,* who in a fast-cutting montage takes down all his photos and packs away all his boyfriend's clothing when his parents come to New York from Taiwan for his green card wedding. It's a funny conceit for a movie but such a hassle in real life, and depressing also to confront the lies I had to tell in order to live the life I wanted.

Of course I didn't mention my dream of making a documentary. I knew they would have thought it a waste of time, just more evidence that I was ruining my life. I didn't need to reinforce those naysaying voices in my head that I'd tried so hard to drown out. Sometimes living a double life is easier for everyone.

As the week went on, my parents and our relatives became more relaxed with one another. Once at lunch, when Bomu wheeled a dish around on the lazy Susan for Dad to try and Bobo scooped up a big spoonful of it, Dad moved in to receive it, but Bobo just deposited the food onto his own plate, leaving Dad hanging. Bomu, sitting between them, nudged Bobo and they all laughed at his rudeness. Dad wasn't a guest anymore, just one of the family.

Spending a week with my parents would normally leave me curled into a defensive crouch, but for once they were out of their comfort zone, and I was in mine. My mom talked about me in the third person as usual, but what she said surprised me. ("Val does all of the talking in the cabs. We don't even open our mouths. They would know instantly that we weren't from here.") My parents did seem somehow out of place in Beijing, like rubber figures among people hewn of wood. She also asked me if I had learned any "authentic Chinese cooking" I could teach her. Bobo talked about me in the third person too. ("Her Chinese has improved so much since she first came. We're so impressed at how capable she is, coming here with nothing and making a successful life for herself.") While their praise may just have been a way to be polite to one another, I lapped it up.

On the last day, Bobo finally took us to see Nainai's courtyard house. Unlike my dad's childhood recollection, it was not on a wedge of land at all but rather at the corner of a quiet hutong and a busy street, across from which was a huge modern office building, which Bobo said was a "Grade A" building and would greatly increase the property value of the house. The shiny modern building and the low, gray houses didn't seem to fit together in the same frame. We walked in through the open red door and confronted not a huge open space but a narrow corridor that ran around the perimeter of the courtyard. After all the families had been moved into the house years ago, the space hadn't been big enough, so they started building sheds in the middle of the courtyard to put coal burners, kitchens, and extra bedrooms.

"My, it's old," said my mom.

Bobo stood in the middle of the corridor with his arms outstretched.

"The Second Door was here."

"I remember," said my dad, and pointing to one of the rooms, said, "I lived there." Walking a little farther, he said, "And Shushu was born here. That was Mom's bedroom."

We walked all the way around the narrow corridor, which was jagged with things constructed only of the simplest materials. A metal shed lashed crookedly together with wire and topped with a makeshift roof patched with plastic held down with bricks. A tarp-shrouded pile of something used as a shelf for small pots of plants and bright plastic soda bottles. Loose, thin underclothes drying on wires. There were no sign of the locust tree, flowering crab apple tree, and grape arbor that Bobo said originally stood in the huge courtyard.

"It's so broken," said my mom as she peeked into a curtained room, reporting that things were piled up haphazardly inside. Mom could have been talking about the house's Confucian unity, which indeed was broken. The layers of other people's used and unused things, piled up like a collage, made distinguishing the original layout of the house nearly impossible, and heartbreaking. There was no way to delete all that mess and rewind fifty years to when the courtyard was empty and peaceful, and my dad a little boy. My dad said he vividly remembered going from this house to Great-Aunt Mabel's house.

Bomu said that the house actually looked better than usual. The government had painted the outer walls for the anniversary and hung up some red lanterns.

A woman wheeled in her bike and went inside, but we exchanged no words. For a moment, I saw us as cartoon characters in a Communist textbook: the evil, well-fed landlords (Americans, no less) coming to survey their property and the noble workers full of dignity.

Outside, Bobo and my dad huddled to one side, whispering about what would need to be done next. My dad looked appalled, as if he wanted nothing to do with this house, its history, and all its complications. The web he'd wandered into was stickier than he'd imagined and I saw he wanted to return to a place where the rules were clear and people actually followed them. I gave up the secret hope I'd been harboring of living there. We snapped some photos to show Nainai, and left.

Just before the fiftieth anniversary, my parents prepared to join their tour. I stood in their hotel room as they packed their suitcases. Before we parted, I wanted to tell them about some of the things I was now beginning to understand about them, little things like why my mom always carried clean toilet paper around in her purse, and bigger things too, about our family's past and the ways it affected us today. Their peripatetic childhoods, recounted as stories, sounded so glamorous to me, but only now could I begin to imagine their reality. So much loss. So much beginning again. And then to have children who were so different than you, who had different values. Plus, could we talk for a second about the absurdity of our situation? My mom had asked me to teach her authentic Chinese cooking. But these weren't things I knew how to talk about with them. I just told them I was glad they'd come, and they told me they were glad to see their relatives after so many years and glad to see that I had friends and what seemed to be a stable life.

Then my dad started talking, surprising me.

"Did you notice how I was able to connect with my cousin? Almost instantly?"

"Childhood companions," said my mom cheerfully.

"No, because—" said my dad, drawing a breath that shook with emotion as he tried to formulate his thought. He exhaled heavily. "My cousin is just that type of person."

"Yes, he's really great," I agreed.

"He's very friendly," said my mom.

"And his father was like that," he said, and then, shaking off his sentimentality, added brusquely, "His father never worked for one day in his life. Rich family. Didn't have to."

On the day of the anniversary, Anthony's parents switched from the hotel in the courtyard house to one overlooking the Avenue of Eternal Peace so they could watch the military parade. Anthony and I joined them. Tanks and missiles rolled majestically down the wide avenue, followed by phalanxes of goose-stepping soldiers, then more tanks, more missiles, more soldiers. Jets cruised in formation through the sky. It was breathtaking and impressive and grotesque. I was relieved to see it through their eyes, as some buffoonish show of might that bore no relation to me at all.

Chapter Nineteen

The Warrior and the Clown

Reporter Wang?"

"Speaking."

"This is Reporter Wang?"

"Yes. Who is this?"

"Guess." It was a middle-aged man with a Beijing accent. I'd interviewed so many people who fit that description.

"I really don't know."

"Are you sure?"

"Yes!" I said impatiently. "Just tell me, all right?"

"It's Zhang Laichun."

"Oh, hi!"

"We haven't heard from you in a long time." It had been a month or so since my Peking Opera story had come out.

"I've been so busy with other stories."

"You should call us."

"I'm sorry," I said, kicking myself for my knee-jerk apology.

"What are you doing on Saturday?"

"Nothing special."

"We'd like to invite you to my father's birthday party at noon on Saturday."

Though I had met many other people since Grandfather Zhang, his words still grated harshly on my ear: *Even if I talked to you every day for ten years, you still wouldn't know anything about Peking Opera.* He had lodged himself in my mind as nothing less than the decomposing heart of Old Beijing itself. An idea had been percolating in my mind.

"Would you mind if I videotaped you?"

"No, not at all."

"Great. I'll be there at noon."

I immediately called Yang Lina. We had become friends, whatever that meant in Beijing. Life here was still governed by *guanxi,* connections, and friendship felt like wampum, something to be bartered for the stuff you needed. *Old Men* had gone on the international film festival circuit and she needed letters and résumés to be translated to and from English, always at the last minute. In exchange for my help, she offered me many things. Her equipment. Her ex-boyfriends. Her advice. *Never date a poor artist. Always use protection.* I refused everything, especially the condescending advice. In America, we learn about sex in elementary school, I said. At this, she erupted into an oddly violent giggle and told me I was even more adorable than ever. If I'd wanted an older sister, I'd gotten one, with all the bossiness and superiority built right in.

Finally there was something I needed from her.

"Can I borrow your camera?"

"Of course. You finally have an idea for a documentary?"

"Yes. It's about this old family that does Peking Opera. The grandfather was crippled years ago during a performance and he has been lying in the same bed for thirty years. He yells at everybody from the bed and they all perform Peking Opera too," I said. I imagined my experience with the Zhangs would be like hers with the old men. I would shift gears, stop pressing them for information, and let their lives unfold naturally.

The resulting film would be a document about the dissolution of Old Beijing as seen through the eyes of one family.

"Do you like Peking Opera?" she asked.

"Well, not really," I said. I thought back to a performance Bobo had taken me to at the Workers' Club, a huge unheated theater whose hard wooden folding seats were filled with the thickly bundled forms of old people. Martial operas are full of exuberant acrobatics, manic backflipping, and spirited swordplay, but of course Bobo had taken me to see a literary opera: a long philosophical argument sung in a slow screech and acted out with tiny but meaningful movements—here a mincing step, there a flicking sleeve—and accompanied by the arrhythmic clanging together of what sounded like pots and pans. The costumes I could appreciate—long brocaded gowns, three-inch wooden platform shoes, headdresses from which sprouted wide fins, colorful flags or pompons on springs—but even they formed part of the crust of Peking Opera that I found impossible to break through. Robots could have been operating the figures from underneath for all I knew. If the theater hadn't been freezing cold, I would have fallen asleep. "But the family—there is something about them that draws me in. Something deep."

"Trust that feeling," she said, and lent me her camera.

My entrance into the Zhang house, I was happy to find, did not make a huge splash. An assortment of relatives was already twittering around the large room and the TV was on, blaring with a Peking Opera performance. I had brought a copy of my article (titled "Peking opera hits low notes") and they gathered around as I translated it for them. The story portrayed them as tragic heroes battling the tides of history and the scrofulous policies of the state-run troupe to keep the ancient art alive. They began arguing among themselves. *You said too much. No, he was just telling the truth. I never said that! This is going to get us in trouble with the troupe. What is there to be afraid of anymore?*

They certainly were in party mode. The room was claustrophobic, and unlike on other days, when the house had seemed a continuation of the street below, tonight I felt cut off, in a hermetic bubble locked away from society. Round folding stools were scattered around the room. I sat on one on the periphery and took out the video camera. I looked at the crowd of relatives chattering loudly to one another and remembered from my childhood how much Chinese sounds like yelling when people are happy. Grandfather Zhang would be the main character of my documentary, of course. He was the nucleus of the family, in the same way my Yeye had been. Supporting characters would include his wife and high-kicking sons Zhang Laisheng and Zhang Laichun. I still had a hard time telling the two apart. I clung to oversimplifications: Laisheng was known in the family as the one who said too much, Laichun for being incomprehensible.

I concentrated on the images in my viewfinder and watched greedily as it took everything in. The other relatives visiting for the day and milling around the room would make colorful extras. Grandpa Zhang's other two sons hadn't fallen far from the tree. One was a producer of kung fu films and the other, the eldest, his face ghoulishly frozen on one side by a stroke, told me about the twenty-part miniseries he had written about his father's life. It made a good story, he said, because their family was still "slightly feudal," which I took to mean that they all, like me, lived in fear of the autocratic patriarch barking out mean things from the bed. The grandmother, overhearing our conversation, insisted that it was my responsibility to find funding for the filming of the miniseries. I nodded weakly.

We ate hotpot together, our chopsticks dipping into the roiling pot in the middle of the table, fishing out meat and vegetables that others had put in. One portly middle-aged relative became drunk and sat rubbing his bare belly after the meal. When I pointed the camera at him, he launched into an extended monologue about how rich and complex the language and lives of a cultured Peking Opera family like theirs was. The liquor made his thick Beijing accent even more incomprehensible. My mind drifted. *And the winner is . . . Val Wang for* Peking Opera & Sons. A bright light shone on me. *Thank you so much for this honor. I never imagined I'd be standing right here. I just had a video camera and a dream—to tell a simple story about the richness and complexity of a family steeped in Peking Opera. There are so many people to thank. Yang Lina and Wu Wenguang for all of your help and encouragement, Cookie for your support, the Zhang family for opening your home to me, my own family in Beijing, and last of all, Mom and Dad for your patience, I told you this whole artist thing would pay off.* When I returned to the room, he was still talking, saying that their language was so full of literary allusions that mere commoners wouldn't be able to understand them, much less a foreigner.

I turned my camera to Laisheng and Laichun. Natural performers, they came alive in front of the camera. They had a spirited debate about what I should do with my life.

"She shouldn't stay in Beijing too long," said one of the sons.

"She should," said the other.

"No, she shouldn't."

"Maybe you're right. Beijing is too complicated, too chaotic for her."

"No, that's not why. She shouldn't stay in any place for too long." I noted the envy in his voice. He turned to me and said, "Your life is about going many places and seeing many things, not like us. We can only do one thing: Peking Opera."

They envied my mobility and I envied their permanence. The Flying Pigeon and the Forever. I thought it might be nice to have a place to call home and one thing I was really good at.

One of the two said, "People say I drink too much." Both of them drank too much, downing glass after glass of *erguotou,* the toxic local firewater whose heavy, sickening bouquet filled the air. I would drink a lot too if I belonged to this family. How could they stand to be in that room together day after day? Didn't they drive one another crazy with the scrutiny, the guilt, the recriminations? Just being there for a few hours made me feel like a fish gasping for air. Maybe, come to think of it, having a place to call home was overrated.

I remembered what Xiao Ding had said about Chinese relationships existing as a series of concentric circles. I was still in their outer orbit; I would have to get closer to make a better movie like Yang Lina had done with the old men.

The family gathered around the grandfather's bed. I turned my camera toward them. Were they about to sing a birthday song and eat the sticky rice cake with the character 寿, meaning "long life," written on it in hawthorn candy, which sat on a side table? The cake was lightly dusted with tiny black specks of soot and all night I had been mentally rehearsing my excuses for not wanting any. They wrestled with something and I saw they were emptying his colostomy bag together. Even this was a family affair. It was my cue to leave. I turned off the camera and said my good-byes. The cake sat untouched on the side table.

Laisheng gripped my arm and walked me outside. I breathed much easier in the cool night air. He told me, "In Peking Opera, I play the warrior. Laichun plays the clown, so he likes to joke. I don't like to joke." The family was right. Laisheng was chatty. He then said that he felt very close to me and was sure that we were good friends. I could barely tell him apart from anyone else in the family and I wasn't sure I felt very close to him, but the polite thing to do was agree, so I did.

Old Men started winning international awards. The Award of Excellence at the Yamagata International Documentary Film Festival. The Golden Dove prize at the International Leipzig Festival for Documentary and Animated Film. The SCAM Award at the Cinéma du Réel festival. A French TV station bought the documentary. International curators, Beijing Film Academy professors, and underground filmmakers showered Yang Lina with invitations to international festivals and private screenings of films. And so of course I was in constant contact with her, helping her to communicate with the outside world. Every time we met she would greet me with an inchoate gurgling of my personal name—Zhenluo!— and a pronouncement of how she perceived me at that moment. Some days it was *You are so adorable and so naïve!* or *You are so well-behaved and serious!* Her idea of me as a prim little violet grated on me; it was so different from my idea of myself as a swashbuckling bohemian. After all, hadn't the fortune-teller said I *zixun fannao,* sought trouble for myself?

She began to throw references to obscure directors into our conversations.

"*Bu-lie-song* is so simple and so strong."

"*Ji-ya-luo-si-ta-mi*'s films about Iran have helped me to see my own culture more clearly."

"I've been watching too many French films and they've made me want to be passionate and sexual." She erupted into her violent giggle again. Unlike most Chinese people I knew whose inner lives seemed to be locked away in top secret underground vaults, Yang Lina's spilled out all over the place like jelly from a powdered donut. It would have taken at least four shots of espresso or a high fever to whip me into the state of giddy, bright-eyed frenzy she seemed to be in all the time.

Bu-lie-song? Ji-ya-luo-si-ta-mi? If I could decode the names, I was sure I would know whom she was talking about. I was American, more modern, more culturally sophisticated, with more knowledge of obscure films than someone who had grown up in a country completely cut off from the world. But even when I found out who they were, I realized with a pit in my stomach that I hadn't seen any Bresson or Kiarostami films, and I had no idea what they were like. Zhang Yuan's words came back to me: Was a fundamental condition of being Chinese to feel inferior—to the people around you, to the rest of the world? Was a fundamental condition of being American to feel superior?

The Zhang family liked to call me on the phone. Sudden and demanding, their phone calls were usually invitations for events that were happening the next day. Often, I already had plans.

"Hello?"

"Reporter Wang? It's . . . Laichun." The Incomprehensible Clown.

Increasingly, the phone calls were coming from him. I tried to dissuade him from calling me Reporter Wang, as I wanted the family to relax around me. He informed me that they were taking the grandfather out in his wheelchair the next day.

"So I'll go out with you?" I asked.

"It's not about whether you'll come or not. His health has been bad and we're taking him to the park."

"Okay, I'll come," I agreed.

"What time will you come?" he asked.

"Midday."

"What time?"

"Ten o'clock?" I did what I could to be tolerant and rational, but I never seemed to know the right answers. He laughed. The acidity of his laughter set him apart from Laisheng. Laisheng was more of a giggler.

"What's so funny?" I demanded.

"Our lives are not alike. Our days have mornings and afternoons."

I understood him to mean that I should come earlier, so I arranged a hurried borrowing of Yang Lina's camera and ended up going at eight o'clock sharp, just as they were carrying the grandfather downstairs.

The family members took turns wheeling the grandfather slowly down the hutong as the rest of the group bobbed around him like tethered balloons. I faced them, walking backward, and shot their procession. We turned onto wider, busier streets leading to the Temple of Heaven Park. When we arrived at a circle of dirt in an isolated grove in the park, Grandfather Zhang gestured with palms up to the empty space and said, "We have arrived at—"

"—our performance arena," his relatives filled in with a murmur.

"—Metropolitan Washington."

We all paused in puzzlement. I assumed he was trying to create a sense of pomp for me, but as usual, his true meaning was nearly impossible to decipher. Laichun took a nearby tree branch and swept dead leaves from the circle and then the grandson began practicing opera forms from *The Ring of Heaven and Earth*. The grandfather sat bundled up under a tree and barked commands at him, ordering him to perform certain moves for my camera and critiquing his technique. I suddenly realized that, unlike my vision of the documentary, they wanted me to shoot a lavish extravaganza showcasing the glories of Peking Opera.

The trees were in fall bloom. In the quiet green, old folks practiced tai chi and other exercises in slow motion. I leaned back and tried to enjoy the show.

In the winter, the Zhang family called several times, but I always found an excuse to decline their invitations. I was busy writing articles, I said. Or my friend with the video camera was out of town. Or I was going home for a visit. In truth, visits to their house were disturbing. I didn't feel like myself there. I never said what I thought, only what I thought they wanted to hear, to avoid disrupting the harmony of their household. Just as my dad did to Nainai, or so my mom claimed. "If she told him that a black table was white," said my mom, "he would just agree." She, like me, preferred expressing her opinion. But for the first time, I knew how my dad felt. It was just easier to go with the flow.

Chapter Twenty

To Know Your Own Life

Crowds of Chinese men in their stockinged feet, their vinyl shoes shucked onto the floor, sat in the departure lounge playing cards and yelling. They would have been smoking had they been allowed. Other people were clipping their toenails or posing for photos in front of the big picture windows. Our airplane sat docilely outside, getting slowly filled with suitcases and gasoline.

I was returning to Beijing after visiting the States, back to my parents' house in the suburbs and then up to New York to see friends. The house I had grown up in seemed smaller every year I went home and my parents unchanging. Despite all the progress I (and we) had made in China, time stood still there. "When are you moving home?" my mom kept asking, while my dad said, "You're not doing anything interesting over there, are you?"

Nainai was the only one interested in hearing about Beijing. I told her about how the city was now and how her relatives were doing. When I went to visit her apartment, I saw that in the middle of Yeye's old study that still held his desk and bookcases there now stood a square table with a mah-jongg set on it. Nainai did seem different somehow, more light-hearted. Home in general felt light without the weight of Yeye. His death had left a power vacuum in the family that no one could or would fill. Nainai didn't seem keen to. My dad aspired to it but did it in middle manager–style, compiling address lists and forwarding *New York Times* columns by David Brooks, with none of the fear-inducing gravitas of Yeye.

I went up to New York, which was so seductive, so frictionless. I kept bumping into the ghosts of myself, versions of me who had moved into that rent-controlled apartment on the Upper West Side after college. I longed for dinner parties, for endless discussions about films, plans, and gossip. I wanted to have a room in Brooklyn with a desk by a sunny window where I wrote. Adventure, history, and truth? Was that really what I'd found in Beijing? All I knew was that both places couldn't exist in my mind at the same time; each was forgotten when I traveled to the other side of the world. The plane ride was a bookend holding everything in place, the dream between two realities. Or maybe it was the void separating the reality of America from the dream of China.

I wasn't eager to go back and face my life in Beijing. Sick of the Entertainment Guide and longing to have more time to do my own stories and shoot my documentary, I'd wanted to go freelance for a while (Wu Wenguang's voice never stopped needling me from within), but I'd never dared. Right before my trip to the States it had happened abruptly, at Sue's instigation. I'd avidly agreed but now I realized that *freelance* was just a polite word for unemployed. I had actually been gently fired. While I was in the States, a friend had e-mailed to say he'd seen Anthony out with another woman. We broke up via a very pricey phone call. I had nothing to go back to: no job, no boyfriend, just the nub of a documentary. I was panicked and dreaded exiting the airport and feeling the tugs on my sleeve of drivers pestering me to take their illegal taxis, and the whole rigmarole beginning for another year.

I told my friend in New York who had given me the orange jacket long ago about how frustrated I was to be returning again to China because it made me feel as if I were doomed for all eternity to retrace the trajectories of my parents and grandparents. It made me feel so determined by my family's past. She looked at me kindly and with a dash of pity for my obliviousness and said, "We all are, Val."

At some point in the airport, the entire crowd rose, unbidden by any announcement, and rushed the gate.

In the breach that Anthony left, new friends entered. I discovered that my neighborhood was actually full of young expats, mostly women, whose stories were startlingly like mine. Cookie lived there with her friend Emma, Rachel lived nearby, and they knew some other Brits, plus a woman who worked at *Beijing Scene*. Cookie somehow knew Gretchen, the woman from the lesbian meeting, who defrosted significantly after she found out I wasn't actually a lesbian, and Becky, who had taken over Anthony's old job at the gallery after he quit to work as a lawyer. We all spoke Chinese, had come to China alone seeking adventure, and found life on the rough-and-tumble fringe of the city to our liking. Most of us had short hair, none to my recollection wore makeup, and everyone's teeth had gone black like mine. They were much more like me than Jade, and I found myself drifting away from her.

Trading stories of our apartments, we found we all heard the same mysterious noises, like the pipes being playfully clanged on and the pearl necklace breaking and spilling its beads, which began to seem more amusing than menacing. We all also had girly neighbors who left their apartments in the evening and came back very late at night. The ones across the landing from Becky's apartment had even chosen English names and she was frequently woken in the middle of the night by the sound of banging and a young woman yelling, "Carol! *Kai men'r!*" Open up!

Inspired by my new friends' apartments, I asked my landlords to clear their belongings off the balcony, save for the giant naked baby doll. I painted the walls of the balcony orange, bought a few plants, and moved a chair out there. It wasn't such a bad place to hang out.

After the big fiftieth anniversary passed, I'd realized there wasn't much to be afraid of in my building. The neighborhood grannies outside my building grew to tolerate me, even occasionally greeting me as I went in and out. I got used to living with a constant, low-grade fear of the police. The policeman still sat regularly outside my gate, but after several times of seeing a woman come up to him, I realized that he was just waiting for his girlfriend like any old schmo.

Flattering ourselves that we were as feisty and devil-may-care as the Chinese grannies living in our compounds, my friends and I began calling ourselves "the grannies," a name that stuck.

Cookie and Emma's apartment became the epicenter of our social life. We ate almost every night at a neighborhood restaurant called Lao Beijing, or Old Beijing, and after dinner, we went to their apartment to watch pirated VCDs that always cut off the last two minutes of the movie, or went out dancing or to the local gay bar, a bare-bones affair called the Drag-On located on a dirt road heading out of town.

Unfortunately, the police were often posted at the gate of Cookie and Emma's compound, demanding identification from whoever came in and out. With vigilance, avoiding them was easy. We just went around back and scrambled over a wall to get in or out. We told ourselves we would rather live in Chinese housing with its faulty plumbing, nosy neighbors, and fear of the police than in sterile expat housing or in the sentimental hutongs of the old city. Gretchen even took a novel approach to her local policeman; instead of hiding from him when he periodically knocked, she would invite him in for a chat over instant coffee, the kind that came in a packet with sugar and milk included. He never turned her in.

This corner of the world was grimy; it was where urban construction grit met dirt that blew in from the countryside. Things combined in a way we had never seen before and the neighborhood felt as if it belonged to us.

A reporter came from Hong Kong to expose the underbelly of Asia's up-and-coming capital of sin and had written for a British newspaper about Maizidian'r with its casual brothels and police crackdowns and growing population of Gen X expats, the newest lost generation. Forget Prague. Beijing was the Paris of the twenties of the *late* nineties. Emma's mother in the UK read the article and called her in a panic for her safety. Maizidian'r had made it.

One day, I likened our lives to those in *Beijing Bastards* and Cookie made a noise of disgust. "That was the worst movie, Val," she said. "Full of wankers."

Cookie knew artists from her time at the Central Academy and Becky and Gretchen worked for rival art galleries, and so we all got invitations to underground art events. The invitations were strictly word-of-mouth and the events were always packed, everyone hurrying to see it before the police shut it down, which happened once in a while. We often found ourselves crammed into a cab looking for an obscure venue, each more unfindable than the last.

One time we arrived to find a blindfolded man standing on a pedestal, naked save for his cloth-wrapped penis onto which a bird was attached via a string. Another time we found a woman sitting on the floor cradling a blotchy fetus and guiding a transfusion tube flowing with oil into its mouth. She was one of the young artists from that first underground exhibition I'd been to the year before, who all used human corpses procured from morgues in their work. It was hard to tell what they were trying to say with their work. Were they expressing the absurdity and degradation of the human spirit in a totalitarian regime? Trying to win a gross-out competition started in the West? Having a laugh at our expense? Even when I interviewed them and asked about the materials they used in their art, they issued only the most gnomic pronunciations. "What did Lu Xun say?" they said, referring to the famous Chinese writer. "'The earth had no roads to begin with, but when many men pass one way, a road is made.'" Chinese art was the new avant-garde, pushing the shock value of art just beyond what artists in the West could or would do.

At one exhibition, I bumped into the Texan art collector, who was happily chomping away on a cigar. He said he'd quit his job at Motorola and was going full bore on his website about Chinese contemporary art. His Chinese wife's solid job at an American multinational financed his quixotic schemes. He boasted that he had the blood of both the philosopher Jean-Jacques Rousseau and Texan horse thieves running through his veins, and I could see both the noble and ignoble at work in him: His website gave China's best artists international exposure, and if it enhanced the value of his own art collection, so be it. His hustle was typical of the art scene, in which critics doubled as dealers and artists invested in lavish catalogs in the hopes that they would find their way into the right hands half a world away.

When he told me he was in the process of staffing up his website, I told him I'd just gone freelance and he offered me what I considered the perfect gig: Every week I would call up an artist and arrange a time to interview him (always a him) and then go to his house and talk for a few hours about his life and work. Then we'd go out for dinner and get drunk, and occasionally he'd try to get me to stay overnight, and I'd refuse. (The Texan hadn't mentioned this part of the gig.) I'd go home and sometime in the next few days write up a small profile, and after I'd interviewed all the artists in one genre, would write a longer wrap-up piece. My meager paycheck was more than enough to make ends meet.

For a series on video artists, I interviewed Song Dong, an artist who combined video with performance work. He began by shooting a video of himself eating noodles as he watched TV, and then projected the video back onto his bare torso as he sat facing a mirror trying replicate his own behavior. The resulting video of his performance is eerie; most of the time his past and present selves are slightly out of sync with each other but once in a while the two snap together, and you feel a jolt. Song said, "In China, you are always taught to experience other people's lives, what it's like to be a peasant or a factory worker, but you are not taught to know your own life."

For his next piece, he took the same concept but instead projected onto himself a video of his father talking about his past as a Communist cadre. A Communist cadre and a contemporary artist; in the way their faces mismatch and meld into a grotesque third being you can feel the distance between them, the tension. The father talking and the son listening. But again there are those brief moments when the two faces nest perfectly and become one, and when they came, tears sprang into my eyes. I told Song how moving I found his work. "In Chinese families, it's rare to have flesh touching," he said. "This was my way of having contact with his flesh. His history, after all, is mine too."

His history, after all, is mine too. Those were words I never forgot.

I began nervously writing my first article for *Business China,* about tampon companies trying to break into the Chinese market. A friend had introduced me to the editor, a Bostonian named John, who liked my pitch. That week, he happened to be coming up from Hong Kong to meet his writers, of which I was now one, and I took him for a drink at the city's oldest rock club, Keep in Touch. John was on the prowl for the inside story and he listened with hungry eyes as I rattled on about sexual modesty, the sanitary plastic fingers enclosed in the tampon boxes, the fact that while only 1 percent of Chinese women used tampons, 73 percent said they experienced discomfort attributed to the use of crappy sanitary pads, and that panty liner sales had jumped 1,024 percent *in the last year.* Tampon companies were running ads with ballet dancers reassuring women that tampons were an "appropriate protection." When I finished talking, John said it was a terrific story. Send it next week. Then he turned the conversation to the lives of young expats in Beijing.

"What can you show me?" he asked.

"My neighborhood's not bad. It's a red-light district," I said.

He nodded eagerly.

"You can meet my friends too." I called Gretchen and Cookie and told them we'd be going to Peter Pan. We walked up the Third Ring Road, onto Maizidian'r Street. "See Arnie? That's a brothel. See the hairdresser? That's a brothel. See that sex shop? Hey, do you need any pirated DVDs?"

Gretchen arrived first. John asked how we had ended up here. I explained that I wanted to write and make documentaries and here was where the craziest stories were. Gretchen explained that she was here on a Fulbright studying contemporary Chinese art and interning at an art gallery on the side, though she seemed to spend most of her time shopping. And how had we met? Gretchen explained that had we met at a meeting of Chinese lesbians where I had been faking it and she had not. Lesbians! John was intrigued. Was this the Underground he had been hearing about? Ah, the Underground. We nodded mysteriously.

Cookie burst into the restaurant, wearing her phoenix-print knickerbockers. Her flaming red hair was wildly unkempt, beyond the point of fashionable, and her fanny pack was bulging like an overstuffed calzone.

"Are you a representative of the Underground?" John asked.

Cookie unclipped her fanny pack and sat down. "I *am* the Underground," she said.

We ate our flavorless pizzas and drank our sour red wine. John looked around, taking in the dingy red-checked tablecloths and the Chinese waitresses struggling with the Italian names.

"Why do you like it here so much?" he asked.

We all thought for a second.

"This place is wicked," Cookie said. She was still working for the international news agency and was becoming a professional at spinning the most lurid version of events. "There are police lurking everywhere and to get home I have to jump the fence in my compound, which is full of prostitutes and punks. A prostitute was killed there just the other day."

"In your compound?"

"Yes, just inside. That's what we heard from Big Sister Bao."

"Who?"

"The mafia don who runs my compound. Plus, the Chinese food here is smashing."

John ate it up. I was starting to eat it up.

"We're all artists," she went on. "Val here is shooting a documentary."

"And Cookie is a modern calligrapher."

"A modern calligrapher?"

"She rips and pastes colored paper to form huge characters and spray-paints characters on wood. She studied calligraphy at the Central Academy of Art before [McNews] claimed her soul."

"You work for [McNews]?" John asked in surprise.

"I was in print, but I just moved to TV. I want to be a camera-woman," she said. "And there's always a rumor of someone writing a screenplay."

"I see. What else?"

"Cheap rent."

"Tchotchkes."

"Massage by blind people."

"You know, I went there the other day and my guy wasn't blind."

"Massage by mostly blind people."

"Ladies Night. This bar nearby had free gin and tonics for women every Thursday."

"They thought it would attract Chinese girls who could only drink one or two."

"Not a bunch of sloppy Western girls."

"We put them out of business."

"We're *hunzi*," said Cookie.

"What's that?"

"Like slackers."

"I know what I like most about being here. Freelancing," I said. "Freedom in general. I feel really free here."

John started laughing. "You're from the United States of America and you come to the last huge Communist country in the world to find freedom," he said, with a combination of pity and admiration that somehow pleased me.

"Funny old world," said Cookie.

"You can find stories from the fringe," he said to me. "You can become *Business China*'s gonzo reporter."

I walked upstairs to my apartment, buzzed on the idea of our lives—or was it on the Great Wall wine that John had put on *Business China*'s tab? I parted the lush red curtains to the balcony and stepped outside for a smoke. All the lights were out in the building across the street. I could see only the blue flicker of televisions in dark rooms and the aged yellow moon hanging in the sky. I stood smoking and listening to the velvety quiet of the night. A knot tied and tightened within me began to loosen. The quiet was interrupted every so often by the gentle rattle of an old taxi or the throaty purr of a luxury car. I saw a mule cart piled high with bricks gliding slowly down the street, a tired farmer at the reins and the hooves clacking a lonely tune on the pavement. The mules came out only at night when they were allowed on the Third Ring Road. A few years in the past, there had been no Mercedes on this street and a few years down the road there would be no more mules. But right now we were double Dutch jump-roping, all the strands of different speeds weaving together in a moment of synchronicity as perfect and fleeting as a heartbeat. A queen could not have felt more content surveying her kingdom. The farmer and mule slowly disappeared out of sight. I exhaled the last of my smoke into the night and went inside.

Chapter Twenty-one
The Decomposing Heart of Old Beijing

I celebrated Christmas with Cookie and Emma, who baked a desiccated nut bread and invited over Chinese friends with whom we played a disastrous round of charades thanks to our dearth of shared cultural references. The millennium came and went. Winter became spring. My freelance career took off. After my tampon article for *Business China*, I did one on the bra industry, then another on the fur industry.

After a particularly infuriating phone call with my parents when they asked yet again when I was moving home for graduate school, I'd had enough. My mom had just gotten an e-mail address and I fired off an angry e-mail.

```
You and Dad are always doubting what I do and telling
me I am doing the wrong thing instead of trusting
that I am responsible and will find jobs to do that
will support me and make me happy. You seem to think
that if I went to law school or graduate school my
life would instantly become better, but that's not
```

```
true. I understand that you're worried about me, but
I wish you would support my decisions and be curious
about my present life more than my future.
```

I readied myself for the impact of their response. Anything was better than their endless needling criticisms.

```
I LOVE YOU JUST THE WAY YOU ARE!!!!!! I will support
you on all the decisions you made for your future.
After all, who will know you better than yourself?
Please keep writing to me, and tell me more about
your life and work in China. I LOVE YOU TOO MUCH.
```

She forwarded it to my dad, and even he grudgingly offered his support.

```
The important thing is to find something that rewards
you with satisfaction, peer respect, and financial
security (whatever the order you would like). Launch
yourself while you are young and energetic.
```

I began to share a little bit more of my life in China with them, sending them clips and links to articles I'd written. I knew they weren't happy with my decisions, but they started keeping their complaints to themselves. But I still didn't tell them about my documentary plans, which proceeded in secret. I scraped together money to buy a video camera, a simple one-chip one, not like Yang Lina's three-chip monster. I was ready to really start making the documentary. But I didn't call the Zhang family. I wasn't as staunch a comrade as Yang Lina. When difficulties presented themselves, I just wanted to quit. The *hunzi* in me was fighting with the ambitious go-getter, and winning.

Then Laichun called one day to tell me his father was in the hospital

with heart trouble. My first thoughts were largely selfish. If the decomposing heart of the decomposing heart of Beijing gave out, my documentary was over. He was my ticket out of the workaday world of journalism
and into the jet-setting stratosphere of art. I kicked myself for procrasti-
nating. I thought about Yeye and the trite but true lesson I had learned
from him: Once death came, you didn't get any second chances. I kept
calling to check on Grandfather Zhang, and when Laichun finally told
me he was out of the hospital, I made a date to drop by for lunch on the
weekend. Laichun said I should come later because he had a midday
performance, but I was adamant on coming for lunch. I wanted my visit
to be a finite activity. A few hours would be enough to get some good
footage without getting drowned in the morass of their family life.

Only the grandfather and the grandmother were home. I had never
seen the house so quiet. The grandmother smiled politely and said that
her sons would be home soon. They seemed excited for my visit. I took
the familiar stool by the bed and saw that my article had been framed and
hung on the wall next to the bed. I asked the grandfather about his
health. He looked the same as he ever did. I turned on the camera and he
immediately launched into a story that I didn't understand.

"A *meng*, when you sleep at night and you see your parents, your
brother, see your home. This is called a *meng*," he said.

"Oh, a *dream*. I know what that is."

"They're not allowed to disclose their *meng*."

"Oh, I see." I had no idea of what he was talking about. But I trusted
that the camera was taking it all down. I entertained myself by staring at his
bald head while trying to connect the viscous words that oozed out of his
mouth with the vivid opera performances trapped forever inside his mind. I
realized that all the camera was capable of picking up were words, useless
words. And the metronymic chirruping of the family's pet cricket. His eyes
rolled past me and I thought he was falling asleep. The door opened.

"Look who's here!" the grandfather said. Enter Laisheng. The Chatty
Warrior. The grandmother sprang into action. She began assembling the

fold-out table for lunch. I got up to help her, but she shooed me away. Laisheng put his leg up on a dresser to stretch and as soon as I pointed the camera at him, he turned on like a faucet. He began complaining about an upcoming performance he had to do as part of the reform of his state-run troupe. The performance would be graded on a scale from "excellent" to "subpar" and in the future the troupe would use the rankings to staff their performances. No longer would anyone be guaranteed work, even those with "excellent" grades.

To him, potential unemployment was just the next tragic chapter of a life that had never properly launched. He said he had been born in the mid-1950s, right as what he called a "natural disaster" forced "food rations" on the country, stunting his growth. (Actually, it was "Mao's disastrous agricultural policies" that plunged the country into "famine.") Just as soon as he was old enough to go to school, the Cultural Revolution started and he was sent down to the countryside to work. Separated from his family and denied schooling, he'd never been properly educated.

"If 'descendants of the Yellow Emperor' don't understand the matters of the 'descendants of the Yellow Emperor,' how can you say you're 'descendants of the Yellow Emperor'? How can you say that you're Chinese?" he demanded.

I nodded. I shook my head. Who was the Yellow Emperor again?

He then spent three years serving in the army. Once he was finally back at home ready to perform, the only operas being staged were the revolutionary model operas, performed by troupes he had no way to join. "Now there are opportunities, but I'm too old. I can't take advantage of them," he said.

"No need to talk about it," said the grandmother, but the warrior was on the warpath already. She peeled a small mandarin and put it in front of me. I didn't want it, but I ate it, peeling apart the segments with my one free hand.

"Does your daughter like Peking Opera?" I asked Laisheng. She was the lazy fake-Pringles eater.

"I don't want her to learn. This is a terrible profession. You'd earn more selling bottled water on the street." He launched into a confusing explanation of a Peking Opera story that ended with the pronouncement, "Those are *stories*."

I nodded.

From the bed issued a roar, "Did you understand?"

"Um . . ." I couldn't tell if the grandfather was being helpful or mocking.

"He said it was a *story* about a benevolent emperor who came down south of the Yangtze to solve the problems of the people." He said *"tanguan wuli,"* which I later found out was an idiom meaning "corrupt officials."

"This is a *story*," said Laisheng.

"I got that part."

"Is it real?" asked the grandfather.

"No?" I answered. I had no idea where this was going.

"Someone once told me the recipe for success was seventy percent connections, thirty percent ability," Laisheng said. "I'm over forty years old now and I'm still a *pusupusu caomin*."

"What's a *pusupusu caomin*?" quizzed the grandfather.

"I don't know," I answered. There was no use lying anymore.

"Literally a 'common person in the grass,' it means just a plain old regular person, without any power."

"Do you know what a *mayi* is?" asked Laisheng.

"Yes, I know what an *ant* is."

He became livid. "I'm just that ant. I'm just that grass on the plain." After a moment, he said softly, "Don't say too much. I don't want to lose my job. When I'm supposed to practice, I practice. When I'm supposed to perform, I perform."

"Say what should be said and don't say what shouldn't," the grandmother said to me. "All of the things about connections. We all know it, but there's no need to say it." She began talking about a story she'd seen on the news about a provincial leader who had been executed for taking bribes.

I had trouble following their instinct for allegory, for using the past to talk indirectly about the present, or for using animals to talk about people. They had to practically spell it out for me: The leaders were not benevolent; they did not care about solving the problems of the people, and anyone who said differently was parroting fictions. Their state-run opera troupe, from the highest level down, was corrupt. Those with connections rose to the top, and the ants, even those who were the true heirs to the art, stayed in the grass.

We sat quietly. The grandmother cleaned the grandfather's ears with a cotton swab, then cleaned her own.

"I want to ask you, Miss Wang, what else do you want to learn?" said the grandfather. "I want you to ask questions."

"Actually, I'm fine with just chatting," I said in my most cheerful tone of voice, trying to defuse the tension that my presence seemed to generate. Why couldn't they just relax and stop putting on an act for me? "I'm not here as a reporter anymore."

"Your foundation is very thin," reproached Laisheng.

I remembered what he or his brother had said to me a while ago and I repeated it defensively now. "My life is about going many places and seeing many things, not like you. You only know one thing: Peking Opera."

"So you know Peking Opera through and through from your one visit today, right?" asked the grandfather.

"That's not really my hope." I groped for a way to deflect his scrutiny. I didn't want to be the center of attention. If I could have directed the scene, I would have been a fly on the wall and the curmudgeonly grandfather would have uttered wise, salty pronouncements about life as the grandmother muttered rueful asides, and they would have bickered among themselves in a way that illuminated the richness and complexity of a cultured Peking Opera family. But instead they just plopped me on a stool in the center of room, lectured me with obscure stories, and slung insults at me when I didn't understand them. Why were they being so obstinate? I'm sure they asked themselves the same question about me. Maybe that drunken relative rubbing his belly after dinner had been right—a foreigner had no way of understanding a family this deep.

Any sensible person would have walked out of the room. But despite—or probably because of—our discomfort, I felt I was onto something. But I would never have had the courage to stay in the room had I not had my camera there as protection.

I tried to explain my vision of the documentary in simple terms. "I'm not only interested in Peking Opera. I'm actually more interested in your family, in your lives. Your everyday lives."

Silence.

I squeaked out, "Our lives are not alike."

"Not alike?" the grandfather boomed.

The room reeked of urine and coal smoke. Spending too much time with Chinese families made me dizzy and, occasionally, gave me migraines. I stared wistfully at the TV, wishing we could just sit and watch it together. I had come to think of the act of communal TV watching as the highest expression of intimacy in a Chinese family.

"Do you know that foreigner on TV who does cross talk?" asked the grandfather.

"Dashan," I said with an angry sigh. I hated Dashan. Cross talk is a traditional comedic art in which two men stand on a stage and engage in rapid-fire, pun-laden exchanges, and "that foreigner" was Mark Rowswell, a.k.a. Dashan. Supposedly his Beijing accent was so perfect that if you closed your eyes you would mistake him for a real Chinese person. But open them and you'd see a tall, sandy-blond Canadian with glasses whose blubbery lips were perpetually parted in the smile of ingratiating naïveté native to North American nerds. Dashan was now cashing in on his fame by starring in commercials for miracle pills that claimed to clear up spotty skin and regulate sleep patterns. "Yes, I've seen him."

"This is like *chaocai*," said the grandfather. "Do you know what *chao-cai* is?"

"Yes, I know." Stir-frying a dish.

"You take a pan, pour the oil in, cut the *cai*: the onions, garlic, meat. You put them into the pan and *chao* it, add some soy sauce, then put it onto a plate and on the table. This is a complete thing, isn't that right?"

"What are you trying to say?" I asked. I had had enough of their riddles and circuitous stories.

"The dish is cooked and I'm sending it to the table for you to eat." Here he paused for effect. "My meaning is to tell you a *complete thing*. But you just want to put in some onions, some meat, some potatoes—you don't even use a pan, you just boil them in water. It's not like a thing at all. I want you to go home and say, *I came to China and met a Zhang Mingyu who told me how Peking Opera developed and how to tell folktales.*" He squinted. "Are you interested?"

"I'm interested in whatever you have to say," I said wanly. Someone had ripped out my backbone and replaced it with grape jelly.

We paused in frustration.

"Do you like Dashan?" I asked. Every Chinese person likes Dashan.

"I don't like him."

"Why not?"

"I like his *thinking,* his *erudition.* Do you understand?"

I understood his jab perfectly: I was too Westernized and should become more Chinese with Dashan as my role model. Some Chinese people, even ones I liked, called me a banana: yellow on the outside, white on the inside. Dashan they called an egg.

"I hope that you grow up to be a skillful, wise woman. You can't disappoint your parents," the grandfather said. His frustration was palpable. "You make me anxious. You've come all this way to China. Just to chat is not enough."

"I can learn things from chatting," I mumbled.

"Oh," said the grandmother in a loud voice. She shot me a pitying look. "She says, 'From chatting I can learn things.'"

I cringed to hear my soft words shouted into the hearing aid.

"What have you learned?" roared the grandfather.

Lunch was ready. Steaming hot dishes were brought upstairs from the restaurant and I gladly moved my stool over to the table. I placed the camera on the table, left it running, and shook out my aching arm. Laisheng poured me some beer and I drank it down greedily. For himself, he took out an enormous plastic container of the local firewater *erguotou,* as big as a jug of cooking oil, and poured a generous glassful. Two liters of *erguotou* could certainly drown out a lot of family madness. Laisheng told me about a Japanese woman he had once met more than fifteen years before.

"She could only speak a little Chinese so I learned some Japanese. If you want to say she is beautiful or that you love her, you say, *Aishiteru. Sugoi kirei* is 'I love you.'" He giggled again and poured himself more *erguotou.* "I'm embarrassed. Quickly, drink some more beer."

He said he used to own his own restaurant and then became a seafood wholesaler. He said that the salt water had suffocated his marriage. "There is a saying in Chinese: 'If a man has money, he'll learn wickedness. If a woman learns wickedness, she'll have money,'" he said. We laughed.

This was the first I had heard of his divorce. Both sons, it turned out, were divorced. They were the kinds of sons who would never detach from their family. *No woman would willingly be a part of this family,* I thought. It revolved unerringly around the patriarch, an ogre who constantly contradicted everyone around him, or at least always seemed to contradict me.

Laisheng said he had a new girlfriend and invited me to their new apartment on Cow Street, in the Muslim area of town. He told me about renovations he was making to his apartment and we idly watched a Hong Kong pop star on TV. At long last, I was less entertaining than the TV.

The door flew open suddenly. Laichun burst in, out of breath and with wild eyes. It took a moment to put my finger on why he looked so strange: His lips were bright with lipstick and the area around his eyes was ablaze with large swooshes of colorful eye shadow. I started in surprise until I remembered that he had just finished a performance. That explained his appearance, sort of.

"People kept staring at me as I biked home," he said. I laughed. "But I didn't care because I knew I was biking here to see you. I biked as fast as I could."

"Really!" I said, reeling from him as one would from the forced, melancholic hilarity of a clown.

After he had cleaned off his makeup, Laichun poured himself half a glass of *erguotou*. "Your Chinese has improved a lot," he said.

"No, not at all," I said.

"Your replies used to come really slowly. On the other hand, my English hasn't improved at all," he said. "I still just know that one word."

"Bye-bye!" chimed in Laisheng.

"You took it right out of my mouth." The family roared with laughter.

"Miss Wang, drink up!" he said, raising his glass. I took a sip, leaving some beer in the glass. Any less and a refill would have been forthcoming. I quietly announced my intention to go. Between the grandfather's ful-minations and Laichun's vaguely creepy aspect, I had had enough for one day. I turned off the camera. Laichun turned to me in horror, or mock horror, I couldn't tell.

"You can't go just as soon as I get here." He then gave me a strange and mournful look.

I went to the bed to yell good-bye to the grandfather.

"It is not enough to just chitchat!" he yelled. He smiled his jack-o'-lantern smile at me as I tiptoed out.

I immediately called Cookie and we went out and got drunk. I told her about my afternoon with the Zhangs. I was just trying to shoot a vérité documentary about them but they were always quizzing me about things I had no way of knowing. Plus the air in the apartment was so stale and they had the gall to compare me to Dashan.

"That sounds like it could really do your head in," said Cookie. "But you know what, pal? I don't think you should worry about it. It's fabulous that you're shooting this documentary. Just keep doing it!"

As the gin and tonics took hold, the sting of the day began to dissolve.

A few days later, I called Yang Lina to talk about my trouble with the documentary.

"The family seems somewhat uncomfortable with me there and I feel somewhat uncomfortable being there."

"Give it time," she told me.

"I want to capture their relationships to one another but they keep talking to me instead!" I said.

"Maybe your relationship with them is the real story then."

"But that's not what I had in mind."

"Don't worry too much. Just keep shooting."

I was determined to prove Grandfather Zhang wrong. I could learn things about Peking Opera. Though I had one of the world's foremost experts on Peking Opera at my fingertips, I began trawling the Internet for information. I learned that the Yellow Emperor was the ancestor of all Chinese people and that there was some debate as to whether he was an actual man who had led a prehistoric Chinese tribe or merely a mythic immortal with the body of a dragon. I learned about an old opera superstition forbidding the utterance of the word *meng* backstage because of Yu Meng, a legendary jester who impersonated a famous scholar in the year 403 BC. I learned that every detail of Peking Opera has a fixed and formal meaning. For instance, the flicking of a sleeve expresses disgust and the asymmetrical face paint of the *jing* character type indicates a criminal character.

One of the artists I interviewed for the Texan's art website had a cat who was pregnant. When I asked what he did with all the kittens, he said that he gave them away to lonely artist friends all over the city, and named which artists had which tabbies. I suddenly realized that I too wanted a cat so that I could be part of his feline family tree. By this time, I understood the importance of being part of a lineage, that there were families other than the one you were born into that you could belong to. I began fantasizing about my cat. A girl cat, of course. Neurasthenic. Spooky. Prone to unexplained hunger strikes and possessed with the ability to read minds and converse with the spirits.

The call from the artist finally came. His cat had given birth a few weeks before, as had her equally profligate daughter. I went over immediately. Eight kittens gamboled around the courtyard, each as tiny as a human palm. Most were white, which I didn't want. One was a calico, a girl, bright-eyed and sensitive but already claimed by another artist. The one remaining kitten was an aggressive orange ball gnawing on a vine with a stubborn look on his face.

I took him.

In the mornings, as I interviewed people over the phone, he sprinted around my room, chewing on every cord in sight and pouncing on invisible foes. I named him Qu Qu'r, meaning "cricket." When I sat down to write, he would climb all over me, up my arms and onto my head, where he would try to perch. If he wanted to play, he nipped my ankles and meowed until I stopped working. At night in bed he did laps around my head. I wasn't getting much sleep, and secretly, I was disappointed. Brawny, blunt, and down-to-earth, Qu Qu'r was not the cat I had ordered up in my mind, and I resented the musky dose of *yang* energy he injected into my house and the way that he scrutinized every single thing I did. I withheld my full affection from him, hoping he'd change.

Then one day I realized that I could either wish he were a different cat, or I could accept him just as he was. And I saw that while he watched my every move, like other family members I'd lived with, he passed no judgment. One neurasthenic female per household was probably enough. To accept him fully was revolutionary. Eventually, he began to sit quietly in my lap while I typed, and when I came home late at night, he ran joyfully to the door to greet me.

Chapter Twenty-two

Facts Are Facts

My phone rang.

"Hello?"

"*Haluo'r?*"

I knew the voice on the other end of the phone. Laichun. The Incomprehensible Clown again. The clown character in Peking Opera, I had learned, is the only opera role that can break out of history, allude to current events, and speak in colloquialisms.

He laughed and said in Chinese, "Miss Wang?"

"Oh, hi." I switched into Chinese too. At least he had stopped calling me Reporter Wang.

"This Tuesday is my mother's birthday. We want you to come celebrate with us."

"Is there a party?"

"No, come whenever you like."

Laichun's voice filled me with dread. I meant no thanks but I said okay. Why did I go back? Filmmaking ambition, partly, but something more powerful. I returned to a guilt-tripping family to whom I would never measure up like spent blood returns to the heart.

It turned out that there was a party, a lunch that I was going to miss because I came in the early afternoon. I brought an ostentatious bouquet of flowers. Overcooked vegetables and slices of meat floated in the cooled soup of the hotpot. Without the unifying distraction of eating, the usual mob of family members sat around limply.

"Welcome, welcome!" said Laichun, leaping up.

I gave the grandmother the flowers.

"What a big bunch of flowers," she said wearily, perhaps dreading the disruption that I inflicted. Sometimes she seemed like the only sane one among them. "How much did they cost?"

"You can't ask that! She's a foreigner!" said Laisheng. He let out a satisfied burp.

"Miss Wang!" roared the grandfather, and then fell silent. The grandmother poured a cup of tea and fed spoonfuls of it to him. I turned on my camera.

"Do you know why there are no bathrooms among the 9,999 rooms in the Forbidden City?" the eldest brother with the half-paralyzed face demanded of me.

"No," I said.

He didn't tell me. He told me instead about a style of Peking Opera that was developed by sword-wielding bodyguards who had worked during the reign of the Empress Dowager Cixi. After losing their jobs when guns were introduced at the end of the Qing Dynasty, they went down south and started a kind of dance that eventually became added to Peking Opera. I nodded eagerly, excited for a Peking Opera story that wasn't long-winded and incomprehensible. The grandfather began snoring. We looked over at him and laughed.

The two brothers carried on a conversation about me right before my eyes, as usual.

"She's not a reporter anymore, is she? She counts as a friend of ours," said Laichun in a strangely lugubrious voice. "I don't understand."

"She just likes to hear old stories," said Laisheng.

Laichun turned to me morosely and said, "Don't bother explaining. It's better this way."

The clock chimed three o'clock. The grandfather let out an animal sound in the background. The older brother said, "Emperor Yongzheng died in the bathroom of the palace, so after him, the imperial palace didn't have a bathroom anymore. It's just that simple."

The grandfather woke up and immediately challenged me to name all the gates of the ancient city wall. I couldn't. He snorted in derision and began a slow trip about the inner wall naming the nine gates. I didn't mention to him that he had named Qianmen twice and forgotten Andingmen. He then recited all seven of the outer gates. I listened as patiently as I could without the heart to remind him that the old city wall had been demolished almost fifty years before.

Laichun looked at me significantly. "I don't even know what to say to you."

"What do you normally talk about with one another?" I asked. "Why not talk about that?"

The family started leaving. Laisheng left to go to the theater. He checked with me to make sure he had the English pronunciation of *ten yuan* right. His job that night was to stand outside the theater dressed up as the Monkey King and to ask foreign tourists if they wanted to have their picture taken with him for a fee of ten yuan.

Laichun sat on a small single bed on the far side of the room. I sat next to him. Here was my chance to capture the family's quieter, more intimate moments. Greenish afternoon light slanted in. I pointed the camera at him and he began talking about the beauty of sculpture.

"China has urban sculptures now. There's one in Qingdao called *The Wind of May*," he said, his description conjuring up the image of an enormous red metal soft-serve ice cream. "You should go and see it. Right now it's—"

"March."

"It's almost May. Imagine the wind in May and then go see this sculpture. It'll be good for you."

"Maybe I'll wait until May to go," I said.

"From an artistic perspective, I think about it this way," he said, a secretive, knowing look passing over his face. "Wind."

"Wind?"

"Wind." He stared off into space. The grandmother fussed with the birdcages before going into the other room for a nap. When he started speaking again, it was slowly. "Miss Wang, you should come more often."

"I'd like to."

"You only come when I call you."

"That's not true."

"I told you already, we're friends, right?"

"Right."

"I've told you more than once: I don't want to take shortcuts. Facts are facts. People make things into things they're not. I'm just a performer."

"What?" His voice was heavy with portent and I didn't like the turn this conversation was taking.

"What was your impression of me the first time you met me?"

"The first time?"

"It was on a screen."

I dimly recalled seeing a scratchy video recording of someone's Peking Opera performance. "Oh, I think I remember. But nothing too clearly." I turned the camera away from him and pointed it at a washbasin across the room still containing a dirty washcloth from the morning, as if to shield my eyes from the car wreck that seemed to be unfolding in slow motion.

"But what were your impressions?"

"I told you I didn't have any impression. Why do you keep asking?"

He let out a laugh. " 'I didn't have any impression.' That's good. I had an impression of you. I became damaged."

"Damaged?"

"My impression of you damaged me. You forced your way into my mind and I became spoiled."

"Excuse me?"

"Sometimes I wonder—where has she gone?" he mused. "Didn't she say she was coming over? My mind has problems. What should I do about this?"

"I don't know."

"Don't you think I'm damaged?"

"No, I think maybe you don't meet many new people."

"Maybe you are like a painting that has entered my mind."

"Maybe."

"I always wonder where she is. My heart has settled into this position. This is not good. Is this good?"

"This?" I wondered how I had missed the signs. The repeated phone calls. The alarming levels of enthusiasm at my visits. The crashing disappointment at my departures. His face with the clown mask he'd been in too much of a hurry to take off.

He laughed again, acid and sad. "This is your response? This is not good." He got up and left the room, slamming the door behind him.

I sat there alone, the video camera still running. His confession made me ill. With it, he had yanked me over the final threshold into their family's most interior room, where my self receded to the point of terror and I became, if only for an imagined moment, part of their family. *Sometimes friends become so close that you treat them like family.* Had he truly imagined I would become his blushing bride? Or was the opposite true— had the clown used me, in that same moment, to break out of family and out of history? He must have felt suffocated by his family too, and my life of floating around must have looked enticing. An escape. I shut off the video camera.

I tiptoed past the sleeping grandfather, back through the lightless rooms and the skinny restaurant, and out onto the anonymous, forgiving street.

I called Yang Lina to tell her what had happened and she burst into laughter that surprised and irritated me.

"That is so great," she said. "He fell in love with you?"

"Yes. It wasn't great. It was horrible," I said. Why had I been expecting her sympathy? "I can never go back."

"You have to go back!" she shrieked. "That's a great story."

"That's the end of the story," I said firmly. "I'm not going back."

"You had no idea the whole time?"

"I had no idea."

"You are too adorable!"

Over the next few weeks, I spent a lot of time at home brooding over what had gone wrong. Yang Lina was right. I had been hopelessly naïve. How had I not seen it coming? Why had I thought I could just squat in the Zhangs' lair, shoot some footage, and emerge unscathed?

Part Five

Chapter Twenty-three

The Marzipan Inquirer

*D*espite, or maybe because of, the spectacular implosion of my documentary, I had a golden summer. I lived the life of a *hunzi*, working only as much as I needed to and going out dancing every weekend. I felt as if I had all the time in the world. The tapes stayed safely tucked away at the back of a drawer.

The Brits were much better at championing the lack of ambition and better at being colonials than us Americans, and I spent many afternoons with them drinking cucumber-soaked Pimm's while pedal-boating around Houhai and Qianhai, the lakes in the center of Beijing. There was always an underground art exhibition to go to or a new bar opening. On the banks of Houhai, a small bar opened. Sparsely furnished with rattan furniture and huge-leafed plants, it didn't have a sign or even a name; everyone called it the No Name Bar. Out the window was Old Beijing—grandpas fishing or swimming in the lake, grannies sauntering by in super slo-mo. It was the romantic old image I'd had of China come to life and I began spending a lot of time there.

But the city in the summer was humid and heavily polluted, so

Cookie and I often escaped to the countryside. One time we took a bus to a temple west of the city to people-watch. Another time when an old friend visited, the three of us hiked up a crumbling section of the Great Wall and slept out on a parapet. We broke up a sign asking in English for an outrageous entrance fee and used it for kindling. Rising up from the darkness of a village below were the sounds of men talking and laughing as they drank. In the morning we followed the ruins of the wall along the ridge of the mountain until we reached the next village, which happened to have a small but functioning go-kart track. It was bathetic, like my life.

One day that summer as I was walking in my neighborhood, I glanced down the length of my street and I noticed that the tops of the tall trees lining the street touched and intertwined, creating a vaulted roof. In the sunlight, the leaves glowed a rich shade of green I'd never seen before in Beijing, and golden shards of light fell onto the cars and people speeding obliviously underneath. Locking eyes with the perfect tunnel of gold and green, I caught my breath. *My god, my street is beautiful,* I thought. But I never saw it like that again.

Cookie's father visited from India. She had always seemed like such an eccentric creature but we saw that she was a carbon copy of her dad: Both were gin-swilling foreign correspondents, both idiosyncratic, both like caricatures of themselves. They even had the same slightly bowlegged walk. He took in our neighborhood, Maizidian'r, with an amused eye and dubbed it Marzipan Street.

His visit coincided with the event of the summer: the rave on the Great Wall. We rode chartered tour buses up north of the city and climbed up a section of the wall to find our DJ friends in an open-air watchtower with their turntables going. House music thumped out over the mountains, and as we danced the night air was clear and cool on our skins. I had never felt more like an invading barbarian, or more giddy. Cookie's dad stood observing us for an article he was going to write for *Time,* and when it got late, he went to sleep in a nearby guesthouse. We danced and drank until the sun peeked over the snaking line of the Great Wall, which hugged the ridge of a mountain as far as the eye could see.

Slowly, I started to wonder if my parents were right—that I should have a proper life with a proper job. My documentary had tanked, the artists were all starting to repeat themselves in the interviews, and it was time to be grown-up and have a full-time job with an official accreditation at a real Western newspaper, even if there was only so much you could say within its narrow columns. I applied for a correspondent job at one of the magazines I'd been freelancing for. The senior correspondent and an editor for the Asia desk took a look at my clips, asked a few questions about my experience, and then about my family background, as people do. I tried to paint as accurate a portrait of myself as possible, assuming they would see how lucky they were to snag a bohemian with street cred as gritty as mine. We sat at opposite ends of a long table.

The editor looked curiously at me after I'd finished talking and said, in an arch, half-joking tone, "You seem to have *drifted* to China and you seem to have *drifted* into journalism. Are you someone who *drifts* through life?" I felt as if he had slapped me in the face. But once I got over the initial blow, I found I enjoyed the tingle it left behind. It was proof that I had completed my transformation into a *hunzi*; I had killed the nerd of my teenage years. Needless to say, I didn't get the job.

Gretchen and I were sitting around my apartment one day, talking about the wonders of our neighborhood, the chicken being raised on my stairwell, and the new fashion of wearing pajamas in public. The dot-com boom was in full swing and average, uninspired expats were coming back from New York with hundreds of thousands of dollars of venture capital that had been thrown at them over breakfast meetings. *The Onion* had also just started and we decided to take matters into our own hands and start our own online magazine, *The Marzipan Inquirer*.

Who would read the publication, you ask? Our friends, probably, both the ones who lived in Maizidian'r and the ones at home who could never quite picture our lives. And tourists. Not the rich Western tourists whom *City Edition* had been geared toward but the down-market tourists—Malaysians, Russians, Albanians—who stayed at the three-star New Ark Hotel in our neighborhood. I had seen them looking out the windows of their giant tour buses as they rolled down Marzipan Street, at what must have seemed a bleak landscape of blotchy socialist apartment buildings and run-down shops. I felt sorry for them, that this was their vacation. (Did they feel sorry for me, that this was my life?)

I began to write articles for our imaginary publication.

Marzipan Street Will Not Be Gentrified!: An Editorial

Interview with the Perambulator: Silent Walker Bares All in Exclusive Interview

Local Woman Wakes Neighbors with Arcane Chant, Again: "Dou! Dou! Dou! Dou!" Revealed as Name of Dog

Support Local Music: We're Not Amateurs, Says Lead Singer Marco, That's Just Our Band's Name

Who needed a proper job when the Internet had the potential to make me into a publishing magnate?

One day, I saw Cookie with a great new haircut.

"Pal, I just went to that *gaoji* salon next to Green Lake Garden," she said. "There's this totally wicked hairdresser there. I told her I wanted a messy haircut and she just grabbed my hair and started cutting. You know how most Chinese hairdressers take hours? She was done in fifteen minutes. I think she was trained by the French guy, Pierre or whoever."

Green Lake Gardens was a *gaoji* housing complex in our neighborhood that was legal for expats to live in. We were the opposite of *gaoji*.

"You went to Eric's of Paris?"

"If you don't get your hair cut by him, it's not expensive, maybe eighty kuai. I'm telling you, pal—go to this woman, Wang Le. She's wicked! I mean, just look at me—aren't I a babe?"

Eighty kuai, or ten dollars, seemed outrageously expensive for a haircut, but if she was really a genius—

"And she even does tattoos. She showed me hers!"

Eric's of Paris was clean and sleek and full of pep, with none of the languor of a Chinese salon. Most of the customers were expats and the hairdressers spoke French as their scissors flew through hair. I was surprised by Wang Le's appearance. Her figure looked as doughy as a tired housewife's and her short wavy hair was tinted a light red, nothing special. A bevy of young men in black buzzed around her. Her pale, plucked, and oddly ageless face had no expression until I mentioned Cookie's name. She lit up and immediately ordered one of her boys to give me a head massage while washing my hair, another to hand me haircutting magazines to peruse, another to bring me water to drink.

"Cookie is so *huopo*, isn't she?" she said. *Huopo*. The word was the bane of my existence. Meaning lively and open and free, it was everything that Westerners were supposed to be and everything I did not appear to Chinese people to be. My hair was a cornerstone of this *huopo* problem. A bad haircut helped me blend in, which had its advantages, but then I looked like a nice Chinese girl, which stung my vanity. But if I got the flamboyant haircut I wanted, I would stick out like a ridiculous Westerner who wanted the rock-star treatment in China. I had to choose. Blend in or express myself.

"I want the same haircut as Cookie. Messy." I jabbed the air around my ears with my upright fingers.

"Are you sure? Cookie looks good with that spiky haircut because her face is round. Your face is angular so you should have a soft haircut," said Wang, staring into my face. "Your haircut should strike a balance with your face."

Had the bonsai found its master? I looked in the mirror and saw that my chin and cheekbones were rather pointy. But ultimately, the tree itself had to dictate its own form.

"No, I'm sure that's what I want." I was ready to let out the inner Val, even if it meant attracting a lot of attention. Or looking like the outer Cookie.

Wang Le worked quickly. I could see she was getting frustrated with my hair. Stiff and stubborn, my hair is resistant to "casual" haircuts. I needn't have worried about looking like Cookie. The end result puffed around my head like a football helmet.

"Oh."

"Why don't you dye it? Totally black hair is unfashionable these days."

"No thanks." I kept waiting for her to show me her tattoo, but she never did.

Chapter Twenty-four

Topless Subtitling

One day Yang Lina called out of the blue and told me she was done with her second documentary and asked if I would help her polish the subtitles that night.

Months had gone by without contact with her. The last time I'd seen her she had also summoned me for help with a translation. I'd gone to Sanlitun to meet her and she'd greeted me with a pronouncement: "You are so pure and old-fashioned!" We'd sat outside under an umbrella in the spring air sipping juices like *xiaojie*s and watching people walk by. Yang Lina never drank alcohol or coffee or smoked cigarettes. She had pulled a book out of her bag and put it on the table. It was an elementary French textbook.

"I'm studying French now!" she said triumphantly.

"French! I thought you were studying English." Speaking English was one of the "three musts" for a young modern in Beijing, the other two being driving a car and using a computer.

"I gave that up!" she said, and told me that a film professor in France had seen *Old Men* and secured her a scholarship to go study documentary production at his university. She was supposed to leave in a few months.

"That's fantastic," I said. Her life was really taking off. I imagined her having a string of affairs with rakish French men, all with broody five-o'clock shadows and a taste for the exotic. She would finally settle on one who could keep her in the manner to which she was accustomed and they would jet back and forth between Beijing and Paris with their adorable bilingual, mixed-race baby. I had met her boyfriend once. He was completely unremarkable, just your standard-issue Beijing *dakuan*—brush cut, dark zip-up jacket, man-purse sprouting from his armpit—just as I knew he would be. His face was dull, verging on the brutal, and we regarded each other with polite suspicion. "I know you don't think he's handsome, but he's very good to me," she had said.

Maybe she was right and I was old-fashioned, and my attempt to work for what I earned was outdated. She was the modern one and I was the relic of the past. Maybe I should go out on that date with her ex-boyfriend Mr. Motorola.

"Zhao Liang told me that I should be paying people for the subtitles they do for me," she said, of our mutual friend. "I never thought about such a thing before."

"That's probably a good idea. It is a lot of work," I said. Most film-makers I did subtitles for paid a token amount, just to acknowledge the help, but she, who had much more money than most, had never even mentioned remuneration of that kind. Every time she called, she needed something from me and she always needed it right away and it always took longer than she said it would and all she gave me in return was a smile—and yet somehow I felt like the luckiest person in the world to have the chance to help her out. She was just one of those people.

"I bet you'll like France," I said. "I took some French in high school and I've always wanted to go." I opened the textbook to a page showing a cartoon of two fresh-faced French youths, one inviting the other out for coffee. One was named Valerie. I pointed to the name.

"Did you know that this is my English name?"

"This name?"

"Yes." I felt like Clark Kent casually letting her in on my secret identity, the American part of me that shed my uptight exterior and performed heroic feats while dressed in spandex.

She said in her sultriest French accent, "Wah-leh-lee? So sexy!" Her giggle turned into a heavy sigh. "French is hard. I don't really study."

"Once you get there, it'll be easy."

"I just don't know if I should go. People keep asking me if I've started my second documentary and I haven't. I threw all of my passion into the first one and don't know which direction to go next. Something more personal, maybe."

"But going abroad is such a huge opportunity. You can't give that up."

"Everything has just happened so quickly," she said. When we finished with the translations, we sat sipping our drinks, lost in our own thoughts. No one who walked by the café was in a hurry. I liked that about Beijing but I wondered if I would still be here long after Yang Lina had left, subtitling other people's movies, taking my time with life, and getting nothing done. I had been in China three years now and showed no signs of moving home. Beijing was my home now.

Suddenly and without explanation, she said, "Deep down, I know that my boyfriend is not the one I am going to marry."

As she drove me home, she floated an idea for her second documentary: the everyday life of a Chinese lesbian. She asked me if I knew any lesbians.

"Yes, I went to this secret lesbian meeting once in someone's apartment." I thought back to the meeting. The women I met there had not been flashy people and I imagined the sexy, curious dancer making a real splash in their midst.

"Lesbian love is so pure," she said, turning to look at me in busy traffic.

"Lesbian relationships are *not* that simple," I said.

After this meeting, she didn't call me for months or even return my phone calls and I guessed she didn't need help with anything. Or had she left for France already? I finally got her on the phone and she told me she wasn't going abroad anymore. She had everything she needed here in China to make documentaries. She had finally started her second documentary but was having trouble with it and didn't want to talk about it. All she would say was that she was flying between her parents' cities, tormenting them. We arranged to go to a dance performance together, but when I waited for her at the theater door on the appointed night, she called to say she couldn't make it. That was the last straw. Of all the things she offered me, the only one I really wanted was her friendship but it was obviously too much to ask for.

So when she finally called to ask me for help with the subtitles, she sounded apologetic. A mutual friend had already done the translation and the polishing would be easy, she said, just an hour of work. She needed it that night. And she'd pay. Of course I said yes.

It was a hot summer day. She picked me up from the supermarket in her car, bearing flowers, and was as giggly, infectious, and mildly patronizing as ever. As she watched me cross the street lugging a heavy bag of kitty litter through the thick summer air, she warbled one of her usual assessments. Today I was "serious and adorable."

At home, Yang Lina sat curled up next to me on my couch. She had her "worried face" on, and as I read the transcript, her glance flickered between my face and the sheaf of papers in my hands, trying to gauge the quality of the translation by my expression. I must have looked peeved. She was so fucking predictable. *Just an hour of work.* This one mutual friend had been born in Beijing, schooled at Eton, and was now back in Beijing hanging out with his punk friends. The documentary, *Home Video,* was about Yang Lina's family, and he had remade the characters in his own image: When they weren't "rather this" or "quite that," they were cursing up a storm. Reading the transcript, I wanted to laugh uncontrollably, or cry. We had hours of work ahead of us.

"How is it?" she asked, her eyes wide with worry. I liked to see her anxious and questioning; it was a nice reversal. Normally, it was she who told me how things were.

"The translation is—" I paused and gave the transcript a casual shake and pointed to a random page, where her glance followed. "Terrible. We need to start over. Do you have the original Chinese subtitles?"

"I should have just had you do it in the first place," she said, the wide eyes of her "worried face" narrowing and her brows knitting to make her "impatient face," a much more familiar look. Watching her was like watching a slide show demonstrating common female emotions.

She stood up abruptly. I noticed her outfit for the first time. It was bland, a man's white button-down shirt, two sizes too large and rolled up at the cuffs, with khaki shorts, but she was the kind of woman who could look stunning even in a potato sack. Her cheeks were flushed with annoyance and she left to go to our friend's apartment to retrieve the original Chinese transcript, leaving me fuming in the muggy summer heat.

She returned soon. I let her in and saw that she was panting and that her cheeks were blushed like a ripe peach.

"I came back as fast as I could. I ran up the five flights," she said, thrusting the transcript into my hands and pushing up the sleeves of her shirt. We went back into the living room and sat down, but she sprang up immediately and declared, "I'm hot!" I picked up the remote control as imperiously as I could and—*beep-beep-beep*—upped the air-conditioning a few notches.

"Do you mind if I take off my shirt?" Her request wasn't wholly unreasonable. Even with air-conditioning, my top-floor apartment felt like the inside of a pizza oven by the end of the day. I asked her if she wanted to borrow a T-shirt. She didn't. She wanted to take her shirt off. What could I do? I wanted to get started. She unbuttoned the baggy white shirt, shook it off, and stood in the middle of my living room with completely bare breasts. She looked at me expectantly. I thought at least she'd have a bra on. I wanted to get started because she wanted the sub-titles done that night and I knew how long it took to—

"Do you mind if I take my pants off too?" Was she au naturel under those khaki shorts too?

"Go ahead."

She shimmied out of her pants and I saw with relief that she had underwear on. She gave a sigh of pleasure to be liberated and settled herself back on the couch. I handed her back the Chinese transcript, which she held in front of her small and upturned breasts. She looked so pleased with herself, and at my discomfiture. I told her to read me the first line. The first part, she said, was the opening text on the screen.

I am the daughter. I was fourteen when my parents got divorced.
My brother was thirteen.
I wasn't living at home then, so there were certain things I didn't understand.
My curiosity led me to start interviewing them, separately.

Ten years before, divorce had been very rare in China and no one in her family had spoken about what happened. Wanting to piece the story together, she said she had gone into the interviews innocently, expecting them to be about dredging up other people's feelings and not her own. The rest of the transcript was just line after line of dialogue and she had to explain to me who was saying what.

"This first part is with my mom. I went to my parents to ask them if I could interview them for the documentary. I went to see my mom first." She snuck a peek at her breasts. I struggled to keep my eyes trained on hers and not to stray south.

"Where does she live again?"

"Qingdao."

"What does she do?"

"She runs a haircutting studio now."

Her mom readily agreed to be interviewed, but her little brother, who also lived in Qingdao, was more reluctant, saying that she was about to unwittingly spark a "family war."

"And last I went to see my dad. He's in Changchun." They were Northeasterners. Northeasterners scared me. Unlike Beijingers, who have a reputation for fighting by hurling empty threats at one another and wearing down their opponents by talking them to death, Northeasterners are known for cutting the crap and just beating you senseless.

She said her dad was the hardest to convince. He said her mom was going to tell a pack of lies and her brother was a lost cause whose later years of life would probably have to be filmed from behind bars.

In the end, all three agreed to be interviewed. She said she shot the whole thing with the camera in her hand, deliberately trying to give it a homemade feel, unlike *Old Men*. But as with her first documentary, she had tried to be invisible in *Home Video,* and she said you caught only one tiny glimpse of her in a mirror.

It turned out that Yang Lina's brother, Xiaofan, who was nicknamed Dayong, played a central role in the divorce. He had witnessed their mom walking with a man he didn't know and betrayed her to his dad. He said he had been under the impression that after the divorce his dad would take him to the big city, Changchun.

Her dad began talking about a day prior to the divorce.

> I said again, "Would you get up? I'd like to talk."
> "So what if I don't?"
> Those were her exact words.
> I remember it clearly, all my anger just sprang up,
> so I pulled her on the ground
> and started to whip the shit out of her with my new belt.

I glanced over at Yang Lina. Her intent expression hadn't changed one bit, as if her dad had just recited what he had eaten for dinner. I felt sick to my stomach and wondered if I should say something, but what would I say?

"Then I asked my mom about it," Yang Lina said.

"She wasn't uncomfortable talking about it?"

"No, she's very open with me."

> *I looked in the mirror and couldn't recognize myself.*
> *My face was all swollen.*
> *Think about the belt whipping my face, my butt, my back—*
> *there were black stripes all over.*

Then her brother told his side of the story, which revealed another betrayal.

> *When I was still in the room, Dad held Mom on the ground.*
> *"Dayong, Dayong," she called for me three or four times in a row.*
> *It was heartbreaking, as if she was begging me.*
> *But back then I really believed that Mom deserved a lesson.*

The documentary continued in this he said/she said/son said–style, telling of the day of the divorce and the day her dad moved to Changchun, alone. Her brother said that instead of taking him along, their dad had called him a "little bastard" and a "cruel wolf" before leaving. Reading the transcript was like watching a police interrogation, ten years after the crime, a domestic *Rashomon*. Yang Lina had probably been watching some Kurosawa too.

Or maybe it was more like reading a play of a therapy session, except that no one in China went to therapy. Most seemed oddly unselfconscious of their own actions and emotions. An American friend of mine joked that therapy might catch on in China if people went in place of their neighbors and told the therapist in detail about their neighbors' deficiencies and problems.

As it went on, I started to feel swamped and yearned to lay my head down for a few minutes. But we needed to finish that night, so I slogged along, working quickly. Her brother continued living with his mom, who sold her blood to be able to bring home extra treats like eggs or candy. He started getting into fights and going downhill at school. From my memory of her family photos taped onto the wall, her parents were average middle-aged Chinese people but her brother had a beautiful face touched with a faint hint of surliness or woundedness.

As he told his story, he became increasingly remorseful.

> *This is how it works: No matter how old you are,*
> *as long as you do something wrong*
> *you will feel ashamed for the rest of your life.*
>
> *Mom has forgiven you for it.*
> *There's no need for you to feel that way anymore.*
>
> *A lot of things you don't understand.*
> *I'm not happy; I've never been happy.*

By this point, Yang Lina told me, both she and her brother were crying. The documentary had unexpectedly recoiled in her face and she said she regretted unearthing so many years of pain, especially her own. However, I had to imagine that reliving what she had never lived in person in the first place was the whole point of making it.

And her regret wasn't strong enough to stop her from instigating phase II of the documentary: showing her family the first part of the documentary and videotaping their reactions. Not only did they have to relive it when she taped the first interviews, but also they had to relive their and everyone else's reliving of it. Yang Lina called her camera her axe, and it did seem as though she was breaking her family apart more than piecing things together. Her project seemed downright sadistic.

Night fell. My apartment cooled off but she didn't put her clothing back on. We kept reading. She showed the edit to her mom and brother first and they debated whether or not she should show it to her dad. Her brother thought she should. Her mom thought she shouldn't, for a number of reasons. She thought it was cruel, she didn't want Yang Lina to seek revenge for her, he was already lonely and sad. Finally, she admitted the real reason: She wanted to stay on good terms with him so he would pay for her house.

In the end, Yang Lina did show it to her dad. He contradicted everything her brother had said. He said he had never mistreated or abandoned him. He had never promised to take him to Changchun and had even given him a choice of whom to live with after the divorce. He had never called him a "cruel wolf," not until years later at least. And the kicker: Her brother had only imagined their mom calling out his name when getting beaten. He had not even been in the room that day.

I was surprised to hear Yang Lina tell her dad she believed him.

My biggest fear was showing it to you.
If what Yang Xiaofan said was true, you would have a different reaction.

I'll tell you truthfully, what he said was all bullshit.
At times my conscience makes me think of him but that's it.
I only think of him from time to time.
Whether or not I think of him—what does that matter?
Not very much.

And that was the end. It was late when we finished. I felt bruised and tired, as if I had just been forced to break up a fight on a lurid Chinese version of *Jerry Springer*. I had seen where Yang Lina had come from. And I could see where she was now: sitting on my couch in only her underpants, the blank at the center of her own story. She was naked, but she had never seemed so mysterious to me as she did at that moment and must have been just as mysterious to herself. She didn't seem to know what to make of her own documentary. She said that when she had screened it publicly, some people in the audience had bawled. Still others said that she was telling the untold story of so many people, especially now that divorce was becoming more common in China. But others had said the documentary was fundamentally flawed because it showed every relationship but the one between her and her family. She'd exposed everyone in her family but herself. Just as she'd been absent when the divorce happened, she was also absent from the documentary, except for that one flash in the mirror and what I assumed was several moments of off-camera sobbing in tune with her brother. Through him, she had tried to feel it, but in the end she had kept herself at a safe distance.

Chapter Twenty-five
The Outlaws Are the Ones Who Become Moral

I jiggled the key impatiently. It wouldn't turn. I rattled the old wooden door. I had kept my key from the time I had lived with Bobo and Bomu because I liked to feel that this was my home too. Now why wasn't the darned thing working? I rang the doorbell but no one appeared. They *knew* I was coming over to see Xiao Peng and Xiao Lu's new baby. I peered through a crack into the courtyard. Nobody. Finally, I called them on my cellphone.

"Hi, are you home? I'm outside the door."

"Oh, that's *you* outside!" said Bomu.

"You can hear me?"

"Yes. We heard the rattling and thought someone was trying to break into the house. We were scared."

"No thief, just me!" I said, and we started laughing. We got along famously now that we didn't live together anymore, though I knew they thought I didn't call or visit enough. "My key isn't working."

"Oh, we changed the locks months ago. You might as well throw out that old key." They had just gotten back from a six-month jaunt to the

States, visiting their daughters in L.A., Great-Aunt Mabel in Seattle, Nainai and my parents in suburban Maryland, and an old student of Bobo's in Philadelphia who took them to New York City for the day.

Bomu came to the front door and I followed her through the courtyard into Xiao Peng's side of the house. He was out but Xiao Lu was there in their small living room, washing their son, Sanbao, in a big plastic tub. A tape of Buddhist chanting played in the background. Per the fashion among young people in Beijing, Xiao Peng and Xiao Lu had taken up Buddhist practices, adopting Buddhist names and playing tapes and burning incense at their small Buddhist altar draped with saffron-colored cloth.

I went back to Bobo and Bomu's side of the house. The TV was on and Bobo was in his big easy chair, leaning back with his pant cuffs hiked up high and his hands on his knees. I took my old position on the couch. The heaviness that used to accompany a visit to their house was gone. After the Zhang family, they seemed normal, loving. Bobo's sternness had defrosted, as had my testiness. I felt almost jovial. And why had this room seemed so claustrophobic when I lived here? It was a grand room with tall and wide windows.

We looked through the photos from their trip. There wasn't a single candid shot among them, or a smile. Bobo and Bomu posed grim-faced under the statue of Lincoln at his memorial, next to the charging bull on Wall Street, on my parents' suburban lawn pushing the lawnmower. The people in the photos were so unlike the ones sitting next to me laughing and offering pronouncements about each place: L.A. ("The air's so clean and there are so few cars!"), suburbia ("Beautiful, but you need a car to go anywhere."), and New York City ("So chaotic!"). They spoke happily about being reunited with Nainai after more than fifty years. My dad had reported that the meeting had actually been slightly anticlimactic after their years of constant phone contact.

I envied them, spending half the year in the States and half in Beijing. It seemed ideal. They also had a whole book of happy photos of their youngest daughter: her posing in front of a car, her posing in a flouncy wedding dress. She was finally married.

After we finished looking through the photos, Bomu left to practice with her neighborhood dance troupe, which was learning a new North Korean dance, and Bobo returned to his TV show. Singers, one after another, came in their street clothes onto a vast stage bedizened with large gold stars and as garishly lit as an intergalactic landing strip. They sang opera songs, rather badly. My time with the Zhangs had not cultivated my palate for Peking Opera, but this was worse than usual.

"What is this?"

"China's First Annual Amateur Peking Opera competition. This is Day Two."

"Day Two? It goes on for two days?"

"No, five days," he said, looking excited at the prospect.

"Why didn't you compete? I bet you sing better than these people."

Bobo threw back his head and laughed. He and his friends regularly got together to play and sing opera songs and, like the Zhangs, had even rented out a theater for an amateur performance. When he showed me the videotape, he'd had to point himself out. He was swaddled in a thick brocade outfit, his face thickly painted. We watched him teeter violently around the stage in his platform shoes until he lost his bout with gravity and toppled over. I had never told him about Grandfather Zhang, whom I think he would have had a lot of respect for. For a while I had been seeing the Peking Opera family more often than I saw my own, but it had been more than half a year since the end of my documentary. Once in a while the Zhang family still called my cellphone and though it made me feel like a cold-blooded strangler, I simply muffled the phone until the song silenced itself.

A tiny girl came onto the stage clutching a microphone, which looked as large as a can of tennis balls in her hands. Pert and innocent as a pebble, she squinched up her face as if in dire pain and began singing with all her might.

"She's the youngest competitor. Only four years old," Bobo said. "Her story has been in all of the newspapers."

I could imagine the state-run newspaper touting her—as well as this competition—as proof that Peking Opera had a future. I thought of Grandfather Zhang lying in his bed, frothing. *The benevolent emperor came down south of the Yangtze to look into the condition of Peking Opera. This is just a* story. *Do you believe it, Miss Wang?*

"What song is she singing?"

"A part by Lin Chong in a story called the *Wild Boar Forest.* Do you know *The Water Margin?*"

"Yes, sort of." One of the masterpieces of Chinese literature about a band of outlaws . . . in some dynasty . . . long ago.

"Lin Chong is an honorable man, a military officer who is framed because a corrupt officer wants his wife. In this scene, he is being escorted through the Wild Boar Forest by soldiers who've been hired to kill him. He later escapes but his wife commits suicide and he eventually becomes a bandit to avenge her."

"You would never guess that by looking at this little girl."

"Usually the rulers are the good characters but when they're corrupt, the everyday people or the outlaws are the ones who become moral. The world gets turned upside down."

"What kind of role is Lin Chong?"

"A *lao sheng.*" Of the four main character types in Peking Opera, the *lao sheng* is the eldest and most dignified. That constipated face had been her attempt at dignified gravitas. The world really was turned upside down. Little girls singing *lao sheng* roles. Old men lying in bed as helpless as babies. She finished her song and the crowd erupted in loud applause. I asked Bobo if her performance had been good. He said yes, but his yes was cautious—she was just a gimmick, after all. Good singing takes years of practice and a deep understanding of Chinese history, that much I did know.

At home, I went searching for an article about her. One Chinese website gushed that "from the first note of her song, the love and hate in her voice were unmistakable."

Suddenly, the Zhang family called me several times in one week. I didn't pick up, but knowing what I would hear on the other end, I resolved to the next time.

Of course it was Laichun, the clown, even though he refused to identify himself. He spoke in the slow, slightly demented (drunk? damaged?) way that I had come to expect of him. My stomach twisted at the sound of his voice.

"How is the family?" I asked.

"Fine," he said, and slurred something incoherent. Finally, he told me that the grandfather had passed away the month before. I offered my condolences. He apologized for being too grief-stricken to call sooner. We left it that I would go to their house if I had time. I thought back to Yeye's death and the way we had all spun out of orbit like planets released from the sun's grip. I wondered if the Zhangs would be happy to find their own lives now or if they would be completely lost without their North Star.

He called back a few hours later. "Didn't we [something-something] earlier?" he asked in a tortured tone, his voice catching right at the crucial word.

Even though I had no idea what I was agreeing to, I said, "Yes, yes, we did."

"You'll come visit if you have time?"

"Yes, I'll come if I have time." I wished I could go to their house and pay my respects but I couldn't. What had happened between us had hit too close to home, and I couldn't bring myself to revisit it, or them. Not yet.

I read that construction had started on a hundred-million-dollar Peking Opera theater inside the Second Ring Road funded solely by local businesses. I could envision the twelve hundred seats of the clean and well-heated theater filled with crowds of young people, the same ones

who could be seen around town wearing Chinese silk jackets embroi-
dered with gold phoenixes and dragons, who were interested in injecting
a quick, painless dose of their own history into their packed schedules. I
imagined child stars singing *lao sheng* roles with all the love and hate that
four-year-olds can muster. There would even be a museum in the theater,
displaying photographs and sculptures from Peking Opera's history, and
I could imagine an enterprising person going up a narrow alley near Tiananmen Square, finding the Zhang family, and re-creating their room in
the theater, just to make sure that the past is really past. More likely,
when their street is demolished along with the rest of the old city, the
Zhang family will just disappear like ghosts into an anonymous concrete
apartment like mine on a desolate road on the edge of town.

Chapter Twenty-six
Not Really "In the Mood for Love"

The unexpected happened: Yang Lina fell in love. He was a penniless writer of forty-five and they were having passionate sex all the time, she said, everywhere, including up on the Great Wall. They were even videotaping themselves. Her boyfriend had found the videotape, but she wasn't ready to break up with him yet because there was the chance that her new relationship was not going to work out. "People who know us say it's only going to last three more months, that we are two crazies and it can't last," she said.

Xu Xing was a sleepy-eyed writer who wanted to transform Yang Lina into an artist. She had been given so much natural talent, he said, she just needed some culture.

"He tells me that Western girls return money that they borrow from their boyfriends and that they think being independent from their boyfriends is important," she told me, as if it would be news to me. Who was more naïve, I wondered, her for not knowing that or me for assuming that everyone knew? "I never think of returning my boyfriend's money.

I always think I deserve to be treated this way. It's his responsibility to give me what will make me comfortable."

She said Xu Xing tutored expats in Chinese to make ends meet and I realized that he had been Anthony's tutor a long time ago, the semi-famous but washed-up writer from the 1980s.

When she finally broke up with her *dakuan,* she had to face reality. She said she had always been sheltered by men and by the People's Liberation Army and now she had to live on a fourth of the money that she was used to. She had been acting and dancing her whole life, but now she was getting too old to dance, and good acting roles were hard to come by. For the first time in her life she had to try to find a job, but of the "three musts," all she could do was drive a car. She couldn't speak English or use a computer. Her car and video camera were getting old, but without her *dakuan,* she couldn't trade them in for newer models.

I was pleased by all the changes in her life, and not only for noble reasons. Witnessing someone falling in love is a wonderful thing, but so is witnessing them getting their long-overdue comeuppance. Finally she couldn't float above me in her bubble of wealth, oblivious to the compromises and anxieties that come with having to work for a living and believing she could solve my problems by playing matchmaker with her discarded exes.

My solitary state still troubled Yang Lina. Her eyes would get soft with pity and she would tell me that one day I would find someone who would love me for who I was, she was sure of it. One day we went together to Yonghegong, the city's big, official Buddhist temple, and jostled through crowds of tourists and Saturday-afternoon Buddhists. Yang Lina was a born-again Buddhist, like Xiao Peng and Xiao Lu, and suddenly, without a word, she bought a fagot of incense, lit it on the altar fire, and stood before a Buddha painted in bright, strong colors with the smoldering spaghetti sticks clamped in her prayer hands. I stood by patiently as she assumed a holy look on her face and bowed three times to the statue.

She then shot me a naughty look and said she had asked the gods to help my marriage prospects.

"I'm very happy alone," I said indignantly. "I have a lot of good friends and that's more important than having a boyfriend."

"This is sure to work," she said, and then stuck the incense in the trough of sand and let the smoke take her prayers up to the heavens where hopefully the gods—evidently the only ones who could help my love life now—would send a man down to me.

One day later that summer, I met Yang Lina at the Starbucks at Pacific Century Plaza. We commandeered an olive-colored velveteen couch by the window and sipped our drinks, coffee for me, fresh-squeezed orange juice for her. On the patio outside, people sat smoking in the thick Beijing air. Yang Lina said she was about to meet with a documentary maker who would be a perfect match for me and that I should go along with her. She felt as if she still owed me for the subtitles, which I had ended up refusing money for.

After taking a gulp of orange juice, Yang Lina pulled out her cellphone and called him.

"Hi, Feng Lei. This is Yang Lina. I have a question. Actually, I have three. Number one: Do you have a girlfriend? Number two: Are you married?" She paused and shot me a coquettish look. "Number Three: Do you have kids?" At this she started giggling uncontrollably. "Good, because I have a friend I want you to meet."

We went to Yang Lina's house. Feng Lei was slim and had a pointy head, shaved close. He wore rimless glasses that matched his thin lips. We barely made eye contact the entire night but this didn't prevent me from tallying his good and bad points. I kept staring at his cellphone, encased in a plastic shell and clipped to his belt (bad) so I could avoid looking at the socks he wore under his sandals (worse). He said he still lived with his parents (bad). Yang Lina told him I had tried to make a documentary about a Peking Opera family but that I'd had to stop when one of the sons fell in love with me. Feng Lei suggested that the story of love sabotaging my documentary would make a good documentary (good). He'd brought a tape of his documentary, *Falling Snow in Yili,* a simple story about a Kazakh girl and her nomadic family in western China. It opened with a scene of snow falling through a block of purplish sky (good).

"This has the depth of film," Yang Lina cooed. "You'll have to pass on some of your technical prowess to us!"

His documentary was simple and deadpan, but not in the comical sense of the word. The girl hauled water from the well. The girl ate dinner with her family. There were few lines of dialogue, whose slight translation mistakes I helped correct.

"Is this a portrait of your soul?" asked Yang Lina.

Feng Lei laughed nervously and said he guessed it was (not bad). The documentary ended with a maudlin poem declaiming that people were like snow—beautiful, mysterious, and transient (terrible). I waited to see how Yang Lina would respond. She told him to cut the poem out.

"Your movie is so profound until then," she said. "You come off as so mysterious."

"But I'm not mysterious," he said with a laugh that both Yang Lina and I agreed later was mysterious. He laughed slightly at every little thing.

"You can pretend to be if you cut this poem out," she said.

"Yeah, take it out," I said.

He laughed. Feng Lei was scrupulous and exacting and didn't give much away. Even if I had swept him off his feet, his expression probably would not have changed very much.

"Zhenluo is cold, but you are even colder!" she scolded him. (She thought me cold?) "If you two had a kid, it would just sit there staring off into space!"

At this, we both stared awkwardly off into space.

Feng Lei owned a small cornflower-blue scooter that looked like a Jet

Ski on wheels, which he rode all over town. He took me from Yang Lina's house to the subway on it, and I straddled the seat behind him, crooking my legs awkwardly so my feet wouldn't drag on the ground, and gingerly put my hands on his waist. On the subway on the way home, I tallied up the points. He wasn't a sure winner but he merited at least another date.

The second time I rode on his scooter he ventured that I should sit sidesaddle. He was taking me out to a used-camera market on the western edge of town where he was going to help me to pick out a manual camera. How romantic! I was going to be the star of my very own movie, finally. But Beijing was no Rome. There were no piazzas, no flocks of scattering pigeons, just wide, dusty streets with buses blowing fumes in our faces. It was summer and over a hundred degrees and I felt as if I were being dipped in sweat, battered in pollution and fumes, and then deep-fried by the sun. The scooter was too big for the bike lane and too small for the car lane, so we wove wishy-washily in and out of both lanes. I clung to the back handle of the scooter like a barnacle and tried my best to flirt.

"How do you load film?" I asked coquettishly at the market. He gave me thorough step-by-step instructions.

"I printed photos and they all have a light stripe on them. What should I do about it?" I asked later on the phone, in my most helpless voice. He told me to go back to the market and call him back if I wanted him to talk to the shop owner.

"What are you doing after work?" I asked. He said he didn't know when he was getting off work. That snow just kept drifting down. I feared that I was having another telephone romance, like with Zhang Yuan, but this time completely devoid of intrigue and excitement. I wasn't yet at the age when I would find a sober and responsible man attractive, and I kept myself interested only by imagining the wickedness and passion roiling beneath his placid exterior, if only I could find the trapdoor. I tried to convince myself that Feng Lei and I were having an *In the Mood for Love* kind of romance—much emotion, few words.

After a while, I suspected stagnation. I complained to Yang Lina.

"You're not just playing around with him, are you?" she asked.

"What do you mean?"

"You can't just go out with him a few times, make him fall in love with you, and then leave him."

"Love?" I said. Forget love. I was just trying to have some fun.

"He's smart not to get involved with you," she said. "You might just get up and leave." Not one to let love—or the lack thereof—sabotage *his* documentary, Feng Lei left for two months to shoot a documentary about a simple fisherman in the Northeast. And so our beautiful, mysterious, transient, possibly nonexistent romance was over.

Yang Lina soon found another blind date for me. She said Zhao Jun ran a website about Chinese independent film.

"I told him, 'She's not beautiful at first sight, but if you get to know her, you'll find she has character.' And then Xu Xing said, 'She has flavor. You have to slowly taste her.'"

"That's so disgusting. I can't believe you said all of that," I said, while thinking, *You think I'm* ugly?

"You're so old-fashioned to be shy about this."

"Arranged marriages are old-fashioned," I said with indignation.

Zhao Jun called and proposed we meet for drinks at a bar near my apartment. I had a drink beforehand with Cookie. As she sat across from me, I thought tipsily, *My friends are the real love affair of my time in Beijing.*

"I don't want to go through with this. It's so moronic."

"But, Val—you love meeting new people!"

I looked at her in amazement. "Cookie, have you been paying any attention these past few years? You're the one who loves meeting new people. I'm shy." Sometimes I wondered if she saw me at all or merely a tweaked reflection of herself.

"Oh, right."

I rode my bike to the Big Easy, a New Orleans–themed restaurant painted a salmon pink and encrusted with intricate wrought iron railings, as though it had been airlifted from Disney's Bourbon Street. It was plunked right outside the gates of the Rock 'n' Roll Disco, a gigantic silver orb that did a fair imitation of Epcot Center. Zhao Jun was waiting outside. He was pudgier and sloppier than Feng Lei. Usually, I liked a man on the mushy side, but he was too much. And his front teeth were black with rot, blacker than mine had ever been. I thought I'd specified "no bad teeth" to Yang Lina.

We went up the spiral staircase, sat at a small wooden table, and ordered beers. It turned out that Zhao Jun ran the film website only in his spare time. For a living, he pedaled birth control pills. Literally. He rode his bike around town from pharmacy to hospital to drugstore selling over-the-counter birth control pills for a Western pharmaceutical company. It was difficult, he said, because the doctors all expected kickbacks.

"Over-the-counter birth control pills? Is that safe?" I asked.

"Oh, yes, it's perfectly safe," he said.

"How can you be sure?"

"The company is Western and very reputable."

"Just because they're Western doesn't mean they're reputable," I said, wondering why I was being so difficult.

"Do you like films?" he asked with a smile.

"Yes. Do you?"

"Yes. What directors do you like?"

"Wong Kar-wai is my favorite."

"I love his films too. And I love Martin Scorsese."

"Yes, Scorsese is good."

We drank several beers. I could not free myself from the droning and familiar rhythms of our conversation, where one person says something and the other agrees. If Feng Lei had given nothing away, this guy was trying to give it all away.

"I feel really comfortable talking to you," he said toward the end of the date.

"Oh, I'm glad."

With a swoony look in his eyes, he told me how lucky Xu Xing was to be with Yang Lina. Okay, Yang Lina was beautiful and *huopo,* but he wasn't—then I realized, he was. He was in love with Yang Lina. I saw that intelligence and personality were not considered beautiful to a Chinese man. Well, rotting front teeth and boring conversation were not attractive to an American woman, so we were even.

Zhao Jun called repeatedly over the next few weeks. When I picked up, I was noncommittal about setting up another date. I resigned myself to never dating in China. The last time he called I was shooting pool with Cookie. I let it ring and kept on playing.

Chapter Twenty-seven
In the Path of the Wrecking Ball

a t the end of the summer the dreaded character 拆 began appearing on a stretch of the shops on Maizidian'r, including the ones right outside my door. Demolish.

I was dismayed—but what a scoop for *The Marzipan Inquirer*! Spurred by the energy of our neighborhood, planning of our publication kicked into high gear. We had to do it before the neighborhood disappeared. We planned the issues:

Issue 1: Welcome to Marzipan Street!
Issue 2: Destruction of Marzipan Street!
Issue 3: Long Live Big Sister Bao!

I grabbed my camera and went outside. The hairdressers had evacuated their salons and the shops were selling off all their goods, their stands spilling out onto the sidewalks. Word got out about the sale and soon the entire street was lined with vendors who had never even had shops on the streets, selling Mao badges, vinyl shoes, gigantic underwear. The atmosphere was festive. After everything was sold, the shopkeepers scattered. Then the demolitions started. Workers with hammers and sticks began tearing down the shops, which were surprisingly flimsy. Brick shacks with corrugated tin roofs patched with plastic sheeting that was held down with bricks, they came apart quickly with a loud popping of glass and cracking of walls. People came to cart away the reusable parts—doorframes, mirrors, glass. Soon all that was left were blank squares on the ground that looked too impossibly tiny to have held all the life that they had.

Weeks later the city painted 拆 on all the remaining shops on my street. Even Peter Pan, the model denizen of the block, was slated for demolition. The same scene played itself out again: clearance sales spilling onto the sidewalk, random vendors from elsewhere, swarms of frugal shoppers, men with hammers and crowbars, smashing glass and falling walls, scavengers in three-wheeled carts, and, in the end, just a strip of multicolored squares on the ground. It happened so quickly I barely had time to react. The first round of demolitions had been exciting and energizing, but the total decimation of the neighborhood was heartbreaking. Without my nemesis Peter Pan, without my whole street, what was I?

The city then eradicated the traces of the shops and turned the empty lots into construction sites. They dug up the road three or four times that year, often working late into the night. Occasionally it had a purpose, such as leveling the sidewalk or laying down new natural gas pipes, and other times they dug ditches and then promptly covered them up again, like an absurdist play performing modernization ad nauseam. The honking below my window was endless.

That summer the city launched their bid for the 2008 Olympics. They began painting the drab facades of the old apartment buildings in pastel shades of blues and pinks to give them new life. They started with the buildings that flanked the roads the visiting dignitaries of the International Olympic Committee would travel, but after the committee had come and gone, the city kept painting buildings like a corpse that couldn't stop twitching. They painted the nice old brick of the building across the road an overgrilled salmon color, and one morning I woke up to see a worker dangling outside my bedroom window on a wooden plank, painting my building the dreaded color. I could hear more workers clattering through the stairwell, taking ladders to the roof and clumping around noisily. When I came home that evening, I found salmon paint splattered on my front door like a curse.

The city built large restaurants and tacky ornamentation in place of the tiny demolished shops. They enclosed anemic rose gardens with tiny wrought iron fences and erected lit billboard advertisements. On the construction lot walls they painted line-drawn scenes depicting satellites orbiting Earth and people using computers, primitive pictograms showing how advanced China was. Tents were erected on the sidewalk, and at the end of the day, exhausted construction workers would collapse onto raised wooden pallets in plain view of the street, their hair gray with dust.

But the new street was a flop. The overpriced Chinese restaurant that replaced Peter Pan was always empty. The four-star hotel that went up in one of the empty lots never opened. The space in front of my building eventually became a long rectangle of grass surrounded by a knee-high concrete wall. You couldn't walk on the grass, but people did throw their empty plastic bottles and yesterday's newspapers on it. One morning I saw a single three-inch platform shoe, black and lonesome, lying in the grass. The city also planted tiny saplings in front of the grass, but like anything not properly rooted into the ground, they fell over in a storm. The whole street felt ghostly and artificial and we lost motivation for *The Marzipan Inquirer.*

The city was changing and it was the first inkling that we were going to change too. Our magic moment was tipping into dusk and I began to understand it would soon be time to move on. To a new neighborhood, or possibly farther.

On my next visit to the States, I saw that my parents were making more renovations to their house. After they finished with the inside, they started on the outside. Calling the forsythias "junk plants," my dad dug them up and threw them out. The red dogwood in the front yard, my mom's favorite, suddenly died. She was busy planting and tending beautiful new plants: a crepe myrtle where the dogwood used to be, peonies, chrysanthemums and geraniums where the forsythias had been, plus new red canna lilies and purple butterfly bushes that attracted monarch butterflies. But all I saw when I went home were the scars on the ground left by the forsythia bushes. The unchanging house had given me a sense of permanence about the world, just as my parents had wanted it to, but when such permanence was revealed as an illusion, I was ill equipped to deal with it. I preferred the house as it had been. Luckily, the pine trees still stood. My parents worried aloud about their dangerously burrowing roots and floated the possibility of chopping them down.

My mom still told me all about her friends' children getting married but I slowly realized that the weddings were a highlight of her social life, a place where she could let loose.

"Growing up, when I was dancing was the only time I could stop worrying," she told me, the only time the responsibility of being the eldest of seven children was lifted. "We went to a wedding last weekend, of our friends the Chengs. Do you remember them? You went to Chinese School with their sons Tony and Billy?"

"No."

"Tony got married. Do you remember him?"

"No, but let me guess—he's a doctor now."

"Yes, an anes . . . aneththe . . ."

"An anesthesiologist?"

"Yes. Guess who he married?"

"Another doctor, named Mindy Yang, perhaps a pediatrician?"

"No, a blondie!"

"Wow, good for him."

"Six feet tall. He's tall but she's even taller. And guess what she does for a living?"

"She's a lawyer."

"No, a helicopter pilot! Can you believe it?"

I laughed. My mom actually had a sense of fun that I'd forgotten about.

They were finally starting to accept that I lived in China for the time being. My mom compared my move to Beijing with her own impulsive leap to America and said that we shared a spirit of adventure. I protested that her move had taken more courage than mine, to leave everything behind for good.

"It's good to know about East and West," she said. "If you come back, you can know about the world."

But strangely, the States was starting to feel like the dream and China the reality.

One night soon after I'd gotten back, as I left Cookie and Emma's apartment complex at midnight, a man's voice called out.

"Hey, you! Stop!"

I kept walking. What a yahoo. Beijing was full of guards dressed up in uniforms, trying to push people around. Once a gated city, Beijing still loved its gates, and with each gate came a guard who ruled his tiny empire like Genghis Khan. The best thing to do was to keep walking until you exited his dominion.

"Young lady, stop! This is the police."

Just steps from the gate, I almost bolted, but not wanting any buckshot in my backside, I turned around slowly. The uniformed man approached and asked which apartment I lived in. I looked closely and saw that he did indeed have a police badge and the cruel, stony-faced visage of Beijing's Finest. Why had I walked out without checking for police first? I was getting soft.

"I don't live here."

"Where do you live?"

"Not here, I told you."

"Where do you live then?"

"Xidan." It was my relatives' neighborhood, all the way across the city.

"What were you doing here?"

"Visiting a friend."

"Take us to their apartment."

My stomach dropped out. Luckily, he and his partner had collared another illegal, a skinny Chinese guy with spiked hair, and he was on the chopping block first. I wandered off to the side, pulled out my cellphone, and dialed Emma's number with shaking fingers. I could barely draw enough breath to tell her what had happened.

"They want me to take them to the apartment I was in."

"Please don't bring them up here!"

"I know, I know, but I don't know what to do. Fuck!"

"Fuck! I'll figure it out and call you back."

"Hurry, I don't have much time."

"My heart is going like a choo-choo train."

I waited nervously, watching them interrogating the guy. His shoulders were hunched in defeat and humiliation and my stomach curdled in dread. What was I going to do? Take him to a random apartment and feign surprise when a total stranger opened the door? Revise my story and say I'd just popped into the compound to buy a bottle of water, which I'd finished and thrown out already? Feign insanity? Did I have the right to remain silent? Would the police take an American to the clink? Would I hold up well under torture? I bet I wouldn't. My phone finally rang.

"Okay, you can go to Big Sister Bao's apartment in entryway 11," said Emma.

"Oh, thank god. How will I recognize her?"

"She said to just go into the entryway and she'll meet you there."

"Okay. I have to go. He's coming back."

With two policemen in tow, I walked as slowly as I could to entryway 11 and up the concrete stairwell. On the second floor I bumped into a woman with a frizzy perm wearing a shapeless nightgown. I paused and raised my eyebrows.

"Miss Wang!" she said.

"Big Sister Bao!" I cried.

She greeted the officers with a familiarity that managed to be both saccharine and oily. "We've met before, haven't we?" They grunted in recognition. She was clearly all paid up on her bribes and they couldn't lay a finger on me. I could have knelt at her feet and kissed her dirty flip-flops. I was ready to part ways then and there, but the four of us all trooped up to her apartment where she poured us tea and we sat around chatting as the TV blared in the background.

"What were you doing here?" asked one officer.

"I was visiting Big Sister Bao. We're friends," I said, my hands shaking in my lap.

"Yes, we're close friends," said Big Sister Bao with a rehearsed air. "She came over to chat with me. She comes over quite often."

"How do you know her?"

"We're friends."

"I don't believe you."

"I'm not sure what there is not to believe," said Big Sister Bao. "We both like to play cards and watch TV. We were just watching a little TV."

The questioning went in the same vein for a while but the officers were unable to penetrate Big Sister Bao's shield of protection and eventually they got up to leave. I got up too, but she put her hand on my arm and sat me down again. She said her sweet good-byes to them as they uttered ominous warnings to me to be more careful next time.

"Don't act so nervous, Miss Wang," she said after they'd left.

I thanked her as obsequiously as I could and hoped she would release me soon. Now that it was just the two of us, she was the one I feared. What price would she demand for saving my life? Her face was shrewd and pinched and she started interrogating me. Where did I live? Who was my landlord? How much did I pay? What did I do for a living? I was too shaken to lie so I coughed it all up like a baby, hoping that there would never be an occasion for her to turn against me. Much as she scared me, I also had to admire her; she was one of the wily ones who made the best of all the cracks and fissures that had appeared around her. She was one of the winners.

Cookie and I, bored one beautiful fall Sunday, decided to bike to my Great-Aunt Mabel's courtyard house, the one the government had given her in recompense for the demolition of her old house, and which I'd visited when my parents came to town.

Several weeks before, Bobo had mentioned that Uncle Johnny was still trying to rent out the house. He said Westerners were willing to pay good money to live in a courtyard house and the prices were skyrocketing. They wanted to charge two thousand U.S. dollars for the sixteen-room house, he said incredulously.

Sixteen rooms. Two thousand dollars. Now that the city was ruining the grotty charms of Maizidian'r, it was time to move on. I asked some of the grannies if they wanted to go take a look at it. Splitting the rent six ways, we could easily afford to pay Great-Aunt Mabel what she asked and the house could even stay in the family. Some of us were considering living elsewhere for part of the year and a house like this would make it possible. One Saturday all of us but Cookie went to go see it; she was busy that day. Bobo met us there and let us in. *His loss might be my gain,* I thought.

The courtyard had been cleared of the ragged vegetation and was immaculately bare. It looked much bigger than the previous time. With the brick walls freshly painted gray and the door and window frames painted maroon, the house almost looked fake, like a showroom or a movie set. The only sign of life was the tall pomegranate tree spreading its branches over the courtyard.

We swarmed all over the house, claiming rooms, talking about what needed to be installed—flooring, a heating system, a kitchen and bathroom, stronger locks—and imagining our fabulous new lives there. Cookie and another friend would take a corner of the massive south-facing living room for their painting and calligraphy and I would take the room with a small office. Maybe I would start to write for real. Maizidi-an'r was instantly forgotten and I imagined the next chapter of my life in Beijing. The Ugly Duckling becomes the Evening Swan.

"Your house is incredibly beautiful," one of my friends said to Bobo. I hadn't told my friends the full story of the house, just that it belonged to my relatives and that Bobo was my relative.

"Yes, it is," said Bobo, and added, with the brisk pride of a real estate agent, "As you can see, the original layout of the house has been pre-served. The big northern room gets excellent southern light. None of the rooms are finished but Johnny will take care of that."

He had hoped to live in this house and I wondered if he was also imagining which room would be used for what, how nice the sun would be in that south-facing room in the afternoon. He was obligated to help Great-Aunt Mabel and I don't know what he got in return, but I couldn't read his face. We thanked him and he locked up behind us. I went home and wrote an e-mail to Uncle Johnny, telling him I was ready to rent the house.

Several weeks later, I was still waiting for a response when Cookie and I made the half-hour bike ride out to the house. We passed under the thundering Third Ring Road, along wide streets with wide bike lanes, past the Second Ring Road, and into the narrow lanes of the old city. I couldn't remember the name of the hutong, so we biked around and around looking for it as swooping flocks of black birds whirred above us emitting their eerie call. The autumn light slanting through the turning leaves dappled the ground with shadows. The curves of the alleys had engraved themselves easily on my mind the first time and I soon located the house.

I had called Bobo but he had been too busy to come open the house so Cookie and I took turns standing on a rickety wooden cart, craning to see over the wall into the house. Neighbors stared at us as they walked by, particularly at Cookie, who was wearing a pair of flowing red pants bursting with bold white swirls. A paunchy, middle-aged man in a blue smock stopped and I explained to him that my great-aunt owned the house and that we were thinking of renting it. He nodded in understanding and then asked if he could borrow Cookie's bike to run an errand for a neighborhood granny standing nearby. Cookie handed it over and he rode off.

"This house is empty," said the granny, clucking in regret. So many other courtyard houses were filled with makeshift rooms housing a jumble of people.

"I know," I said.

"The owner of this house lives over there," she said, gesturing to a neighboring house.

"No, this house is owned by a relative of mine," I said.

She didn't believe me and we argued back and forth good-naturedly until the neighbor returned. After thanking us profusely, he then offered us his ladder so we could climb into the house.

"Really?" we asked.

"I've done it before," he said. "No problem."

We readily agreed and he came back with a tall A-frame ladder and together we maneuvered it so we could climb up one side and down the other into the courtyard. As we scrambled over he laughed and said that in England, where his son had gone to study, this kind of thing would probably be illegal.

Touched by an illicit magic, the courtyard looked even larger this time. I could just see Qu Qu'r padding around the place as if he owned it. The old pomegranate tree was just beginning to drop its leaves and the ground was covered with the brown husks. I showed Cookie where she could do calligraphy and where I would write. The neighbor, who likely felt responsible to show China to the foreigners, picked two pomegranates off my great-aunt's tree and presented them to us as gifts. The forbidden fruit felt heavy with the secret of our day. We climbed out and biked home. I put the pomegranate on my washing machine and waited for Uncle Johnny's e-mail. It sat there full of promise like the fateful pomegranate that Hades gave Persephone.

A month later, his reply came. "Sorry," he wrote, "but I have decided to rent the house to an Angolan-Korean couple." I was furious. I realized that he had never intended the house to stay in the family. He had wanted a piece of real estate, nothing more, and I got a taste of how Bobo felt. I wondered how years of this kind of treatment sat with him. Perhaps if I'd eaten the pomegranate I would have been cursed—or blessed—to spend half of my days on this side of the world. As it was, I was free to go.

Later Bobo told me that Uncle Johnny didn't end up renting the house to the couple. He said he preferred renting it to a company. Families are too much trouble, he had said. They come and then they go, one after another. I remembered my sentimental urge, years ago, to write about my family's houses, and now I felt it again. I understood that vengeance can be an equally powerful source of inspiration. *I want to write stories that will last longer than your house,* I thought.

Part Six

Chapter Twenty-eight

The Shade Provided by the Branches Is Gone

*B*eijing was changing. The edge of the city pushed farther outward. The Fifth Ring Road opened and the government initiated a five-year plan to relocate a third of the people living in the old city to apartments in the suburbs and to preserve only twenty-five small zones of hutongs. The pace of demolitions picked up.

Beijing went into overdrive to win the 2008 Olympic bid. Ten thousand children jump-roped in unison on Tiananmen Square to support the bid; People's Liberation Army soldiers climbed the Great Wall. The government declared the official color of the city gray and when the bid committee came to inspect the city, they spray-painted the grass green. Beijing won, of course, and erupted into a rapturous party. And a few months later, China entered the World Trade Organization. Once that happened, the city felt palpably different, as though a page had been turned. Gone was the feeling of zany, zigzagging promise; all the energy suddenly started moving in the same direction, toward the money. I could just picture all the bright-eyed business majors in the States learning Chinese as they'd learned Japanese in the 1980s.

Cookie got an official journalist's accreditation and a raise and was kicked out of her apartment. She and Emma moved to a more expensive apartment in the old city. The three-story buildings of her compound in Ju'er Hutong were built around a central yard in the style of a courtyard house but were separated into apartments with modern conveniences. The place had won international social housing awards and was teeming with young expats. We had always refused to live there and made fun of people who did. Who needed to be overcharged to bask in the romance of Beijing's past, in its feudal tranquility? But Cookie loved it. Just as she used to rhapsodize the squalor of Marzipan Street, she would not stop talking about the beauty of the old hutongs and bragging about her two balconies. Becky moved back to the States. Even after everyone else moved away, after the dot-com bubble crashed and *The Marzipan Inquirer* became a vague memory, Gretchen and I stayed in the neighborhood. Even there, life continued to change in minute ways. When the monthly gas and water meter check rolled around, a stranger dressed in a jumpsuit holding a clipboard knocked politely at my door, calling out his mission, and issued me a computerized slip with instructions to pay at the bank. Then he left, strangely uncurious about my apartment. I felt like a relic of a lost time but life was easy and time passed quickly.

Then 9/11 happened, and I felt as if I had been roused from a beautiful dream and forced to stare into a rippling infinite void. A string of thoughts detonated in my mind: America was over—I could not go home—I would become a nomad, one of those people who wander homeless through whatever country will have them. I knew people in Beijing like that: Leo the engineering grad from years ago, as well as an anti-Marcos Filipino stranded after Marcos declared martial law. But America wasn't that much a part of the world yet. After my worst fears about its demise didn't come true, I just wanted to go home.

Even though Beijing felt like home, I started looking for a way out. I had to face facts: I was a Flying Pigeon, born with wings and cursed to be free. Home would never be a single place I could point to on a map.

But the city exerted a powerful magnetic effect on me and I needed an equally persuasive reason to leave. An idea that had hung patiently around the edges of my mind came front and center: I wanted to be a writer.

So I dug the tapes of the Peking Opera family out from the back of the drawer, forced myself to watch them, and wrote a story about it. I sent the story out with applications to writing programs in the States, and waited.

Offhand things my parents had said came back to me. My dad told me, just once, that he had wanted to be a writer but his dad had forbade him to, and he had become an engineer instead. My mom told me that at boarding school she had published stories that were thinly veiled fictionalizations of the lives and loves of her fellow classmates. She'd even fictionalized her own name, giving herself the nom de plume Bai Yun, or White Cloud. She said that if she hadn't had to worry about getting a steady job after college in New York, she wouldn't have majored in math but instead done something more artistic. What would they have become if they could have stayed in China? What would China have become?

Suddenly a hidden dimension of our story seemed to reveal itself: By becoming a writer I was doing what they had never had the chance to do, what they had sacrificed so I could do. *You can be anything you want to be in life.* I had taken them at their word and maybe it wasn't only their disapproval I was shouldering, but also their hopes for me, and their fears and envies, which were a much heavier burden to bear, if also somehow easier.

And the more I saw of the changes sweeping through Beijing, the more I understood how my parents' peripatetic lives had left them with a feeling of perpetual instability, even after their house was paid off, their children through college, and their retirement account plump. Their decision many years ago to move to a house in the suburbs with no history began to make sense. A place whose story you were free to write, a place that would never break your heart.

Then one day an e-mail came out of the blue from my dad.

Subject: White Pines

A crew of nine arrived Saturday around 7:30 am. In 10
hours they chopped down 27 trees and fed the branches
and trunks into a shredder which filled six truckload
of mulch for dumping. Sad to say that the yard looks
now bare and empty. The shade provided by the branches
is gone. We have to get used to the sun light and
clear unobstructed view of neighbors' houses. It was
gut wrenching to see the 27-year growth ended in
mulch in seconds in the shredder. They will be back
soon to finish the two biggest trees, grind the stumps,
and prune the dogwoods in the front. Since they gave
us one of the lowest bid we had to be a little more
tolerant and patient. Those Hispanic day laborers
were hard working and dedicated.

Heat and humidity returned to Washington after we
enjoyed a reasonably mild summer.

I was furious with my parents the next time we spoke on the phone.

"There was nothing we could do," said my dad. "That many pine trees don't belong to this small lot. The yard can support maybe five trees, small trees. Pine trees are too big. We learned it after twenty-five years, unfortunately."

"Aren't you sad about it?"

"I miss the look of the trees, but I don't miss the pine needles dropping that I have to scoop it up," my mom said. "Sooner to later it's going to drop on someone's house—that house or my house. It was just going to make more trouble for us."

"There's no use being upset about it," said my dad. "There was nothing else we could have done."

"Why couldn't you have just let the branches fall where they would and let the roots bore into the house?" I asked. I was proud of our pine trees for being too grand to be contained in a trim suburban plot and of my parents for daring long ago to dream so big. And I also had to admire their instinct to adapt to change, which twenty-five years in the suburbs had not dulled.

Eric's of Paris closed and I followed Wang Le to her new salon, willing to give her another chance. The salon was a dingy space attached to a three-star hotel, and I got a slightly better haircut for about half the price. It still looked helmetlike but was coming closer to the thing that I couldn't put it into words. Business was slow and Wang Le seemed depressed to be there without any French atmosphere or lively expatriates.

The next time I called, the salon said she had moved on, so Cookie and I followed her to yet another new salon. The price went in half again. She kept moving farther and farther south in the city, a move that usually meant one's fortunes were going south too.

The salon was located on a dusty side street across from a construction site. It had the same shoddy look as my original neighborhood salon, but Wang was still wearing her Eric's of Paris T-shirt. It was summer, hot, and she immediately had her boys bringing us water. Even her coworkers looked familiar. A Cantonese hairdresser named A Di had a pompadour of crispy reddish hair and long pinky nails. I watched as he coiled, pinned, and sprayed a woman's hair into a French twist at the back of her head. When he was done, he twirled her chair around and I saw with horror that her smiling face was framed by long, stiff ringlets. Wang whispered to Cookie that she was getting four thousand yuan a month, almost five hundred U.S. dollars, just to be a salon consultant. She didn't even have to cut hair. Half of the salon was for haircutting and the other half for massage. Fleshy middle-aged men sat with closed eyes as young women stroked their faces or tattooed their backs with their tiny digits.

"You have to try the face massage!" said Wang, pushing me toward the chairs and ordering one of the women to massage my face with coconut lotion, but midmassage, she grabbed my hand and asked, "Do you like to eat noodles?" The three of us flew down to the basement where a cook was making *zhajiang mian*.

"My husband's *zhajiang mian* tastes much better than this," whispered Wang between slurps of noodles. "He puts much more meat in it. They're stingy here. And this has no taste because they forbid us to eat garlic during work."

Cookie and I feigned dismay at this rule.

"Actually, it's a good idea. If you want to be cultured, you shouldn't be breathing garlic in customers' faces," she said. "Anyhow, you should come to our house; we're in a courtyard house not far from here, and my husband will make *zhajiang mian* for you."

We went upstairs. When Wang suggested that Cookie dye her hair, she eagerly agreed and soon it was a reddish color that pleased them both.

When it was my turn, Wang scrutinized my face, pulling my short hair in all directions and letting it fall. She said that if I wanted my hair to stick up straight, I should get a perm. A perm! Bad adolescent memories surfaced.

"Not with curlers, just with foil on the ends."

"No, no perm."

"If you don't perm your hair, it won't stick up."

Then all of a sudden, I said yes, and the next thing I knew my head was covered with a bumper crop of foil-wrapped sprigs of hair, and toxic chemicals were burning through my scalp. Afternoon sun flooded into the salon and I couldn't tell if that funny feeling in my chest was extreme peace and happiness or a panic attack gathering steam before erupting.

Wang took out the foil, rinsed my hair, and sat me in front of the mirror. I put my glasses on. My hair stuck straight up, but in a crinkly, crispy sort of way that seemed to be the hallmark of this salon. I looked as if I'd been electrocuted, then deep-fried. All I could think was, *Damaged, damaged, damaged.*

"It's called Exploding Fireworks," she said proudly. "Really *huopo*."

I nodded, trying to hide my crushing disappointment. I could always shave it in the morning.

"Do you know how you should do your hair in the mornings? You should take a pillow like this," Wang said, holding the imaginary pillow flat on outstretched arms as if presenting us with a crown, "and rub it all over your head." She bent down and thrashed her head around wildly. "It makes great effects."

"She's completely mad," said Cookie.

But the next day I looked in the mirror and somehow, my hair didn't look half bad. Angular and jarring and unbalanced. Every day I grew into the haircut more and more, and by the end of the week, I felt as though I belonged to myself finally and not to some tribe of Cantonese karaoke stars. At the eleventh hour, Wang Le had divined my inner character and even when people stared at me on the street, I didn't care.

I called my parents with the news that they'd been waiting for since I moved to China.

"I got into grad school!" I said. "I'm moving back in the fall."

"Oh, Val, that's wonderful," said my mom. "What are you studying?"

A tiny part of me wished I could say law or medicine but mostly I was delighted to tell the truth. "Writing."

"Journalism?" asked my dad.

"No, creative writing. I've been *doing* journalism for the last five years, remember?"

"Oh."

"Where?" asked my mom.

"At Johns Hopkins."

"Close to home!"

"Yes," I said, not sure what *home* meant anymore. I had deliberately chosen a place close to both my parents and New York but I wondered if it would be too close for comfort.

"We can help you with the tuition," she said.

"No need. I got a full scholarship. Plus a stipend."

And with this, I was at least partially redeemed in their eyes. And I felt relief. My double life had become more tiring than it was worth, and like with many things one hides from others, my desire to write had been hidden from myself as well. I had mixed feelings about returning. China was where the best stories were, not to mention my entire life and all my friends and contacts, but to write about it, I needed some distance. I was willing to barter my Beijing life for what I wanted more: a writing life.

The chair of the writing program said he didn't support the writing of memoirs, only traditional nonfiction, so what was I planning on writing about? I panicked. I hadn't infiltrated the inner circle of Falun Gong leaders or taken up the cause of any political dissident or exposed any humiliating government scandals. Nothing important had happened to me in five years. I'd been a *hunzi,* befriended a few artists, failed to make a documentary. How could you write about that?

What's more, I found out that I had mistranslated a long time ago and the foundation on which I'd built my life was shaky. *Zixun fannao* does not necessarily mean "seeks trouble for oneself"—it can also mean "worries oneself over nothing." Instead of finding adventure, history, and truth in China, had I merely been plumbing my own anxieties, neuroses, and self-deluding fictions?

I had to find an important, relevant topic to write about and do some interviews in the few months I had left. There was one story that had been in the Western press that I did know about: the demolition of the old city. After seeing my own family's house demolished, the sense of urgency to document the city before it disappeared had stayed with me. And now that I was leaving and would be losing the city in a different way, writing about it felt even more crucial. The city as I knew it could live on, on the page at least.

Whole neighborhoods were disappearing overnight. The demolitions happened so suddenly. First, 拆 would appear on the wall, large and circled. Next would appear handwritten lists of possible apartments—their addresses, size, cost. Families picked new apartments and moved out. Giant earthmovers moved in, gnashing through roofs, smashing down walls, and reducing the intimate capsules of houses into big uneven yards, which stayed suspended, for a period of time, in states of half death. I went to see the demolition sites. Only the outlines of houses were left: fragments of walls, looking like Kit Kat bars snapped open, worn wooden doorframes standing alone, no longer separating inside from outside. I walked over sturdy wood beams and old stones, flimsy plaster and jags of glass, straight into the homes of strangers. I looked at the peels and cracks of their walls, at the years of cooking grease and dust, at the faded posters that they had decided were not worth taking away, the occasional shoe. Just as in Maizidian'r, I was surprised at how little space each house took up. How could it have been enough to contain all the life that had existed here, all of the time that had passed? The demolition sites drew in people who hauled away reusable parts of the city, brick by brick, beam by beam.

I took cluttered and incoherent photos and tried to talk to residents who were moving out. They weren't eager to recollect their pasts in these old, decrepit houses and seemed to be thinking more about their roomy new modern apartments.

Only a few devoted to the old houses protested for their preservation. And soon their focus shifted from the idealism of preserving the old city, which most saw as impossible, to the pragmatism of getting adequate compensation for the demolished houses, enough to buy new apartments elsewhere and move on with life. I met people who had filed lawsuits against the city government and development companies for violating their land-use rights, sometimes in groups as large as twenty thousand. I met a lawyer who had filed mass civil suits and won. I met an activist who wanted to stage a huge march to Tiananmen Square to protest and was looking for the protection of the international media. But I didn't want to find a hero. I wanted to find an ordinary family who felt comfortable talking about their old house, their memories, about this way of life that was disappearing.

Chapter Twenty-nine
I Hope to Bring This Tape to You in Person

I trooped off to Bobo and Bomu's house one day, minidisc recorder in hand, and sat down with them in the high-ceilinged room that had been my bedroom when I first moved to Beijing. Bobo sat in his big easy chair, which was covered with a protective sheet and doilies. On the wall next to him, a big reed butterfly covered a blotch of crumbling paint. Bomu stood doing bouncy dance moves and gently pounding her thighs with her fists. I hoped she would chime in with her comments too. Four years ago when I'd lived with them, they'd been cagey when I probed them about the houses, but when I approached them now as an interviewer, they readily agreed to answer my questions. Somewhere along the line we had grown close.

There was an element of panic to my questioning. We were both leaving soon for the States—me to go to school in Baltimore and them to visit their daughters in L.A., and this might be the last time we'd meet in this house.

Bobo said that years ago he borrowed a video camera and a car and shot a video to show his aunts the condition of their houses in Beijing; he pulled it out for us to watch. He said it showed all four of the family houses: Great-Aunt Mabel's big house that had been demolished, Nainai's house filled with squatters, the house we sat in now, and their original family house that I'd never seen. He lifted the doily on the VCR, popped the video in, and pressed play. We saw a shaky shot of mottled gray walls; someone biked by. It took me a second to recognize Qianbaihu Hutong, where Bobo and his family lived for almost fifty years. The video was stamped August 1993—almost ten years earlier.

"The hutong looks horrible," said Bomu, ever concerned about appearances. You could see the blackened side of a house and, if you knew to look, the edge of a public toilet. But once the camera panned to the front door, those annoyances were forgotten, and she sat down to watch. Bobo, tilted back in a laugh, stood in front of a wooden door flanked by carved stone figures.

"That was back when you still had hair and didn't have a stomach," Bomu said. "That was back when the door wasn't painted red yet." She didn't need to mention that that was back before the house had been demolished to make way for a parking lot.

Bobo stood awkwardly for a moment before turning and walking in. The camera followed him and we went ten years, or one hundred, into the past. This trick of time is the magic of courtyard houses. They are able to conjure the lives, so different from ours, that have been contained in their walls. Watching the video, I felt as if I were seeing their courtyard house for the first time, feeling exposed to the sky but also enclosed on four sides by the house. We saw the apple tree that we picked apples from my first fall in China and, hung from a bough, a cage containing two small yellow birds. The courtyard was green and blooming.

"How big the lilies were," said Bomu wistfully, "and the grapes, how sweet."

The video trailed Bobo as he walked through his daughters' rooms, filled with tiny knickknacks, and into the airy northern room bathed in light. The family was gathered stiffly on the couches as if waiting to greet relatives in person. Their older daughter, in her twenties, was sitting in a long white dress, while the younger daughter hid behind the refrigerator. Xiao Peng must have been filming.

I imagined Nainai and Great-Aunt Mabel sitting in their comfortable apartments—in Leisure World in suburban Maryland and the Upper West Side of New York City, respectively—and watching the tape. Did they feel sadness to have left or relief that they were not still there?

Xiao Peng drifted in to watch with us. His side of the house was a mess: The roof had caved in, showering his bedroom with dirt. Through the hole in the roof, you could see the sky. Xiao Lu and their son, Sanbao, were at her mother's house until the hole could be repaired. I already knew how Xiao Lu felt about the courtyard houses: She had grown up in a courtyard house shared by many families and would rather live in an apartment. She didn't think preservation should stand in the way of the city's progress.

With a sweet, cloying smile into the camera, the older sister said, "I hope to bring this tape to you in person." She left for L.A. not long afterward.

"She's so beautiful," said Bomu. The sister then ordered her little brother, Xiao Peng, to stop shooting and show himself, so Bobo took the camera from him and Xiao Peng sat down on the couch. He was skinny with a big grin.

"Look at how spirited you looked back then," said Bomu. "Not like now." The present-day Xiao Peng shrugged apathetically and said nothing. But back then, he spoke freely into the camera, telling his relatives in America that Beijing had gone through big changes, that cars filled the road, and that he was going to study hard for his classes at Beijing Film Academy and send them his projects so they could see his progress. "This house can't compare to the U.S., but it's considered all right here," he said. The older Xiao Peng laughed a little bit at himself, but not too much.

"I look horrible," Bomu said with false modesty. "Those front teeth are so big." She was still slim and graceful, the type who compels people to say she must have been a great beauty in her youth. Everyone was laughing in the video, not speaking anymore, and Bomu laughed in person too. "Things were so much fun back then. Not like now."

It was true; I rarely heard them laugh like that anymore. I assumed they missed their daughters, just as my parents missed me. Bobo, Bomu, and Xiao Peng didn't agree about much these days, but they all said that things seemed better then. Then they all lived together in a whole court-yard house with an apple tree in the yard and a room for each person. Bomu said she spent all day cooking dumplings, sesame seed cakes, meat buns, *hongcai* soup, whatever that was. But these days she was too tired to cook. Xiao Peng was often out at night; he had stopped coming home when Bobo called, sometimes even refusing to answer his phone. Just like his grandfather who had been left behind when Nainai and Great-Aunt Mabel went to the States, he was the one left behind while his two sisters made new lives abroad. He had never managed to get a visa.

I asked Bobo if he liked living in the hutongs.

"I like living in the hutongs. Why? Because every nation has its own national culture," he began, his pointer finger going up and his eyelids fluttering in a teacherly way. I reached over to pause the videotape. "Now, if you look north from the Forbidden City, the whole view is courtyard houses, like a single roof, and you can go there and say, 'Ah ya, this is the emperor's majesty.' You don't just knock down old houses and build tall buildings and say you've built a modern city. When you're done with it, how will it be different than Shanghai or Tianjin or New York or Paris? What difference is there? There's no difference."

Bomu interjected, "Courtyard houses are dirty."

"Of course, courtyard houses require more work than an apartment building. You have to clean the yard."

Bomu refrained from mentioning that she was the one who did all the cleaning. "And going to the bathroom is not convenient."

"Yes, going to the bathroom isn't convenient. But if you can renovate, then all these problems go away."

"The country should do renovations. We don't have the money to. The roof just fell down, and dirt is all over. It costs ten thousand kuai to fix," she said.

We started the video again and it moved to Xiao Peng's old room hung with posters of scantily clad girls, the same room I stayed in when I came to Beijing to look for a job long ago.

I asked something I'd wanted to know since that time. "What happened to the house during the Cultural Revolution?"

Bobo stiffened and began speaking in a somewhat robotic voice. "The Cultural Revolution was a mistake in the course of Chinese history. The government chased out of their houses the 'five black elements'— landlords, rich farmers, counterrevolutionaries, bad elements, and rightists—and moved in people without homes, poor people. People like us who had houses were considered moneyed and were chased out. You didn't have the right to live in your own house anymore and you had to live in a small room somewhere else. Your house was given to the 'five red elements'—the workers, farmers, soldiers, revolutionary cadres, and revolutionary martyrs."

"Did you have to move out?"

"The house was handed over to the government, but because I wasn't the landlord—your Great-Aunt Mabel was—we were allowed to live there. They said, 'You are of the capitalist class and if you close the door, you might be engaging in espionage,' so they moved in a family of workers and we had to leave the door wide-open."

He said a family of six lived in the eastern wing of the house for twelve years. The parents worked for a construction company.

"Did you have any contact with them?"

"No."

"None at all?"

"No."

"They lived there for twelve years and you didn't have any kind of relationship with them?"

"Our educational levels were not the same. Our living conditions and our habits were not the same."

"What was their attitude toward you?"

"They were the power of the revolution, we were the opponents of the revolution. How could they have treated us well? It wasn't possible."

"Did you ever see them after they moved out?"

"Their oldest son was a student at our school. After coming back from the army, he became a worker too. They all became workers. Not a single one of them studied hard and got out of that life."

I remembered another question that had been nagging me for years. Bomu had enigmatically mentioned a bathroom that had existed in the house at Qianbaihu. What had happened to it? I imagined something ominous and meaningful.

Bobo shook his head angrily. "Before, the eastern wing had a bathroom, with a toilet, a sink, and bath. When the workers moved into that wing, they demolished the toilet, crammed tiles in the drain, and clogged it up. After they left, even if I had wanted to fix it, I couldn't have. It was clogged beyond repair."

"Oh," I said, disappointed by the senselessness of the answer. It was even more mysterious than the question.

Bobo turned back to the TV and restarted the video. Nainai's house came next. It looked pretty much how it looked the day we visited with my parents. A shirtless man came out of one of the rooms.

"This is how poor people live," Bomu explained. This was how most people who live in courtyard houses now lived, in a *zayuan'r* with other families. The video then moved onto Bobo's father's old house, the one we sat in now. It was like watching a store security camera of ourselves, with a ten-year time delay.

Bobo said that at the start of the Cultural Revolution in 1966 his father had been forced to move out and live in a single room nearby, measuring 130 square feet. Bomu said it was lucky he'd already sold off three-fourths of the house before then or there would have been even more trouble. Neither mentioned his gambling or his multiple wives. Nor did they mention that during the Cultural Revolution Bobo's younger sister had been accused of hiding jewelry for Great-Aunt Mabel and had committed suicide by throwing herself down a well, leaving her young daughter motherless; my dad told me that story later.

After the Cultural Revolution ended in 1976 and Deng Xiaoping came to power, the workers were moved out and the houses returned to our family. Bobo's father was finally allowed to move back to his house in 1981.

We then saw scenes shot from a car driving along the Avenue of Eternal Peace past Tiananmen Gate. It looked like an old *National Geographic* vision of Beijing: The wide avenue was clogged with bikes, and a few yellow breadbox vans were starting to ply the roads.

The video ended with exterior shots of the old family house, which Bobo said was no longer in the family. The government had taken it over and then turned it into a dormitory, and since the shooting of the video, it had been demolished. You couldn't see much of it—just a two-story gray exterior wall. I had never even heard of this house. Nainai had grown up there, Bobo said, and so had he. They had lived there with their extended family and their servants. He said it had been a grand house with a courtyard big enough to drive a car around in. There had been a rockery in the center, as well as his grandfather's huge fishbowl full of goldfish.

"In the past, when your Yeye lived here, when my Yeye lived here, when my aunts lived here, we used to always sit outside in the summer. You could watch stars in the yard, you could eat watermelon, you could drink tea and talk," said Bobo.

"Old Beijing habits," said Bomu.

"Before the Cultural Revolution, we always ate out in the yard at

Qianbaihu also. Then, there wasn't any TV to watch. We would all sit out in the yard and talk or play cards."

"Why don't you sit in the yard now?" I asked.

"Now the yard here is too small. If we sat outside and ate, no one could even bother trying to come into the yard. That's one thing."

"Also, the pollution is bad," says Bomu.

"Scientific advances have enabled me to install an air conditioner, turn it on, close the door, and be cooler than I am outside," says Bobo, speaking theoretically because the voltage in the hutong was prohibitively low to install an air conditioner. "I don't need to go out anymore."

"Were you sad to leave the house at Qianbaihu?"

Xiao Peng had been listening the whole time, and while I could tell he thought my questions were stupid, he couldn't resist putting his two cents in. "I didn't feel anything because I knew it wasn't our own house. It's not like losing something that's your own. Anyhow, the atmosphere of the hutongs when I was growing up is already gone, destroyed by tall apartment buildings. Sanbao will probably become accustomed to living in a huge city. I just regret that he won't experience traditional Chinese community life. Before, every room had people living there."

"It was too crowded," said Bomu, laughing.

But Xiao Peng was serious. "It was too crowded, but life had a mood that was important."

"People had feelings for each other," she said. "People took care of each other."

"Our living conditions are much better now, but if you ask how that time was, it was also really good," he said. "There's nothing specific that's worth recalling. There's nothing that's negative either. Life is just like that."

Xiao Peng was still a character straight out of *Beijing Bastards,* a tough guy who never made a big deal out of anything. Owning a house, owning a story, or not owning either—what was the difference?

He was right, in a way. Some of my questions were stupid. I was asking an outsider's questions and making a story out of something that was just life. I thought of the things that they didn't need to explain to me: the feeling of biking through the hutongs at dusk or of stumbling into a freezing outhouse at three in the morning, the smell of burning coal, the taste of warm *baozi* and the fear that they are stuffed with human flesh. Living in these courtyard houses had made me feel a part of my family as nothing else had.

I wondered where my relatives would live when this house was demolished, which would happen eventually. Bobo and Bomu were getting used to the idea that they would be exiled from the old city where they had grown up. They had gone to look at newly built villas in the suburbs, modeled on the kind of suburban house I'd grown up in.

"Not bad," Bobo said. "But the prices are 'not bad' too."

Bobo and Bomu had lived through so much; the demolition of their homes and their way of life was just the next thing that they had to adapt to. I tried to adopt their equanimity about it, tried to see what was happening less as destruction and more as change, a mere swapping of set scenery that we would improvise new lives in, but I couldn't. I felt more ready than ever to leave. And actually, they were leaving too. We were all ready to start over in America.

Without telling Bobo and Bomu, I visited Nainai's courtyard house before moving back to the States. I wanted to talk to average Beijingers who lived in a *zayuan'r*, who didn't have relatives in the States, and who didn't own their own houses. I didn't tell my relatives because I didn't want them coming along and censoring what people had to say. I went also because I wanted to know some history of Nainai's house from the people who had actually lived there.

I found the house, just north of the Avenue of Eternal Peace. The front door was open and I walked in cautiously. I knew what to expect this time and the place looked merely rundown, not heartbreakingly ruined. It was the end of summer and the house seemed to be peeling apart from the heat, layer by layer. At the end of one corridor, an old couple sat on stools in the shade, fanning themselves. The woman asked me what business I had there. I explained that it was my Nainai's house—yes, she was in America—and I'd come to take a look. She asked me if I was related to the man who took care of the house. Yes, he's my Bobo, I said.

I asked the granny if she liked living here. Her middle-aged daughter, wearing a housedress and round metal glasses, came out carrying a metal pail. The granny said she liked it, yes. Her daughter disagreed, saying, "There's no shower or bathroom. It's cold in the winter, hot in the summer. It leaks. I don't like living here." The roof, originally a sea of gentle upside-down-U-shaped tiles, was patched haphazardly. Her mother conceded that it leaked.

"We have to pay for all repairs by ourselves," the daughter continued, and her mother was forced to agree again. Her daughter added, "This house is beyond repair."

"Beyond repair," echoed the mother, but her affection was unwavering. "It's convenient to go in and out."

They told me they'd lived in the house since the Cultural Revolution.

"There must be some stories from then," I said.

"We've forgotten all the stories a long time ago," said the daughter.

"All of the stories?"

"What stories are there?" she said. "They let us live here, so we live here." It reminded me of what Xiao Peng had said about not feeling anything when the old house was destroyed because it hadn't belonged to them. None of us had anything else to say. The daughter filled the bucket from the outside spigot, the water drumming loudly onto the metal. I asked their surname and they said Fang.

On the way out, I met a girl with pigtails wearing a strawberry-print dress. Around eight years old, she'd been living in the house for two years and liked it because it stayed cool in the summer. She kept two white rabbits in a plastic crate outside her door. I helped her feed them some lettuce, took her picture, and then left.

Bobo and I talked about what was going to happen with Nainai's house. He didn't want to be her proxy when demolition time came. He would rather my dad or uncle come in person to deal with it.

I wondered aloud if Nainai would choose a new house or cash. I said I preferred for her to choose a new house. It would be wonderful to have a courtyard house in Beijing that I could always return to. Choosing cash would mean that our hold on the land was gone and would disperse, dollar by dollar, out into the world.

"Are you going to come take care of the house? Who's going to come?" Bobo asked. "It's better to just get a lot of a little bit of money and give it to Nainai." He paused, unsure what constituted a lot or a little bit of money anymore, to an American or a Chinese person. Or what constituted enough money to compensate for the loss of your family home, the loss of your last toehold in your homeland, the loss of a life you never got to lead. "She'll be able to spend the money for two years," he said, and laughed bitterly. "You could even negotiate," he said, and the thought made him laugh again, this time not as bitterly. "Your Chinese is good enough."

"I'm too young," I said, chiming in with my own laughter. No one in the government would take me seriously.

He didn't protest and we left it at that.

Chapter Thirty

Your Face Is So Magnificent,
but the Back of Your Head Has Rotted Away

*R*ight before moving back to the States, I called Wang Le's cellphone to check that she was still at her latest salon so I could get my last haircut. She told me she had just quit the day before, without further explanation. I was dismayed. How could I go back to the Cantonese hairdressers of the world right before I moved home? She offered to do a house call.

"No, that's too much trouble," I said. "I'll come to your house."

"But my house is so run-down; it's a *zayuan'r*," she said, and added, "I'm embarrassed to have you come over."

"I'm not embarrassed if you're not embarrassed," I said.

"Well, then, I'm not if you're not," she said.

"You don't like living there?"

"It's terrible, we hate it."

A bell went off in my head. Of course. Here was the family I had been looking for. I told her about my project and asked if I could interview her and her family. She readily agreed.

"You don't mind talking on the record?"

"I'll tell you everything. What do I have to hide?" she said. "Come in the afternoon so you can eat my husband's dumplings."

She picked me up at the intersection of Dongdan, one of Beijing's oldest and busiest shopping streets, and a road so new that I wasn't sure it even had a name yet. Cars hurtled down the fresh, unmarked pavement. We turned off into the hutongs and headed toward her house. Old people sat outside on tiny stools, gently fanning themselves in the heat. Children and cars were the noisiest things around, yelling and honking and vexing one another's passage through the narrow hutong. Inside the house, the passageway was only a wingspan wide and we walked along over loose tiles set crookedly into the earthen ground and wooden planks laid over pools of standing water. She kept repeating the same apologetic refrain, "It's so ugly, so dirty."

Seven families lived in the house and for privacy had covered over windows with old newspapers or calendar pages and hung doors with bead curtains made of popsicle wrappers folded like origami and hooked together with paper clips. We saw no one until Wang's next-door neighbor came out in his wifebeater tank top. He didn't say hello. Wang's family had just a small corner of the courtyard to themselves. On top of a tarp-covered mound was a pile of drying pumpkin seeds, crawling with flies. Wang's husband, tall and genial, greeted me from the doorway.

We entered their space, just one tiny room crammed with beds: On the left side of the room was a bunk bed and on the right were two single beds that had been pushed together to make a larger bed; in between them was only a narrow gap. The room fit together like a 3-D jigsaw puzzle: The top bunk was stacked high with large cardboard boxes, and on other high shelves more boxes reached up toward the lofty ceilings. Concrete floors made the room feel chilly and dank even though the summer air was stifling. By the door was another small bed on which Wang Le's ninety-two-year-old mother-in-law, skinny and toothless, perched cross-legged. I almost didn't see Wang's son, who was wedged into the corner behind the bunk bed, playing a computer game showing brown brick dungeon walls.

"This is my son. He's twenty-two," said Wang. "Do you think he's too fat?"

After we drank some orange soda, Wang pulled down a box full of her haircutting supplies and we went out into the courtyard to prepare for my haircut. She ordered her husband to boil water to wash my hair, and when the shampooing was done, I rinsed it over a painted metal washbasin on a stand, which he emptied into a tall metal pail. The pail, in turn, would have to be emptied in the drain outside. Her husband noticed the flies crawling on the pumpkin seeds and yelled to the granny that he was throwing them out. She had been peering out of the window at our activities.

"What?" she yelled back.

"I'm throwing out your seeds!"

"Why?"

"There are flies all over them."

"Oh, flies," she said. "All right."

He went inside to prepare dinner and Wang Le covered me with a red haircutting apron and began to cut. As she jerked my hair to and fro, I could see the crooked flagstones below and the sky and the large tree above. The summer day loosened its humid grip and the air was perfect. I mentioned this and Wang seemed surprised.

"You think it's nice out here?" she asked. She complained that it was too small. "If I took a stool and sat out here and you took a stool and sat out here and we stuck out our hands, we'd be able to shake." Mosquitoes started biting our legs, but the haircut, as usual, didn't take very long. We rinsed my hair out again in the washbasin and went inside to eat, leaving my fallen hair on the ground.

They had set up a folding table between the door and the beds and offered me the seat of honor on the bed. Her husband brought out a steaming plate of pork and celery dumplings. Though I knew it was hopelessly sentimental, I couldn't help but glow from my al fresco haircut, the deliciousness of the dumplings, and the overall romance of hutong living.

Wang and her husband started talking excitedly about the new apartment they wanted to buy. This was my cue to take out my recorder and ask them what was wrong with living in a courtyard house. So many things, it turned out. The beams of the house were rotting. You could see the sky through the crumbling roof, and rain poured down into the house, as did dirt. Rats ran *huala huala* on the roof at night. The room was stifling in the summers because there was no air circulation, but if you opened the door, the mosquitoes came in. The drains didn't drain and there was nowhere to shower. Every night around nine o'clock, the room reeked of excrement.

They were living in this room only temporarily while the government demolished and reconstructed the courtyard house that contained their original room. There, the beams had rotted to the point that they feared the house collapsing and killing someone. That house had been built during the Japanese occupation in the 1940s and had never been restored. Wang's husband's family had been assigned to live there in 1957, and the rent, thirty yuan per month, had barely grown since then.

"They should have knocked these houses down a long time ago," said Wang. "They're not fit for humans to live in. Nowadays, the doghouses that rich people buy are more beautiful than these houses."

Her son complained that the government cared only about its facade, about fixing up big avenues and restoring relics and temples while the common people went hungry. I wondered what he and Wang's husband did for a living, if they did anything at all.

Their old neighborhood sat right behind the International Hotel, a five-star hotel on the Avenue of Eternal Peace. "From the International Hotel, which is so magnificent, you can look down into our one-story houses, which are just like slums. If the government wants to improve its facade, it should fix the slums," said Wang. "Your face is so magnificent, but the back of your head has rotted away."

To demonstrate this discrepancy to the people in the hotel, she wanted to hang a Chinese flag on the roof of the house. I had no way of telling her that the guests in the hotel, looking down at the flapping flag, would miss her furious irony and see only a charming scene. Half of the time, I myself idealized the courtyard houses as a peaceful and humane escape from modern life.

She said if you wanted to shoot a movie about the past, you could just bring over the crew. "You don't even have to fix it up. You can immediately come and shoot this scenery that we've inherited."

The Beijing government had stipulated that each person should have a minimum of 160 square feet of housing, but the four of them together lived in a room that was not even 200 square feet, and they complained that no one in the government had come by to investigate. Why should they bother? Wang said she had a friend who was married to a Communist cadre and they had plenty of houses.

Wang's son had burned his hand while working as a cook and, lacking health insurance, was out of a job. China's cradle-to-grave housing and health system was unraveling as a result of state-run companies downsizing in preparation for China's entry into the World Trade Organization, and her son was among the many laid-off workers who idled their days away, living off meager savings and hoping things didn't get worse. He complained about a news broadcast he had recently seen; one segment said China's basic economic level had reached the "moderately well-off" level, while the next was a story on people starving and suffering from some natural disaster.

Wang started lamenting, "The Communist Party spreads such beautiful propaganda. What do you mean Beijing's population has reached the '"moderately well-off" level'? This is fucking bullshit." Gone was my charming hairdresser and in her place was a Beijinger with years of pent-up grievances.

"Oh no, she's gotten started," said her son, laughing.

"I may be poor, but I used to be a pretty cultured person. But if they don't let me be cultured, I'll curse them. I can't take it anymore," she said. She turned to her husband and said, "You worked for the Communist Party for thirty years and what did you ever get? Since we were young, the Communist propaganda has always said that we are living under the red flag, growing up in the heat of the sun. Up until now, I have yet to taste the sweetness."

She said they had just put a deposit down on a three-bedroom apartment in a newly built compound south of the city. The 990-square-foot apartment cost around one hundred thousand yuan, just over twelve thousand U.S. dollars. Wang showed me the advertising flyer, which someone had handed them on the street. It showed a bird's-eye view of a cluster of around twenty buildings, edged by green fields. Above the buildings was a blue sky filled with clouds, and the following text was superimposed on it:

> People who live in the city all dream of, at the end of a busy day at work, returning to a space that they can completely call their own: home. But faced with unattainably high prices, your dream may just turn into an illusion. Qin Yuan will help you to transform your dreams into reality. The low price of 1,130 yuan per meter will move you greatly.

They were planning to visit the apartment the next day and buy it before the price went up. The way it worked, they told me, was that developers would sell apartments while they were still building them and use that money to finance the construction of later buildings. Unbuilt apartments were the cheapest, then bare concrete apartments, then renovated ones, and so on. But it was a delicate balance; the newspapers were rife with stories of people who bought early and were cheated by unscrupulous developers who ran out of investment money and were never heard from again.

I asked if I could go with them and they agreed. The compound, almost an hour's drive south from the western edge of the city, seemed achingly far away, but it was the best they could afford with the little bit of money Wang had saved from years of work. She wasn't happy about it.

"Beijingers don't want to leave Beijing. To grow up in Beijing your whole life and, in the end, to be chased into the mountains—" she said, not knowing how to describe the horror of their exile. After the Cultural Revolution, the countryside symbolized a place of hardship where city people were "sent down" as punishment. "They are making us into peasants. And now the peasants, or people with power or influence, can come into the city."

"Peasants at least have land that they can work on. If we go out there, we'll have no work to do. How about this: We go and 'Develop the West,'" her husband said, referring to the government's plan to offer subsidies to those willing to move from China's richer coastal areas to the underdeveloped inner regions. "Give me some land then—"

"We're not afraid of hardship," she cut in. "We'll work the fields!" I had a vision of Wang in her Eric's of Paris T-shirt and perfectly made-up face hoeing in a bean field.

She turned to me and, in another fit of wild dreaming, pitched an idea of opening a salon in the States.

"You can be the boss and I'll work for you," she said. "I can cut hair all day long. We can make lots of money and come back to China to spend it! I have about ten more good years in me. What do you think? What kind of invitation letter do I need?"

"I think it's very difficult to get such a visa. I don't . . . I've never done it before," I said.

Her husband looked embarrassed. "It's not that easy. You have to prove how much money you have in the bank, in U.S. dollars. You have to have a business plan. And now America is restricting Asian and Middle Eastern visas."

"Well, just look into it," said Wang. "Think of all the money we could make."

Wang's entrepreneurial spirit had taken her a long way. She started cutting hair when she was twenty-one and after ten years of working in one of Beijing's large state-run salons, she quit and opened her own salon. The year was 1987 and Deng Xiaoping's "reform and opening-up" policy encouraged private businesses. Wang's salon was the first shop on a new commercial strip on the north side of Beijing. She decked out the tree in front with strings of tiny lights and opened for business. Working long hours, she earned about thirty times her old salary. Wang kept on top of new trends, learning how to stencil in eyebrows and to do tattoos. After ten years of owning her own salon, she was hired at Eric's of Paris.

After four years at Eric's of Paris and then hopscotching through various salons, she had somehow become one of the Beijingers who just idled at home. It didn't fit her character.

"If I had the chance to go to the U.S., I would definitely go," she hinted. "It's not that I want to forsake my country, but I'm *kanpo hong-chen*." Disillusioned with human society. The idiom alluded to the tradition of people retiring to the isolation of the countryside to live a monastic life. "But I'm not willing to go be a monk or a nun. I want to live life."

We finished eating, I paid her her Eric's of Paris rate for the haircut, and we made preparations to meet the next morning.

"Granny, what do you think about that? We're going to be living in an apartment!" her husband said.

The granny didn't answer.

"Maybe when we move we'll have a new mood," Wang said. "The only sure thing is that there's going to be a change."

The next day, I arrived at nine o'clock sharp at the office of the housing developers, on the fourth floor of a two-star hotel, where we were all going to catch a shuttle bus to the compound together. There was no new mood yet. The air was already thick with cigarette smoke. Wang and her husband were sitting around a small table listening to the entreaties of a tanned and gaunt young man in a slightly baggy suit who addressed them as "Big Brother Wang" and "Big Sister Wang." They were visibly angry. He was smiling overconfidently, wolfishly almost, and apologizing in a loud voice. He, or someone at his company, had sold the apartment that they had put a five-hundred-yuan deposit on. It was a south-facing three-bedroom apartment situated on the ground floor so the aging grandmother could easily walk in and out. There were no more ground-floor apartments in the size and orientation that they wanted. Wang Le suggested an apartment on the third floor. Her husband looked astonished that she would even consider it. She gave a shrug.

Agent Wang made a great show of returning the money to them and offering cigarettes all around, including to me. He tried to draw me into conversation by noting the coincidence of our common surname, but in this country at least, I didn't find it much of a coincidence. At least he didn't try to tell me that five thousand years ago we were family. Agent Wang said he had also sold the apartment that Wang Le's brother had put a deposit on. As her brother took his deposit back, Agent Wang pumped his hand unctuously while saying, "It was good cooperating with you."

Eight of us had come along to view the apartments: me, Wang Le, her husband, her brother, and her two sisters, plus her younger sister's husband and five-year old daughter, Niu Niu. Her younger sister, skinny with a puff of hair in the front like a rooster's crown, already owned three homes: one villa and two apartments. Her husband, a Communist cadre who was chain-smoking and talking about raising pigeons, casually mentioned—as if he were talking about matching sweaters—that if other family members bought apartments there, they would too. I wondered if her sister was the "friend" married to the Communist cadre who Wang Le had alluded to yesterday.

Wang Le asked to see the official certificate of their company to verify that it was legitimate, but Agent Wang laughed away her concerns. "The investor is from Beijing. If he were from Guangdong or Hong Kong, you'd never be able to find him if something went wrong," he said, and then added what was to become a refrain of our trip today, "You rest easy."

We had been waiting a half hour by this time and we asked him when the shuttle bus was coming. He went behind a partition and, when he emerged, told us that the road to the compound was closed.

"But aren't there public buses that go there?" asked Wang's older sister. "How are they getting through?" He went back behind the partition again.

The family began milling around the room. Agent Wang came out and, seeing them examining a poster depicting the same bird's-eye view of the compound that was on the flyer, said that only three of the twenty buildings had been built, but in three more years the whole compound would be completed. The cadre scoffed and said he bet that even if you gave them thirty years, they still wouldn't finish building it. Wang Le used this opening to jockey for a discount.

"You rest easy," said Agent Wang. "We'll get you the best discount." He assured us that the delay was due to a little engine trouble and that they were fixing the bus, but minutes later, he admitted that he had no idea what was going on. He concluded that we probably couldn't go today. Wang and her husband shrugged, resigned to the inefficiency. I wanted to yell at him but knew it wasn't my place to.

"Then you find a way!" said Wang's older sister. She was pudgy and shrill and I was relieved to see her taking control of the situation. "I think I've spent too long working in a foreign company. I can't stand this way of doing things. People have come from so far away to buy your apartments and you can't even find a bus to take them there."

He went back behind the partition and, within minutes, announced that the bus was here. We got in and headed toward the highway. Wang sat in the back to play with Niu Niu. After fifteen minutes of driving on the newly paved highway, we turned off onto bumpy country roads.

"This road has been bought by the developers. By 2008, when Beijing hosts the Olympics, this area is going to be villas with golf courses," said Agent Wang, pointing out the window. All that was there now were fields of green and low brown warehouses storing bricks or window frames or boxes of beer. We shared the narrow road with huge blue cargo trucks and bouncy motorized tricycles called *bengbeng* cars. The whole scene was glazed with hazy summer pollution and I couldn't decide what would be worse: this desolate countryside or villas filled with Chinese yuppies. After a half hour, we reached the compound.

There are two words in Chinese that translate into "apartment building": *loufang* and *gongyu*. *Loufang*, where I lived, borrowed their featureless design from the Soviet aesthetic and you could tell from the outside what the inside would be like: cramped and dark with concrete floors and a dusty balcony crammed with broken sinks and naked baby dolls. Too many people would live there fighting with one another in the too-small space, watching China Central Television while sitting on a thin, hard couch still covered in its original plastic. *Gongyu* were just the opposite, striving instead toward the Chinese ideal of Westernness. The Grecian detailing and garish paint jobs of the *gongyu* indicated the openness, sophistication, and hardwood floors inside. I imagined lives of ease filled with DVD watching and joyous family gatherings.

With this idea in mind, I expected to be greeted at the compound by a statue of some galloping horses or maybe some freestanding Corinthian columns, but the small cluster of dirty concrete buildings we drove up to just screamed *loufang*. The buildings were painted yellowish with thick blue stripes. They already looked run-down without ever having been lived in.

"What do you think of the exterior?" said Wang's older sister.

"It looks like a steamboat," said Wang Le. Other than scrawny marigolds growing in the dirt around the buildings, there was little sign of life. The languid whirring of cicadas and hollow metallic clanging from the construction site in the compound were the only sounds. Summer heat had started to rise off the pavement.

"Well, it's no villa," said her younger sister in a shrill voice. "Far from it."

The compound had rows of padlocked garages that were, oddly

enough, the exact same size as their current house, 200 square feet. Wang anxiously asked Agent Wang if all the parking garages had already been reserved.

"You rest easy," he said. "We'll get you the parking space."

The eight of us followed him and his great ring of keys from apartment to apartment, all just dusty concrete shells empty save for the occasional lacquered wood nightstand to imply a bedroom or an asymmetric tchotchke-holding shelf to imply a living room. Agent Wang took us to apartments on the ground and third floors. Wang's husband kept hinting that the ground floor would be more convenient.

"She can't be the only consideration," said Wang of her mother-in-law, "because in a few years—"

Agent Wang took us to see a finished apartment. The heavy security door unlocked with a clang and a lone man in a wifebeater tank top opened it. He was unshaven and heavyset and I felt as if I had seen him somewhere before. Afraid to track dirt into his new house, we stood at the threshold, breathing in the cool rush of air-conditioning and craning for a look. I could see fancy kitchen fixtures and a big plush sofa. The bright, immaculate apartment looked as if it had been dropped from outer space into the concrete shell and the man shuffled gingerly around in it. The only other person we saw at the compound was a cloth-slippered worker covered head to toe in dust, working in another apartment. In the midst of construction rubble, he had laid down planks of wood and bamboo matting to make a bed, which was then shrouded with a ghostly mosquito net. I imagined how quiet it must be here at night.

Agent Wang used great pomp to state the obvious. He threw open doors and announced, "The difference is that this apartment is *larger* than the other one we just saw." His already loud voice was amplified to an unbearable volume by the bare concrete walls and seemed to get louder at every stop. Wang told me he used to be in the army.

"You should lower your voice," she said to him after we had seen five or six apartments. "You must be tired."

"It's no problem!" he yelled.

We went outside to get away from him. The inside was stifling and clogged with dust, the outside sticky and sweltering. We were exhausted not only from the heat but also from the effort it took to imagine the future when their lives would be relocated into these vast and empty steamboats. I was thirsty, but we hadn't brought anything to drink, an oversight that might have actually been for the best since none of the toilets were working yet. Wang's younger sister had brought a big bag of drinks and snacks for Niu Niu, who slurped and chomped her way through them.

Wang was confused by all of the different apartments that seemed so similar and asked me my opinion, but they had all blurred together in my mind. In such heat, there was a great possibility of making the wrong decision.

"I asked Niu Niu for her opinion and do you know what she said?" Wang asked as we stood in the atrium of one apartment. I was about to laugh until I realized that she was dead serious. "She said, 'All three of our houses have living rooms right as you walk in.' " I waited for more insight, but no more was forthcoming. Wang looked as worried as a child.

"What are *you* looking for in a house?" I asked her.

"I've lived in such a small place for so long. I'd like to experience the opposite. I'd like a big house," she said, and added hesitantly, "One that's not too high up."

Agent Wang kept fielding cellphone calls and coming back to crow triumphantly, "We've sold another one!" while holding aloft a piece of paper on which was penned the magic digits of the sold apartment. I caught Wang consulting again with Niu Niu. Outside one of the apartments, Niu Niu crouched down, lifted up her skirt, and urinated on the ground.

Suddenly, Wang and her husband decided to buy a two-bedroom apartment on the ground floor of one of the buildings, even though the apartment was smaller than the one they had originally put the deposit on and wasn't south-facing. The master bedroom looked out on a six-foot-high wall, beyond which was a big rusty industrial building that, according to Agent Wang, was a natural gas plant. He was about to X off the apartment in his book and call in another sale into the head office when Wang paused, uneasy. She was worried that she would have to keep the shades drawn all day to block out the sight of the plant, darkening an already dim apartment. Agent Wang assured them that the plant would be demolished in a few years and transformed into green space. Her sisters joined her in criticizing the apartment. We went outside and stood in a tense circle in the dead heat.

"I want a third-floor apartment," Wang said to her husband. "I don't want to live on the ground floor." He was shocked by the directness of her declaration. The sisters asked me and I reluctantly agreed with them. The view from the ground floor was oppressive.

"Even our American friend thinks it's too low," said her older sister.

Wang's husband shook his head angrily. For him, his mother was the unalterable factor in this equation and he assumed Wang thought so too. Her sisters encouraged her to look at more third-floor apartments. He conceded defeat to the trio of sisters.

"You do what you want," he said, sitting down. "I'm not even going to look anymore."

"I'm taking my money and buying what I want," she shot back before going upstairs. "You don't have to live there."

Out of her husband's earshot, Wang began fuming about his intractability.

"He's lived in courtyard houses for fifty years. He can't change his habits now. He's like a peasant, walking in and out of our ground-floor house in his slippers. Of course he thinks it's convenient. I do all of the cleaning," she said, as she gazed out the window at the bean fields below. "I don't want to say ugly things, but she doesn't really have many years left. And she doesn't *ever* go out, even now."

We prepared to leave. Agent Wang, sweaty but undefeated, smiled wolfishly and said he knew they could resolve their problem. But how could they? They would have to choose between moving upward toward Wang Le's dream apartment or staying on the ground floor with its familiarity and her husband's filial obligations. I realized with a flash that they were just like my parents: my dad who would sacrifice everything for Nainai and my mom who wanted to live a more unfettered life. I thought back to the wording on the flyer that led them here in the first place, about one's dreams ruined because of *unattainably high prices*. Did Wang Le or my mom ever imagine the true price of their dreams? Did they really think they could convince their husbands to pay?

"That's what I want to do," said Wang as we passed by a small shop set up in one of the garages. "Open a small shop out here."

I was glad to see that she had not stopped her dreaming.

As we waited for the bus, Wang's brother went back to buy popsicles and said the shop owners asked him why anyone would buy a house out here. The bus finally came and I gobbled down my sweet red bean popsicle before it melted all over my hand. Wang tried to get a 5 percent discount from Agent Wang, repeatedly saying she'd sent him all these customers. Her younger sister tried to persuade her to buy an even larger apartment—on the third floor, of course. Wang's husband sat silently. In the end, they didn't make any decisions.

As I held the bare wooden popsicle stick with my sticky hand, I watched Beijing's countryside roll by the window. It lulled me into a sense of peace, laced with a sadness that it would probably be gone the next time I came, whenever that would be.

Chapter Thirty-one
Qu Qu'r in America

a few workers arrived at my apartment one day armed with cardboard boxes, razors, and tape. They were led by a man in a polo shirt named Polo Ding. The movers dismantled my life in a single hour, putting it all onto a slow boat from China.

After they left, I sat down on the couch. The apartment looked exactly as it had when I had moved in that hopeful, frightening day years ago. Empty, just me and my two suitcases, as if those years had transpired in the blink of an eye. I thought back on all that had happened. This trusty apartment had seen it all. I would have been excruciatingly sad had I not been completely numb.

As I sat there, the emptiness of the room began bleaching out my memory and I feared that I would forget the Beijing of my twenties when I went back, just like every time I visited the States. Would getting on that plane delete all that had happened to me, like a tape erasing itself as it rewound? Would I forget whom I'd met, what I'd been a part of, whom I'd become? The city had made me, but I sensed the freedom of the last few years slipping away from me. I thought of the curse of the fortune-teller: I'd constantly want to return to China but I would come back only once. I couldn't even begin to imagine how Nainai and Yeye, or my parents, had felt right before leaving China many years ago knowing they might never return.

Gretchen was leaving too, going back to study anthropology in New York. She said Big Sister Bao had recently shown up at her door, unbidden, wanting to buy her furniture for cheap. Somehow she'd sniffed out Gretchen's departure.

"She asked about you. She said, 'After saving Miss Wang from the police, she doesn't even have the decency to say hi when I pass her in the yard.' She even did a little imitation of you mincing right by her," said Gretchen, reenacting Big Sister Bao's version of my walk complete with a prissy pushing up of glasses. I felt bad. I would have said hi but I had no recollection of what she looked like, my memory having kindly deleted all but the shell of that experience.

Cookie was staying in Beijing. She would soon become a camerawoman, what she had wanted to be. She'd been sent to Pakistan for a stint already and was headed to Afghanistan when I left. She would eventually go to Iraq too. We said good-bye sadly and promised to meet again, if not in Beijing, then in New York or London, or Bombay or Ouagadougou. Somewhere. But as I sat there, I wondered if I would ever see her again.

I looked over a newspaper article I'd recently stumbled across, detailing a serial killer who had actually been loose in our neighborhood several years before. Starting the year I moved in, he picked up fourteen prostitutes in his white cement truck, some near the bridge over the Third Ring Road and some near the Rock 'n' Roll Disco down the road, and then brutally murdered them. The Beijing night hadn't been as tranquil as I'd assumed. He said he was filled with hatred for prostitutes after finding out his girlfriend of a year and a half was one. He had a fond memory of each of his victims: "Number Eight had the longest hair. Number Eleven had the shortest. Number Nine was the tallest of all. And the fattest one was also the one with the worst Chinese. I think she was

Russian," the article quoted him as saying. Even before murdering her, the man had to stop and insult her Chinese. It was sick and strange. These women lived all around me but their lives were so different than mine, so truly dangerous.

Just the week before, I had bumped into Yang Lina as she was dining alfresco with a group of people at Le Petit Paris on Sanlitun. I hadn't seen her for a while. A mutual friend had told me that she had cheated on Xu Xing with a Palestinian, stopped working on her third documentary, and was staging an experimental play with her new boyfriend. She had gained a lot of weight, he said, and now wore these shapeless Palestinian dresses. When I saw her on Sanlitun, her face did look fuller and she wore a colorful dress shaped like a tent. I told her I was leaving soon and I wasn't sure when we would meet next. We talked about the Olympics and wondered where we would both be in 2008.

"I'd like to come back then," I said.

"Oh, you'll come back," Yang Lina said with a giggle. "You'll bring your husband and kids!"

"In six years?" I said. "I won't be married then, much less have children."

"No, you'll be on your second husband by then," she said, and we both laughed. It was much more likely that she would be the one divorced and with a child. Yang Lina had been like a big sister to me, in the true sense of the word: helpful, condescending, bossy, a force of nature to look up to and to differentiate myself from. I would miss her.

One recent afternoon I had also dropped by the No Name Bar for the last time and had been surprised to see Zhang Yuan scouting locations for his new film. We said hello. I tried to be cold and dismissive but when he turned his attention to me, I just wanted to sit down and tell him everything, about the home I'd made in Beijing and the pain of giving it up, but also about my relief to be leaving, and how the twin feelings of exile and escape mingled strangely together. I even felt tempted to tell him how much he had meant to me so many years ago. To avoid doing that, I asked about his new film. He told me that it was a romance called <i>Green Tea,</i> about a bookish young woman with glasses who is pursued by a guy—a bit of a bad egg—who's intrigued by her mysterious inner life. He paused to clock my reaction. In his eyes was that old teasing look that I could swear was saying, <i>Resemble two people we know?</i> Or was his look saying, <i>A little presumptuous of you to think my film is about you, no?</i> It was confusing. In any case, it didn't resemble my version of the story at all, which would go a little more like this: Lonely tomboy stalks loutish director who has been using her for publicity but who becomes repelled by her desperate fantasizing. All that had happened between us, and a sharp memory of my naïveté slashed into my gut, sickening me a little. I'd come a long way since then. But before I had time to say anything, he'd disappeared into himself as quickly as he'd appeared. Had he just been pulling my leg again?

Back on the couch in my apartment, I saw Qu Qu'r creep into the room, belly to the floor, sniffing from side to side and squawking in bewilderment. Something was missing. He remembered, and with him by my side, hopefully I would too.

I went to see my relatives to say good-bye. We reminisced about my living with them long ago and they kidded me one last time about how much I had eaten at that first meal. I told Xiao Lu about the fortune-teller's curse and she said, "Do you know why you won't come back so often? Because you will be married with children, and it won't be so easy." I took photos of Bobo and Bomu out in the courtyard. They posed under a tree, ramrod straight and smile-free, but once the shutter clicked they relaxed and started laughing, and I snapped again. The two photos are like "before" and "after" shots of our relationship. They went inside and I sat down for a minute on the brick planter I'd sat on in the dead of the night so long ago. I looked up at the apartment building looming above and heard in my ear the ghost of Elliott Smith's voice, which seemed so sad and so untrue.

There's nothing here that you'll miss
I can guarantee you this is a cloud of smoke

• • •

That Christmas was the first I celebrated with my family in five years. Being back in the States made me uncomfortable; it was like being dead, or asleep. My long-coveted thrift-store outfits were waiting for me in the closet, but putting them on made me feel twenty-two again, as if my old self was waiting there for me, and so I left them on their hangers. My parents didn't ask any questions about China and it seemed they wanted to erase all the years I'd been away, all the distance I'd put between us. I'd gone so far from home to develop away from their scrutiny, and now I was upset that they hadn't witnessed my development and didn't know who I was.

My mom's comment about the adventurous spirit that we share has been added to her canon of stories. We both went halfway around the world alone when we were just young women. "She's just like me," she says, and not just about our adventurous spirit. We are also friendly, out-going, and any number of other positive character traits of her own that we don't actually share. There is more wishful thinking than anything else in her observations, though I do believe I got from her my instinct for turning every tiny thing that happens to me into a story.

She continues to tell the one about the mysterious man with the gift of the Gruen watch, though it has become *A Timex, wow!* and she has added some extra details withheld from me before. *I was young and stupid and instead of asking him to meet me in the lobby, I went up to his room.*

To my surprise, Nainai and I formed an unspoken bond. In the years since Yeye's death, she had mellowed and I saw a new side of her personality: impish, gently ironic, knowing. I wondered who she had been before she married him. She could still communicate with a single look but her message was now one of love and acceptance. She took a shine to Qu Qu'r, calling him my *mao erzi,* or cat-son, and filled me in on the latest gossip about our relatives around the world, all of whom she kept in constant touch with.

One afternoon she and I sat at the kitchen table of my parents' house, looking out the sliding glass doors at the neat backyard in its wintry bareness. Where the pine trees had been were now short holly bushes, which my parents said would grow tall enough (six to eight feet) to block the view of the neighbors' yards but not tall enough to endanger the house. My mom told me the hollies were called China Boy and China Girl. My parents had finally mastered suburban moderation. I asked Nainai about her courtyard house in Beijing. She refused to open her mouth when a tape recorder was running and I had to wait until she wanted to speak.

"It's very terrible shape. What to say about it?" she said in English. "You've been there. You tell me about it. What it's like now?"

"It's run-down," I said. "I want to know about it before, its history."

"History?" she said. "No history."

"Did you have a car?"

"Of course!" she said.

"What kind of car?"

"It was a jeep," said my dad, listening nearby.

"No, how can you remember?" she said. She told me they had had a car and a chauffeur. They also had a cook, a nursemaid, a laundress, a maid, and a doorman.

"A doorman?"

"Who's going to answer the door and the telephone otherwise?" she asked. Even now when the phone rings at home, Nainai instinctively orders people to pick it up. And having a cook would explain why the only dish of hers I remember from my childhood is brownies. "Your daddy used to wait by the door for Yeye to come home from work. He would sit in car . . . ," she said, then switched into Chinese. "He would ride in the car just that short way from the door to the garage." She corrected my dad. "The jeep was in Qingdao, not Beijing. I used to drive the car. The American soldiers stationed there weren't used to seeing a young Chinese girl driving a car. Cars back then weren't automatic. I was always stalling out and the American soldiers would yell, 'Hoo hoo!' I was so nervous I stopped driving. Then the Nationalists left and it was all over. The cars we just gave away."

She didn't know what she was going to do about the house when it got demolished, whether she would take the cash or try to get a new house. She almost sold it a few years ago, but the owner of the adjacent house wouldn't sell, so the deal was off.

"I don't want to sell the house now," she said.

"Why not?" I asked hopefully.

"The house is very"—she searched for the word—"*zhiqian*." Valuable. Bobo had told her the house was in a good part of the city with high real estate prices. He would be visiting in the spring and they could discuss it further then. She said he would be bringing a video that showed both the house that she lived in before she was married and the one she lived in after she was married.

"You never saw the video?" I asked. "I thought he sent it to you years ago."

"No, I've never seen it. Have you?"

"Yes, I saw it."

"What does it show?" she asked.

I paused, unsure of what to answer.

Unexpectedly changing the subject, she told me about an article she had just read in a Taiwanese newspaper about six people in Taiwan who received organs from the same organ donor. One got an eye, another a heart, another a liver, lungs, a kidney. The woman who got the eye could see again. I nodded impatiently, anxious to return to our conversation, but in her own way Nainai had never changed the subject. She said the six had originally all been strangers, but their families all knew one another now. They are like family, she said, because they all received something living from the same donor.

Epilogue

*a*fter a year in Baltimore, I moved to New York. I finally had the room in Brooklyn—two rooms, actually, one a study with a desk by a sunny window where I wrote. Or at least tried to write. The sounds of the neighborhood clamored for my attention: horns and sirens and gunshots and music, dogs barking, ice cream truck jingling, neighbors laughing and yelling, kids whooping as they popped wheelies, drug dealers hooting like birds. Every Sunday, and many weekdays as well, a neatly bearded West Indian man in an immaculate olive suit and hat would wheel his amp under my second story window to warn all within earshot about the Second Coming of Jesus. "Boom-shallack!" I scribbled into the margins of a draft. "My heart shall not fear!"

To my surprise, my parents became China junkies, joining group tour after group tour and seeing all the parts of their homeland that they had never seen before. But my relationship with them remained vexed, as they continued trying to micromanage my life via telephone. *How many blocks do you live from the subway? When it rains, are there big puddles? When is the book you are writing coming out?* One day my mom called to tell me about a PBS documentary she'd seen about Chinese-Americans who had moved to China to work, starring people I knew from my time there. "Why don't you do something like that?" she asked.

I had the shell of a new life but my heart was still living in the past. After a few years of writing, I decided that it was time to visit Beijing, even if I dreaded seeing what had changed and even if the new city would overwrite the one that had existed in my mind since I left. My boyfriend, Graham, was also coming, a few days after me.

When I walked out of the airport into the humid night air filled with cigarette smoke, I felt as if I had come home. I might have been gone for weeks instead of years. I wasn't even jet-lagged. Yet the differences made themselves known quickly. No one tried to offer me an illegal cab ride into the city and the dour primary color palette of the homegrown cars on the streets had burst into a rainbow of shiny imports. Even the wheezing red-and-cream city buses were gone, replaced by chipper green, yellow, and red electric buses. All I could see was the new: new office towers, new malls, new cars, new companies, new restaurants, new spas, new bars, new bar streets, new streets, new young expats. Beijing was growing up. In many ways the city had become a more cosmopolitan, probably more interesting place with more points of view and more connections to the outside world. But a yearning for all that was missing tugged at me. Entire neighborhoods were gone. Gone was the wild, enchanted feeling that hung over the city in those days. Gone was the tranquility of the No Name Bar—its success had spawned a whole street of gaudy imitators who brought neon signs and noisy drunks to the lake. Gone also were many of my friends. I kept half expecting to hear my phone ring and for Cookie to be on the other end asking me to meet her at the Lao Beijing restaurant in our old neighborhood, but she lived in London now.

I took a walk on my first day there, forgetting that Beijing was not a city for walking. Down dusty streets past construction sites, competing with cars for space on the road, not recognizing any of the buildings around me, and forgetting how the streets connected to one another, I walked and walked as the muggy August air wound around me. Defeated and desperately thirsty, I stumbled into an old neighborhood, the kind that used to be everywhere in the city. Narrow lane. Brick houses with leaky tile roofs. Tiny restaurants containing only ten tables. I bought water from an old man chain-smoking alone in his tiny shop. There were bicycles and bike repairmen and a man sleeping on a big piece of cardboard, a chess set sitting next to him untouched. I had never been so happy to hear someone hocking up a juicy loogie or to smell the ripe, fetid stink of a public toilet. I caught a glimpse of myself in a passing pane of glass and saw that the tomboy I'd been writing about had disappeared and been replaced by a woman with long hair, wearing a skirt. On the brick wall of a house at the edge where the neighborhood abruptly ended, someone had painted big black characters reading 大村变小村, A BIG VILLAGE HAS BECOME A SMALL VILLAGE. I took a picture and moved on.

I went to find the people I'd been writing about. When I called Yang Lina, I was not surprised to hear an automated voice tell me it was an "empty number." I got her new number from a mutual friend and visited her in a new apartment she'd bought. The intervening years had been difficult for her: She had gotten married, had a daughter, and gotten divorced, and hadn't made any more documentaries. Running through her usually bright, strong voice was a new note of sorrow. Money had made everyone in her generation crazy, she said. It had ruined their lives. Her mother was raising her daughter up in the Northeast, and she was starting on a few new documentaries, mostly about groups of women.

As for the subjects of my own documentary, I no longer kept in touch with the Zhang family but I did wonder what had happened to them. One afternoon, I took a walk down their street; the narrow alley had been widened several years before, and now the small shops and restaurants on both sides were in the process of being demolished and the whole area remade into a pedestrian-friendly shopping and hotel district designed to mimic the intimate dimensions of the original neighborhood. I stood outside their restaurant and looked up into their apartment above. It looked emptied out, the windows flung open to the street.

Wang Le's number was also disconnected and Cookie told me the last she heard she was working at a salon "on that really long road which was *chai*'d and made into a modern road" that ran parallel to Wangfujing. I spent an afternoon biking down the road, poking my head into all the hair salons asking for her, but she was nowhere to be found. All this thinking about her made me want to cut my hair short. A branch of the British salon Toni&Guy had recently opened and I went there instead and emerged looking like any woman with a pageboy whom you might see on the streets of London or New York.

Graham arrived and I took him to see my relatives. They were refreshingly unchanged. They still lived three generations all together in the same courtyard house and we still sat and watched TV together and they still made jokes about how much I'd eaten the first time we met years ago. The newborn baby had transformed into a rambunctious little boy who, as we sat quietly talking, rode his scooter in circles around the room at top speed, barely missing the TV, people's toes, and the stools with glasses of tea perched on top. And Xiao Peng, who played a Game Boy all through dinner, seemed to be shrinking in years. Though my relatives and Graham had no common language, they liked one another, as I knew they would. They accepted him more easily than did my parents, who didn't mind that he wasn't Chinese but couldn't help disapproving of us living together. Bobo took us to see another courtyard house that Uncle Johnny had bought, which he had renovated impeccably and then rented out to the Inner Mongolian provincial government.

While I kept pointing out to Graham all the new things he should ignore, I began to see that many of the city's particularities had remained the same. The city still moved with the same drowsy, frenetic pace of life as before, and Beijingers were still gruff and loquacious with the same take-it-as-it-comes attitude. Under the new upholstery of the city, an indestructible something had endured. Graham noted gently that perhaps it was as much the passing of my own youth that I mourned as the city itself.

In 2008, I returned to Beijing for the summer to work for NBC News during the Olympics. The fortune-teller's curse: broken.

Cookie was also going to be there for the summer and we decided to live together. Bobo told me the tenants in Nainai's courtyard house had finally been evicted (more details than that were not forthcoming) and I told him I might want to live there with my friend that summer, so I went with him and Bomu to see the house. We walked in and I saw that the courtyard was wide-open, all the makeshift rooms in the center having been demolished. But the house was a wreck. The yard was filthy, trash strewn everywhere, red firecracker papers dotting the ground. Half the roof tiles had fallen off, and where they hadn't, tall yellow grasses sprouted straight up. Laundry was strung across the courtyard, and Bobo casually mentioned that a friend of his was living in the house to look after it. Not to worry, he said, they'd left the best room for me. The grayish walls of "my" room were blotched with water stains in some spots and patched with newspaper and checkered cloth in others, and dust lay thickly on every surface. Even after a good mopping the place would still look pretty grim. The toilet was predictably small, dark, and pungent, the squatter merely a slat cut in the concrete floor, and needless to say, there was no shower. I didn't disguise my unhappiness with the situation and Bobo smiled and laughed in a way that made me feel he was disguising other emotions. This wasn't the gentle, fictional Bobo I'd been spending so much time with in my writing, but the real one. Prickly and still a mystery in many ways. I met his friend, a man whom my dad would have characterized as rustic, with crooked teeth and an unctuous smile, and I understood that I would be living with him the entire summer, as well as with his friend, a sesame cake maker. On the way out Bomu mentioned a policeman lived there too. It's safer with him here, she assured me. I suddenly had a pang of compassion for Uncle Johnny.

Cookie and I instead rented an apartment in our old neighborhood, in a *gongyu* that hadn't existed when we'd lived there. An enormous neo-Roman triumphal arch stood as the entrance gate, inset on each side with a soldier easily twice our height clad in full battle regalia. The building had an elevator and we even registered officially with the police. The city, on its best behavior with fresh flowers everywhere, was unrecognizable. It was a simple and happy time and we got to be young again for a summer before saying good-bye to it—the city as we'd known it, our youth. I realized China was a place I could return to, a place my parents could return to, as long as I accepted that none of it could ever be counted on to stay the same.

I took Bobo and Bomu to see a show at the new multimillion-dollar Peking Opera theater that had opened inside the Second Ring Road and was surprised to see the theater full. I also finally met their two daughters, who were back for a visit. The younger daughter had two sons and the older daughter was divorced, or so Nainai had told me. Bobo and Bomu now wintered annually in L.A. and hoped to bring Sanbao to the States in a few years.

After the Olympics were over, Graham came again, and at Cookie's suggestion, we went to visit a miraculously preserved Ming Dynasty town down south in Anhui Province and stayed at an inn run by a Shanghainese poet.

The Pig's Heaven Inn was just as beautiful as Cookie had said it would be. It was an old wooden house with soaring proportions built around an inner courtyard set with plants and a huge ceramic fishbowl. While architectural details like the intricate wooden latticework of the doors and windows were perfectly preserved, the inn also had a pleasant sense of growth and decay, of time passing. We were the only ones staying there and we spent days wandering around the alleys of the walled village of Xidi, which felt as picturesque as Beijing had years ago, more so even. The whitewashed buildings all had baroquely carved lintels and dark roofs with flying eaves. Most ancient villages like this had been demolished during the Cultural Revolution; Xidi had been preserved by one official's patronage, a fluke of history. The village felt unreal as a dream but Graham is an anthropologist and I wanted to sell him on China as a future field site. Once he was hooked, I would do the bait and switch and show him the real China.

Our birthdays fall near each other and we'd brought presents to exchange. After dinner we sat upstairs on a balcony that overlooked the sea of tiled roofs of the village. We could have been hundreds of years in the past, save for the occasional solar panel on the roof. Mist painted itself poetically onto the hills in the distance. Graham handed me a small box, saying he was giving me a selfish present that was more of a present to himself. Even after I opened it, it took me several moments to understand what it was. My twenty-three-year-old self would kill me if she knew I was going to end a book about her with a marriage proposal in a storybook foreign locale. But there were so many things about life she could never have known.

The night before our wedding, my parents sat me down for a talk in their living room. Dread curdled in my stomach as I had flashbacks to other talks they'd held with me in that room. I hoped the words "marrying an alcoholic and going on a honeymoon on a sinking ship" weren't going to come out of my dad's mouth. They didn't. He said kindly, "We wish you all the happiness in the world," as my mom nodded her agreement. He continued, "But if anything goes wrong, you should know that you can always come back to us." Go back to them? I was shocked. I had been on my own since graduating from college. But to them, I'd been their ward all these years, until I got married and they could pass on the responsibility. We'd been operating under such radically different ideas of family and independence, and each been oblivious to the other's point of view. It was no wonder we'd had such a hard time. To my surprise, after the wedding the familial pressure I'd felt my entire life lifted.

My parents had long since stopped asking about my book, and I never told them about my struggles to finish and sell it. One night I stayed over at Nainai's apartment, and in the morning as we sat outside before I left, she said to me without prelude, "I hope you can make your mark in the world." I nodded, and she said she knew it wasn't easy. This encouragement was her last gift to me before she passed away the next year. She was ninety-five.

Her courtyard house in Beijing she bequeathed to her three children. They held on to it for a few years as the houses around it were sold to a state-run developer who planned to knock them down and build a complex of high-rises. My dad's younger brother, who lives in Singapore, took on the task of dealing with it, relieving my dad of the burden. My uncle wanted to trade the courtyard house for another one so we could retain a family home in Beijing, just as I wanted, but my dad and his sister had no interest in that. Just recently, under pressure from the developer, they sold it. Bobo said Nainai told him over that phone before her death that if the house was ever sold, he would get a cut of the profits, and so he has.

With Nainai gone, and now our house too, a crucial part of our connection to China is lost. My parents talk on the phone with Bobo regularly and I get back to China as often as I can, but I wonder, as time goes on, will Xiao Peng and I have as strong a relationship as our parents and grandparents did? What will take me back there? What will take my children back there?

Marriage gave me the accepting family I'd craved for so long and it primed me to do the most square thing of all; our twins were born in 2012. After I birthed out almost fourteen pounds of baby the natural way, words I'd been waiting years to hear finally came out of my mom's mouth: "I am so proud of you." (If I'd known all these years that that's all it took.)

Just as Yeye's passing irrevocably altered our family structure, adding August and Maurice to our family tweaked ancient patterns we had no way to intervene in ourselves. I see more of my parents than I have in years, and we even vacationed together in the summer, renting a beach house together for a week.

On the last night, as we sat in the kitchen after the boys went to sleep, my dad began telling the story of his journey to the States when he was sixteen, which I'd never heard in full before. His family of five set sail from Jakarta in December of 1956. They first hopscotched around Asia, stopping off in Taiwan to get passports, taking another boat to Yoko-hama, Japan, then a train to western Japan, and finally boarding a Chi-nese freight ship bound for America. The only other nonsailor aboard was given the luxurious guest suite at the front and they were given a window-less room in the back, which was freezing in the winter and, by the time they got to the Philippines to pick up a load of iron ore, boiling hot. We were roasting like peanuts back there, he said. The ship then took a month to get to Hawaii. It was mind-numbingly boring, Dad said, so he and his siblings roamed all over the ship and got to know the entire crew of twenty. The sailors stitched together a volleyball out of scraps of cloth and, when it flew overboard, just made a new one. Yeye befriended the captain and got them moved to a room closer to the front of the boat. They sailed through the Panama Canal and finally arrived in Baltimore in April of 1957. They took a train up to New York City and wandered around 125th Street with all their worldly possessions in a few suitcases, not knowing what they were going to do.

"Didn't you have a plan?"

"A plan? There was no plan."

"I thought Yeye had a job here."

"No, no."

"You just came."

"Yes."

They bumped into a Chinese man and struck up a conversation. He took pity on them and let them stay in his apartment for a few nights. He even lied to his wife, telling her Yeye was his cousin.

"Was his wife Chinese?" asked Graham.

"No, she was black. She was very welcoming. Without that man, I don't know what we would have done. Just to have a place to stay for a few days was a tremendous help.

"The man was from Tianjin," my dad said as an aside to me.

It seemed I'd been doomed to retrace my parents' steps in ways I'd never even known. What had gone through my dad's mind when he'd heard years ago that I would be moving to Tianjin? It must have seemed a meaningful coincidence and, knowing him, not a positive one. Closer to a bad omen. But now I understood parts of his story that no one else in our family did. As usual, though, he shifted quickly out of sentimentality. "That man had been in the U.S. forty years. But his English still wasn't very good."

"That's a crazy story."

"Anyhow, that's why I don't ever want to go on a cruise ship. Mom always wants to take a cruise. I say no way. It's like being in prison."

"Why did Nainai and Yeye decide to come, if they didn't have a job or much money?"

"It was Nainai's idea. Like many Chinese people, she was a little bit fascinated by America. So Yeye agreed."

Could Nainai ever have foreseen the changes that not only China but also America and our family too would undergo? No more than I can look into the future another half century and see where everyone ends up. Nainai and Yeye made a lucky gamble coming to the States, but as China rises, perhaps the pendulum will swing back in the other direction. All I can do is what my parents and theirs before did and so on up the chain: Give the boys the best start I can and hope they forgive my missteps. They are enrolled now in a Mandarin-immersion day care where they are getting excellent "eaah training," and I sense that somewhere out there, Yeye is finally laughing.

Acknowledgments

Thank you to Bobo, Bomu, Xiao Peng, Xiao Lu, and the whole clan in Beijing for welcoming me despite my barbaric ways. Thank you to all the grannies, *hunzi*, and other friends in Beijing who lived this story with me, and to the Zhang family for opening your home to me.

Immense gratitude to everyone who helped me along on this long journey of writing, especially the following: Rebecca Barnes, Nick Poppy, Jeff Alexander, Jonathan Ansfield, Ann Finkbeiner, Chip Brantley, Heather Dewar, Sally McGrane, Shanti Avirgan, John Sanchez, Blue Chevigny, Justine Kalb, Margot Meyers, Ben Ryder Howe, Carey Goldberg, Krista Van Fleit Hang, Eric Han, and Jo Lusby and the Penguin China office.

Thanks also to the Brooklyn Writers Space and the Writers' Room of Boston, and all the kindred spirits found there.

Thank you to Gillian MacKenzie, the very best agent a writer could have, for your smarts and savvy and good cheer when I waver. Thanks also to her assistants, Adriann Ranta and Allison Devereux.

A huge thank-you to my editor, Lucia Watson, for sharing in the vision of this book with me and for keeping me on the path when I strayed.

Thank you to Gigi Campo and to the huge crew at Gotham who turned the file on my computer into a beautiful book out in the world: Brian Tart, Lisa Johnson, Lauren Marino, Megan Newman, Susan Schwartz, LeeAnn Pemberton, Dora Mak, Mikayla Butchart, Spring Hoteling, Beth Parker, Gina Chung, Farin Schlussel, and Allison Prince. Big thanks especially to cover designers Monica Benalcazar and Stephen Brayda.

Finally, thank you to my family. To my parents, Allan and Lisa Wang, for long ago giving me the choice to either "read a book or look at the wall" and for so openly sharing your stories with me. This book has been a long way of delivering a short message: I love you. To my brother, Chris Wang, for being so perfect growing up so I didn't have to be. To Carol and Richard Jones for your unwavering support.

My deepest love and gratitude is reserved for Graham Jones, a prince among men, for always listening with love, care, and humor, and for the way you believed in this book and in me. Without you, well, I just shudder to think. And finally thank you to my princelings Augie and Momo for simply being.